SELECTED ESSAYS

ALSO BY WILLIAM WALLIS

Poetry
Poems
Biographer's Notes
Four Valley Poets (with others)
Ruth
Asher
Eros
Dutton's Books
Joshua
Twins
Simple Gifts
Selected Poems

Prose
A Meeting of Cultures
Essays on Lakota History and Culture, Literature and Music

A Dream of Love Fulfilled
An Interdisciplinary Introduction to Opera

Drama
Hanblecheya, The Vision

SELECTED ESSAYS

William Wallis

Stone & Scott, *Publishers*
Sherman Oaks, California

SELECTED ESSAYS

First Edition — Second Printing, 2004

With gratitude to Martin and Rita Horn

Printed in the United States of America by Delta Printing Solutions, Valencia, CA

Library of Congress Control Number 2002 131313

ISBN   1-891135-04-X

Book design by Lynn Eames.

PREFACE

As a poet, one who practices the soul's search for meaning through language, I have always valued the essay as a supremely useful means of sharing information rationally. It is a flexible, powerful, and creative tool of expression. Before selecting these 22 compositions from a group perhaps three times that large, it seemed to me that I had recorded more ideas and experience in poetry than prose. Now I am no longer sure. At all accounts, these essays cover the same years as my *Selected Poems, 1969-99*, and explore the same thematic chord: the search for love in passion; the slow emotional healing from a difficult childhood; religious belief; dealing with death; and a passionate love of poetry, music and music drama.

The *Early Pieces* were written while searching through the glorious dustbin of Europe (1978-85). *The Lakota Trilogy* and the Kafka/Niebuhr study were products of my doctoral and post-doctoral studies in Lincoln, during the 1970s. The essays contained in *On Conversion to Judaism* are pieces from an unpublished manuscript written between 1988 and 1990. Most of the *Personal Essays* and *Scholastic Pieces* were written for my students, echoing and illustrating their writing assignments. *A Bookstore* was written to preface a small volume of poetry describing my life in the San Fernando Valley in the early 1990s. *An ESL Publishing Project* and *An Introduction to Lyric Poetry* were meant to serve as pedagogical aids. The section on opera contains a selection of essays from my book on romantic opera, *A Dream of Love Fulfilled* (Stone & Scott, *Publishers*, 2001).

These essays might have remained scattered across thirty years and two continents, except for that singular need for order than typifies one dimension of the mind's domain. A related dimension is responsible for the urge to share knowledge through teaching. I dedicate this collection of thought to my students, with the hope that it may aid them in their search for meaning. Each honest essay is, it seems to me, a doorway to truth. Through that doorway is self-knowledge.

Valley Glen, 2004   *William Wallis, Ph.D.*

TABLE OF CONTENTS

For my students

1

EARLY PIECES

ANNIE

May 5 is Dutch Liberation Day. The allied forces reached Amsterdam in September 1944, too late for all but a handful of Holland's Jews. Those who survived knew the smell of blood and sewage as my generation knows cheese and tulips. We honor those who did not survive by recognizing the seemingly iridescent presence of a Dutch girl whose life ended at Bergen-Belsen shortly before that death factory was closed. To me, however, Anne Frank will always be a resident of Amsterdam. Each year the startlingly clear adolescent voice of 263 *Prinsengracht* echoes faintly through the street festivals in Amsterdam as televisions re-run the American film about Anne.

The neatly scrawled, dark paragraphs of Anne Frank's Diary form the most crystalline record we possess of humanist naivete's struggle for faith against the social cancer that engulfed Europe the first half of this century. But even Anne understood that, despite our need to believe that man is essentially good, Hitler's appearance was as logical, historically speaking, as nuclear weapons. Himmler was Hitler's narcissistic Einstein, and the Jews of Europe suffered ten years of Hiroshima in slow motion. It is too simple to say that twelve hundred years of hero worship led the German people to accept Hitler's psychotic vision of Western values, but like a handful of ashes, this generalization takes on weight and strength enough when Anne speaks to us again each year.

I am an American student, thirty, studying my craft in Hanover. I am an opera singer: I carve and hew my expression from the air supporting and caressing unseen muscles in my throat. I did this on the stages of America before I came to Europe to retrain my lyric baritone as a tenor and during this first year the only place I am truly happy is in a space defined by my thought. As many of my generation in America, I am over-educated and rarely happily employed, restless and dissatisfied with too much in myself and in the world around me to relax for long in one place or at one kind of work. I came to Europe, as hundreds of other young American artists have since America was discovered somewhere to the west of France, with hopes of beginning a career in the theaters and opera houses here, where the occupation of artist is more simply accepted as legitimate vocation. Unlike many who have come, however, I have no real plans to return to America, which is haunted for me by the ghost of my father, who sat at the end of the long line of Puritan backwoodsmen and who rejected my unscientific nature at first glance. It was always easier to deal with other people's ghosts, and my highly-personal, thoroughly American education has better equipped me to understand the ghosts of Europe—Jewish or Gentile—than my own. One sees clearly from attic prisons.

I visited Amsterdam in May 1978 with an American Jewish friend who was born and raised in the Midwestern United States, where I was educated. Rachel is twenty-one, and it was partially through her wide-open, optimistic eyes that I came to an understanding of what has passed through Amsterdam since 1935.

Many Dutch, old and young, hate the Germans. It is not just because of the German occupation of Holland from 1939-44, although that is important. It is the essential rejection of the land by the sea. It is a fear of and disrespect for what is assumed to be a genetically based tendency, or a willingness to disregard basic human values when it suits a political or commercial purpose. It is far more than acting superior; it is the nationalistic muscularity and the aggressive attitude that sustains it, which allowed a political regime to twist the spine of half of western humanity under its steel boots.

Like many middle-aged and old people now living in Europe, the middle-aged Dutch also hate themselves for surviving while so many innocent died. This is a phenomenon most clearly observed in the survivors of Hiroshima and Nagasaki. But my Dutch friends are young, and they carry a new, transmogrified hatred. Again, it exists not just because of the occupation and war, for they understand that almost any person or people will disadvantage others to some degree to get ahead, but because they feel that freedom, basic human freedom, is a secondary, functional concept in a circular German value structure that is perpetuated with a cold precision.

How must such a people see themselves? The particular nature of the German mirror causes the native viewer to believe that she or he is stronger, more correct, and superior to the other, the background. (After the last European war, everyone hoped all such mirrors were broken, but some were inevitably pulled from the rubble. A people cannot change; its style undergoes metamorphosis.) To look in the German mirror causes self-hatred among many non–Germans because the reflection of reality is so strongly and clearly distorted. One hardly replaces lost harmony with such an image: one creates new and refined dissonance, one refines the nightmares.

I call this hybrid, ongoing, second-generation self-hatred *Annie*, short for Angst, anguish, Aginbite of Inwit. Almost everyone I know carries a bit of it in his or her psychic pocket. Many artists rattle it, like gold coins.

■

Before I left New York in March to work and study in Hanover, I had read in the *Times* of Neo-Nazi activity in Hanover, where I have German and Canadian friends. As early as the middle sixties American opera singers were leaving secure positions in Europe rather than have their children educated in schools where Hitler is either ignored entirely or praised as the political and military genius who created the German system of roads and the Volkswagen, and where Hitler's creation and handling of "the Jewish Problem" is too unpleasant to mention. (German youths flock to films about Nazism and Hitler now, partially because they have little or no factual knowledge of these phenomena.) It is more than the history texts, or course. As I walked through the Zoo district of Hanover recently, I heard a strident chorus of children's voices from a gymnasium's open window pushed high and straining even higher on the refrain of a popular marching song. It was bright edge of searching hysteria.

And on Saturdays the new redbrick streets of Hanover's *Lister Meile* near the stern remnants of *In der Steinriede*, are filled with bitter, pale eyes, which glare from alcoholic faces hung over thick, stiff bodies. *Die Deutschevölke* have not healed well internally from World War II. Many Germans limp and not from the war alone, but from the occupation of Germany itself.

The new generation? The only observable generation gap is one of mode, not behavior. Some psychologists and sociologists attempt to explain the recurring phenomenon of the German ethos as one in which the "social character" of the German people is not fully matured, is maladapted to the atomic age: they cling to dangerous, older types of social character; for example, absolute sovereignty of state.

My mother, who probably never read the ancients, would simply say, "But most all people are good." And she, as Tevye says, would also be right. The German people were for the most part depressed to a state of inactivity and had to be lied to and taunted before they would approve of Hitler's war: once committed, there was no way out till the very end. Besides, the eye of a hurricane is a very pleasant place to be once you've forgotten how you got there and how you will have to leave. Mirror sales were up.

After World War II, Germany emerged from the alternating hysteria and depression of Europe's masculine menopause in ordered, massive, sun-set ceremonies that celebrated the joy of superiority. It only takes a very small percentage of a population to coerce the remainder under such circumstances, and there is little guilt residue for such a majority after the conflict. They have followed the tanks and read the newspapers as they were told. Their orders came from above. Whether these orders are to advance on a heavily shelled French fortification or to pull the switch which releases gas into a chamber crowded with women and children seems to make little difference. The orders came from above, thus absolving the guilt of those below.

(This reference to hierarchical order is also accurate pictorially. At Waterloo, Gettysburg, Calcutta, Auschwitz, Mi Lai, all orders to act came from messengers on horseback, on elephant, in jeep, or from a disembodied voice over a short wave. In *War and Peace*, Tolstoy argues that all such orders are ultimately dictated by the force of history which used to operate about ground level. His ultimate symbol for order and peace in the same novel, however, is the sky.)

A word comes from somewhere, millions die, and that is and was all. It can be seen as that simple from several perspectives, but it is quite another matter for the historian, philosopher, psychologist, and even the professional soldier. For example, there are those military historians who argue that Lee lost the American Civil War because of his compassion, his inability to order the destruction of exposed enemy forces. Grant did not suffer from such a fault.

Was Hitler's god or moral sense or whatever it was that made him act to destroy others, the same nocturnal figure who whispered to Truman before Hiroshima and Nagasaki, to Grant before Chancellorsville, to Napoleon before Borodino, and to whomever it was who spoke to Calley before Mi Lai? And who made the call that first set the Auschwitz machinery of death in motion?

■

The train from Berlin to Amsterdam was crowded and Rachel and I stood most of the seven-hour trip. After arriving at the *Bahnhof* we were intercepted by a British expatriate and led to Fat City, a hostel run by French and Israelis. The rest of the first day in Holland we explored Amsterdam on foot, took a canal excursion, and visited the Anne Frank House.

Just inside the door of *Anne Frank Huis* we took "Brief Guides" in four languages: English, French, Hebrew and German. Tourists collect keepsakes; performers collect multiple images of important phenomena. At first I resented the brutal clarity of the clippings and cartoons from Dutch newspapers 1935-1945, the accompanying captions, and the photographs of the remnants of Bergen-Belsen and Auschwitz. I had seen such photos, of course, but these all seemed new and were printed in startling heavy black and white, obviously meant to unsettle.

I had been impatient with Rachel in Amsterdam, with her absolutely indiscriminate interest in every word, article of clothing, every brick which she thought was "really" Dutch, but my heart went totally out to her as she moved very slowly along the wall displays from one to eighteen with only partially hidden shock written all over her, from head to toe. Jews were depicted in the Dutch cartoons as diseased, sub-human, evil, the source of all Europe's woes. It was all painfully clear.

By the time we reached the room where Anne slept and where she had carefully pasted the photographs of American, French and German movie stars to the thick walls, we were exhausted. In front of Ray Milland the dam broke and Rachel's mascara ran. By then it was almost closing time and after a brief glimpse into the attic room where Anne wrote her diary among potatoes and onions, we were thrust out into the rainy street with a handful of French and American sightseers. They disappeared quickly into the grey evening.

A man who had been shooting film with a small but high quality hand camera inside the house stood near us capturing different angles of the house front. After a moment he walked to the great church down *Prinsengracht* and disappeared into the shadows. I saw him there ahead of us, shooting, as we walked slowly in that direction to return to Fat City. Then Rachel stopped and leaned against me. She was sobbing. I held her close and kissed her many times softly. All this was caught by the filmmaker. I was glad: the world is full of people unable or unwilling to share their capacity to love; Rachel isn't one of them.

At Fat City, one seeks repose sixteen to a room in the middle of the red light district. Our room was over a disco and on Saturday night, May 1, was directly across a small courtyard from a group of Israeli students. Only the dead sleep under such conditions.

■

Maryke is petit and shy, a young artist whose smile and sudden full-hearted bursts of excitement shatter all cultural walls. On Sunday she chose to show us the small towns and sand hills of northern Holland. We were late for tulips. The brilliant covers had been gathered up into knee-high rows and piles that dotted the parallel sections of brown and gold on either side of the narrow road. The bulbs had been harvested. (That so much beauty could be incidental!) Anne did not write of tulips, though she had seen them hundreds of times. She writes of potatoes and men, the necessity of silence and the acceptance of limitations. Yet she too was torn up, piled, shipped off, and finally planted in a mass grave. The allied forces came too late to find all the flowers of Holland.

We pass through clusters of shanties and tents where city dwellers escape Newtown and old people dream their way into dry seas. The dikes are high and the thick grass is swarming with tiny, flying insects. At a small village I try *palling* for the first time and love it, but instinctively avoid the herring.

Margret, Maryke's warm, grave roommate, points out again and again the varying land and water levels of the countryside, as if fascinated by the idea of reclaimed land. Soon a large new area of the sea will be drained and settled to relieve the overcrowding in the Amsterdam area. Despite her relative difficulty of speaking in English, she points out various sociological, political and practical difficulties involved in such reclamation.

Later we four walk on the beach, two couples constantly changing to exchange impressions. Margret and I talk over historic perspectives, returning again and again to the German ethos. I give her my impressions of Cohn's *The Mind of Germany*, which she has not read; she recommends Mosse's *The Crisis of German Ideology*. In periods of silence, Rachel gathers seashells and pockets them. (I remember photographs of my childhood at Lake Johanna in central Florida: I am three, blond, in overhauls with a small bucket of shells clutched in one hand.) As we continue on, I become fascinated with throwing shells back into the shallow water.

Small groups in yellow windbreakers pass by us occasionally, singing. Margret says they are Germans, who flood northern Holland in the spring and summer months. From her tone I begin to understand the strength of the Dutch underground during Nazi occupation. The rhythms of her speech are indistinguishable from those of the waves at our feet.

Later, at Maryke and Margret's we eat good cheap Chinese food, and Maryke and I speak of translating her poetry for New York publication. We decide to correspond and begin work on a photography-poetry volume. She gives me a beautiful panoramic shot of Manhattan taken from the World Trade Towers. It is entitled "a memory of a memory."

We sleep that night on the floor, surrounded by photography and poems. I dream of black tulips growing near a red stream, and everywhere swans are singing abrupt, muted passages.

■

Monday night Peter takes us walking in Newmarkt, whose narrow, redbrick streets have become a nocturnal classroom for a generation of American and European undergraduates. Along the crowded, narrow sidewalks moustached figures (always dressed casually but expensively) whisper throatily that any desiderata is available. In the small windowed rooms facing the street all the black-lit forms of paradise stretch lazily and settle deeper into velvet cushions: small boats on a brick sea.

Rachel watches it all pass, fascinated, closely scrutinizing the whores. Her reflection in the panes contains a half-smile of self-discovery. Who would not want an existence of total pleasure: nights of constant, knowing surrender; days of sleep and shopping for new clothing. Who would not, in a passing moment, want such a life of passionate surrender on the narrow streets of Amsterdam? I watch her reflection in window after window, reaching through her narrowed eyes for Anne. She trips occasionally on the swollen brick street.

(Remembering kissing Rachel at *Schwarzer Bär* in Hanover, waiting for the bus and singing popular folk songs, near us two red-haired women spoke French and laughed softly in the cold night, *Hu Nunpa*/Two Legs laughing in the wind as he danced before the village maidens causing delight among the Lakota and the spirits, there in the flood of Hanover's bitter evening, moving sparking the everyday rhythms of Eire and France and old middle America, wrapped in each other's coats, lost to old lovers, living only in the immediate joy, the warmth of each other and the night's soft sounds, the many languages and meanings unvoiced, and kissing endlessly, laughing, smiling, singing through moist lips into each other of the loneliness of a foreign land, tasting tongues made dull by the strangeness of words forgotten and the first urges of rebirth in learning.)

Peter moves rapidly ahead of us from window to magazine shop to window, cat-like, constantly turning to observe us. He knows we are running on empty. His tone is both ironic and charming: Perhaps this will please you in our charming Amsterdam? Or perhaps we could purchase this for the lady? His irony is the price my generation pays for Chamberlain's blind naiveté. Empty, empty.

The sins of the father are not always visited on the sons. The second and third generations must struggle harder to realize their innate inheritance. My German friends, who are for the most part not artists, say that hatred still exists because "one generation is not enough to forget." But Peter has searched and knows that most of the Newmarkt drunks sleeping in their own excrement are Dutch, French, Belgian, and American, not German. His free dance through the neatly garish streets for two foreigners is graceful and sweet to me. I wish I could bring New York to him as he is bringing Amsterdam to me with his gently mocking dance through Newtown.

Later, as we cross *Prinsengracht* on the way to Peter's apartment, Linda Ronstadt's voice drifts from an attic window: "There's night life / it's like life / but there's no one else in it."

■

On Tuesday I decided to return to Hanover, then on to Berlin. (Rachel went on to Paris.) I felt I had to return to my studies. Although comparatively young for one establishing himself in my somewhat rarified occupation, I have felt time slipping away more rapidly since I turned thirty. I have come to opera late, but its demands are such that my restlessness and indecision have been somewhat quelled by it. It has also occurred to me that my restlessness may well be permanent.

The train ride back was dull: businessmen and grandmothers. At Hengelo where I changed trains a pedestrian had been struck by a car. It was hard to believe that the human body could so damage a machine of metal and glass. The windshield was completely shattered and the hood and right fender dented deeply. A young man with long brown hair and a thin beard is being carried into an ambulance, his forehead heavily taped, his right leg buried in an inflated splint. He mumbled in English. An hysterical travelling companion carried his backpack to the ambulance and got in beside him. In her other hand she waved two futile train tickets. I remembered seeing two other student travelers in new casts in the Amsterdam Bahnhof information line.

As the train pulled out from Hengelo, I realized I had left Maryke's gift in the luggage rack on the other train. Or was it gone before I gathered my things? I could not remember—the accident. I had addressed the envelope it was in, so perhaps someone will send it. Peter would say, "No, it's gone, no one will send it. Forget it."

But I cannot forget it, any more than I can forget Amsterdam. The photograph will return in time. If it does not, by then it will matter less. But I will not forget Amsterdam, and I write these words (though they too may finally be lost or useless) for myself first, because I feel—and I feel little enough—when I write. I write for the German People, because sometimes since Amsterdam I feel that among the Germans I know only the philosophers and artists have active conscience; and with Tillich the great tradition of German Philosophy died: too many books burned, too many families decimated, too many hearts burst.

I also write for Anne, whose voice makes us sit together, united in all nations, through the movie year after year. This movie and others, less worthy, will take on increasing importance in Europe in the next few decades. I am learning to understand that when my Dutch friends are shocked at my criticisms of Bergman's *The Serpent's Egg*, they are allowing their heart to over-rule their aesthetic judgement.

"It is beautiful," Maryke argues defensively, "every frame like a photograph!" And Peter says, with measured emphasis, "This film is very good. We must be reminded of these things. Now is the time for such films. These people are coming back!"

There is no reason to fear another Hitler. If for no other reason, the commercial style of western politics will not allow it. Once a product backfires, politicians and demagogues don't use the same methodology again. Whether the phrase is Hitler's or Nixon's, the public will simply laugh, and one can't be laughed at and win too often. The political paradigms of conflict, so firmly dictated by the superpowers, are too deep and cold now for another Hitler. His style, the essential bile of a spirit that has slouched its way intermittently from Toulon to Bucharest since the Thirty Year's War, now serves as a negative training ground, an obstacle course for international politicians, most of whom strive for the Dag Hammerskjold image: the broad intellect, the sensitive conversationalist.

My intellectual generation's pessimism concerning political solutions to human misery has allowed me to put little faith in political systems. The murder of our President, his younger brother, our greatest black pacifist, and others unsettled the foundation of faith in politics. When murder becomes chronic, something dies in the living who remain behind. Perhaps the sixties brought us a little taste of European history first hand. In the seventies, the purgation of Nixon Presidency served in large part only to emphasize the ideological profligacy of most major politicians in America.) But we absorb these outer signs, the verbal and physical gestures of these figures of "evil" or "unethical behavior," and we redesign our patterns of expectations, our criterion for the charisma requirements of our "new leaders": the next one won't be anything like Hitler.

And why bother anyone now with this unpleasantness? It is over. Perhaps not. The exiled Jews who have returned to Hanover and other metropolitan areas in Germany feel that the 1977-78 desecration of their cemeteries is only the beginning of a new cycle of hatred. Because of this, and other phenomena less obvious, Hitler's heritage should be a part of all our memories, or "collective conscience" if you will, a part of our post-Greek culture and our holy thought. We must carry him on our backs, live with him, understand him and through him the dark flowers of our own civilization. Like the Jewish hero of *The Man in the Glass Booth*, I now sing the responsibility for Hitler's sins. In this way I feel I am stronger, more pure in mind and free in body, and in this way I know—if I consciously analyze it—I am miming the guilt of my knowledge into expression, and will perhaps someday soon create art from it. It is for others to create new bombs.

Perhaps much of what I write about is not so, much of what I think I see is not there, and I invent guilt in order to create. I have a very real fear of being reductive in this regard. But I do know that when I cannot envision Annie, when I cease to find Rachel, Maryke, Peter, and Hitler within myself, I will cease to understand myself. Then my search will be over and Hitler will be free to appear again, and there will be more Annie. I sometimes dream of the turn of this century and Yeats's rough beast.

If I were locked up in a high, dark, room I would, like Borchert, scratch my words into the plaster.

Hanover, May 1978

9

FALLING OFF THE EARTH

Although I have been preoccupied with racism since my childhood in Georgia and southern Arkansas, my impression of it did not solidify until high school in the early 1960s. I began to understand the nature of the beast at Watson Chapel High School, which lies in what was then a semi-rural community on the outskirts of Pine Bluff, the second largest town in Arkansas. Pine Bluff was also 70% black and about 50% slum. It is located half way between Monticello, fifty miles to the south where I spent my boyhood, and Little Rock, the capital city, which lies 50 miles to the north. Between the ages of fourteen and nineteen I moved north over these one hundred miles from College Heights (Grade School) to Pine Bluff (high school) to Hendrix College just to the north of Little Rock. This northward migration was—as my Lakota friends would later tell me—a journey toward self-knowledge. One of the most important mirrors in which I was to study the changing images of my self and those close to me during this time was the racism that enclosed me like a dark cloud. This is the story of a troubled kid who fell off the edge of the earth in southern Arkansas and existed there for an endless time in reduced form, crushed down by what he came to think of as a kind of evil.

In 1957, Little Rock High School had been integrated, but there had still been no attempt to integrate my small high school outside of Pine Bluff by the time I was graduated in 1964. Long before this I had glimpsed through the crystal eye of childhood at the division of the races in southern society and the inherent physical and emotional violence that rural and semi-rural life in Arkansas seemed to foster. Racism appeared to most people I knew to simply be an ingrained fact of life, but I never assumed that it was natural or normal—things were supposed to be. For one thing, the New Testament said that things should be different. I knew the points of the fundamentalist sermons well: those who believed were equal in the sight of God and would have everlasting life, and those who did not would burn in hell. But life was peaceful around Monticello and College Heights with respect to racial violence; if life was hell for the Black workers in the area, it was a calm hell.

It was in high school at Watson Chapel, fifty miles to the north of the tall pines and pink tomatoes of the Louisiana border country that I was to experience the *nastiness* of southern racism. I choose the term *nastiness* because of its arresting connotations of childish fear, adolescent prudishness, and adult vileness. These qualities tainted most of the southern personalities I encountered during my formative years. In this group I place all of the politicians and businessmen with whom I had contact then, and most of the educators. I suspect Arkansas was no worse than any other Southern state at that time, and was probably better than some, but its racism was that particular combination of perversity and pride that misshapes young sensibilities. This was the case at every school in Arkansas I attended. At that time, Arkansas fell short of furnishing its youth with good examples. I found one or two, and they were enough to save me from the sickness surrounding me. Most of the young people I knew were, it seemed to me, sick unto death long before a treatment for the virulent disease of racism appeared in their lives.

My memories of the cultivation of social violence and racism in the south are interwoven, but I became aware of the violence seemingly inherent in southern society before the racism that still chews at my soul. Suppression and teasing thrive in the rural south, certainly at the schools where I attended. (I have since studied children, including my own, and this kind of viciousness and the need to degrade others is not inborn. They had to be carefully taught. Kids will be kids, but not like the kids I grew up with.) Junior High and high school students of both sexes worked out social and personal problems in behind-the-schoolhouse rituals of conflict, usually arranged and refereed by an acquaintance or friend. Often as I approached school at 7:30 a.m., I would see a loosely arranged circle of young males enclosing two wildly swinging youths. Darting in and out of the circle was the figure of the manipulator. This was the one who had probably instigated the fight, and now danced into the flexing circle he had created, half-coach and half-referee. There were white puffs of breath in the heavy November atmosphere and the dull grunts of blows landing to the torso echoed against the dull yellow bricks of the schoolhouse. Any resulting bruise or black eye was worn as a decoration.

Such fights could start for any reason. An older tough might pick a fight to release the tension of an argument with his father, coach or teacher. I was often challenged simply because my father was a teacher, or because I took my studies seriously. In grade school, outside Monticello, I managed to avoid direct conflict for some time, and when I finally did fight it was with my best buddy. After the coaches made boxing gloves available on the school grounds during regular school hours, Wayne, my only real grade school friend, and I once allowed ourselves to be goaded by one of two older bullies into sparring with each other. Wayne, a particularly good natured and gentle boy, was unwilling, but the older boys forced him into the worn gloves with shame and shoving. I also gave in to their insistence more easily than the good-natured Wayne. The older boy pushed us into each other again and again, and we pretended to punch each other. Finally, we were allowed to go our way. To be manipulated like this was debasing, but it could have been far worse. We were, after all, only thirteen years old, and we were whites among whites. Still, he had been my best friend.

Schoolyard fighting was a sport, an instrument of social equality and a release from the nightmarish amount of aggression generated by southern society—the last Pentecostal fortress, the last bastion of Puritanism in the United States. Schoolyard violence was accepted by students and parents as simply the way things were, like the townsfolk in *The Lottery* accept the drawing from the worn black box. It was just the way things were or had always been. Then when I was fourteen, we moved to Pine Bluff, and there, in the more pronounced mixture of urban and rural that typified Watson Chapel, the conflicts took on a more serious tone; weapons, for example, were used more often than in College Heights, and the words *death* and *kill* wormed their way into the threats, including those that led to fights which at this school occurred "across the highway."

When I was a junior, an 18-year-old eighth grader threatened to kill me "if I ever crossed the highway" because he "didn't like the way I looked." This was at the time a very popular goad. I believe to this day that only the serious intervention of my friend Don Pyatt saved me from at the very least a bloody beating. Don's fiery red hair, hair trigger temper, and formidable bulk must have seemed an unlikely complement for the stringy 95 pounds that hung on my six-foot frame. This friendship is one of the indelible memories of my high school years. It was the fellowship of Don and a small group of young men that pulled me through the fights and degradation of the "educational" experience Arkansas had to offer. And then there were the sweet, prudish Southern girls, caught between the sultry desires so evident in their hallway strut between classes and the Sunday school rules driven into them since birth by their mothers, who were as often as not sixteen to eighteen years older than their daughters.

And there were a few teachers who helped me grow. But these teachers didn't talk about the fights that were so real and threatening to me as a student; and there was no talk about the fights that were so real and threatening to me as a student; and there was no talk about racism among them. In a way I'm glad. What if those one or two who were so incredibly important to me had admitted condoning the racism that most of my teachers openly embraced? Racism hit me hard at Watson Chapel, and from all directions.

Integration in Arkansas (and the South) officially began in Arkansas at Little Rock in 1957 when Governor Orville Faubus' State Police and President Dwight David Eisenhauer's National Guard circled each other in the schoolyard at Little Rock High School. At this time I was in the fifth grade at Drew Central Elementary School at College Heights, one hundred miles to the south. Even in grade school I heard talk, mostly in the form of jokes, about "Niggers." I had no contact with Blacks at school or on the adjacent college campus where my father taught. There were of course no black students there to have contact with.

After we moved to a rural community about a mile from school, I got to know the rural black workers who harvested crops and dug wells in the area. I began to talk to them as they worked, and after a time I worked with them picking cotton and doing odd jobs. I liked their gentle humor, music and food. I liked them because they accepted me for what I was: a skinny kid who liked reading and listening to others, but who didn't say much. With them it was okay to be quiet, okay just to sit and watch and think. I felt accepted by that rural black community, and the peaceful, laid-back quality of their life seemed to me a chance to relax and learn. My first real thinking occurred at this time—as I shared meals with Southern black laborers at lunchtime or suppertime and relaxed with them after work. I was able to see myself as they did, as an individual who had a natural place in the world. They were an accurate mirror, a mirror reflecting what I thought to be natural rather than social values, a mirror without distortion. I was just a kid who read and thought, one in whom reflexive thought was awakening. I felt then that they understood and found this acceptable. I was neither patronized nor excluded; I was simply let be, and included when I wanted to be. I was able to be myself. It was okay to be a white kid among them. My need to learn and to experience unquestioning companionship were two very human matters they understood perfectly and shared with me. I was treated as an equal in a community of brothers and sisters. I did not experience this sense of equality anywhere else at the time—certainly not at school.

This occurred between the ages of eight and thirteen. It still seems strange to me that I was never castigated by the adults of College Heights who knew of my interaction with the black community of laborers and their families. Perhaps it was thought that no harm would come of it because the blacks down there "knew their place." Maybe they thought my behavior was beneath comment, unworthy of their concern. But when I moved to Watson Chapel to begin the eighth grade, my associations with blacks elicited a very different violent reaction.

After moving to Watson Chapel, I worked summers and weekends at a nearby egg farm. Its violations of minimum wage laws and unsafe working conditions—at sixteen I injured my back permanently hoisting crates in an ice locker—is secondary in my mind to this small company's general fair and equal treatment of black employees. Among the blacks who worked there was my friend Jim, a veteran of Korea and a member of the Arkansas National Guard. Jim was a good, kind young man, who was quick to laugh amidst the hard work. We made delivery runs together on slow days and sometimes I dropped him off home on my last run of the day. One day when we went by my high school, we were forced off the road by a group of seniors and burning cigarettes were thrown in our faces. I wanted to call the police, but Jim absolutely refused. The next day in school someone held a lit cigarette to my neck. I still have a tough little semi-circular scar there below my left ear.

Aggressive driving and fistfighting were not the only informal sports in the Arkansas school system. There were other ways to prove your manhood. The most offensive was a variation of *chicken*, where two cars jousted by rushing headlong at each other, one car *chickening out* before the collision, but passing as close to the other as possible. The other sport was simple and depended on several factors: a speeding car, a brick or pipe held at the end of a hand outstretched from the car, and the absence of sidewalks in the slum areas of Pine Bluff so that pedestrians were forced to walk in the street. This sport was called *nigger-knocking* and only the most daring men on campus risked it. The reasoning that justified this sport was simple: if the fathers could don white hoods and blowtorch *uppity niggers*, who was going to begrudge the sons a little youthful fun down in *niggertown*?

It is from the very existence of this sport that the extreme importance of personal dignity became obvious to me. At the same time the plethora of social forces that dedicated themselves to the diminishment of Southern blacks became equally apparent to me. I knew hate in others; I learned to hate.

By the eleventh grade, it seemed to me that I was suffocating in the dark hallways and yellowed classrooms of Watson Chapel. I grew to despise school and hated going there. I dreaded seeing the small groups of students who would gather on the schoolgrounds before school and talk in hushed, seemingly reverential tones about their or some else's forays into *niggertown*, whispering about how many *niggers* had been *knocked* the night before, whether the daring heroes had been pursued, and other details of the sport. Later, many of these young men would use the same tone when they were debriefed after hellish patrols in Vietnam, where they found their very lives were in the hands of black soldiers. The sport that was being developed to a fine art in Vietnam during the early 60s was *American-knocking*. Education is a never-ending experience, and often generational in essence: the sin or grace of the father is visited upon the child.

Two events occurred during my junior year at Watson Chapel that derailed me and made my remaining time in Arkansas hateful. These events occurred in realms that seemed worlds away from me, but penetrated me in such a way that they crushed me into a corner of myself I had not known existed.

The first event occurred on the day President John F. Kennedy was assassinated. The news was brought to my English class by my dear history teacher, Mrs. Reagan. She appeared in the doorway like a ghost and sobbed, *President Kennedy has been shot in Dallas.*

I will never understand what happened then. With the exception of a few of us who were struck dumb—my mental image was of Abraham Lincoln falling forward heavily in his theater seat—the entire class rose to their feet and cheered loudly. This went on for some time, but after a while my English teacher hushed the class—by this time some of us were crying or in shock—and said grimly, *If I'd've known they were going to do it, I'd've bought 'em the bullets!* Her face was drawn up into a simian mask, with eye openings slicing through heavily rouged cheeks. Her false teeth were perfectly even, her green-grey eyes glittered joyfully. The class cheered even more loudly. It was the first time I had seen her genuinely pleased about anything. I glanced over at Susan Bradley, who stared at me out of a deep shock, her eyes hollow with incomprehension. I remember the rest of that day in great detail, from the instant I slumped forward in my seat from the force of Mrs. Reagan's words to the time alone in my dark room that night when I attempted to get out my thoughts in verse for the first time.

The second incident involved the attempted integration of nearby White Hall High School, another satellite school on the outskirts of Pine Bluff. This attempt failed. Don Pyatt and I found out about the failure by word of mouth in one of the tight, whispering groups that formed before school. The younger brother of one of the boys who had run Jim and me off the road that day told Don and me that both the black girls, who were sisters, had been taken from the school by force the day before and their faces slashed and their n-s cut off. This was the first time that the nasty stench of racial violence filled my senses. I first began to conceive of the presence of evil in the world, and to feel that some actions place the perpetrator outside the realm of forgiveness. The stories of hangings, blowtorchings, and *nigger-knocking* no longer seemed far away. They never would again. I can still see Don bucking back, head high and eyes blazing in his powerful stiff-necked way, from the picture those words formed in him. I still clench my hands and cling to concrete ideas so as not to fall off the face of the earth when I think of it.

These words had a violence and a force of truth that words have rarely had for me since. So I understand those who now argue that language is a violent medium and that western metaphysics—language, history, philosophy, and thought—is too faulty and violence-prone to be allowed to go on as it is. The reportage of the horrors of this century have driven us both to depend upon language as the only potential messenger of the unimaginable horrors man has perpetuated on man in our time, and at the same time to despise it as the medium of this horror. We want to say, *Let he who delivers this message die.* Better yet, say the deconstructionists, let the medium of the message itself die. We are slaves to language. We hate it as the southern slave hated and feared the master, and the countless victims of terrorism in the last twenty years have feared and fear the terrorist.

After graduation at Watson Chapel, I attended Hendrix College at Conway—thirty miles north of Little Rock—for one year. As freshmen we were hazed unmercifully. The South is nothing if not reductive. Like Iktome, the spider man of the Lakota mythic universe who reduces all men and women to hungry paradigms of frustration and rage or passive slaves, the Southern mentality drove me painfully into myself. My sophomore year of college, I began study at Southern Illinois University at Carbondale. We lived in Carterville, a few miles from Carbondale. No blacks lived inside the Carterville city limits, and blacks were not allowed in town after dark. How far north of "Bloody Williamson" County did I have to go, I began to wonder, to find some relief from this sickness? The answer is still not clear to me.

Where were the Medicine Men and healers who brought us through this, who fell forward and bucked back? They were there throughout the entirety of the quiet horror: the black workers who took in a lonely white kid, teachers like Mrs. Reagan, friends like Don Pyatt—all those whose elemental decency overcame their desire for acceptance among their peers, and somehow in themselves. I was attracted to the blacks of my childhood world as the other, equally lonely and estranged spirits looking for a truth not yet recognized in the fallen world where we found ourselves.

Hanover 1979

2

LAKOTA TRILOGY

These essays examine *lakol wicohan*, the Lakota Way or perspective on life, as it was before the white man came, as it was during the period of conflict with the white man, and as it exists in the hungry present. The first essay will trace the metamorphosis of Lakota culture through the past one hundred years. The second and third essays will serve as brief introductions to Lakota literature and music.

LAKOTA HISTORY AND CULTURE
Before the White Man
A Brief History

A century ago the Lakota Nation was a great nation. Its realm included parts of what are now the states of Nebraska, South Dakota, Wyoming, and Montana. Its borders were formed by the Platte River in the south and the Heart River in the north, the Missouri River in the east and the Big Horn Mountains in the West.[i]

The Lakota or Teton Sioux ("Dwellers of the Prairie") were the westernmost division of the Great Sioux Nation, as distinguished from the Nakota who lived in the central part of the region and from the Dakota who lived in the easternmost part of the region. The main difference between these three divisions—then and now—is that they speak different dialects of the Sioux language.

Between 1650 and 1680, small bands of Sioux moved westward from the Mille Lacs region in what is now Minnesota. They were under pressure from the combined forced of the Cree and Assiniboine, who were supplied with guns by the French. They were also attracted by the great herds of buffalo that roamed the plains. The Sioux, until then a more sedentary hunting-gathering people, became a nomadic hunting and warring society.

Although nomadic, the bands of the western Sioux Nation, the Lakota, assembled each summer to decide matters of national importance and to give the Sun Dance, the most sacred of ceremonies.[ii] It was a complicated ritual, involving many rites. It was a gathering for all people of the western Sioux Nation, not an assembly of representatives. This summer meeting symbolized the unity of the Sioux people. These gathering gave the entire Sioux Nation cohesion and force in affairs of the Plains Indians. It was also a time when dancers received visions for which they were greatly honored.

As the Sioux secured territory to the west, they became great warriors in the plains. They carved out a territory from lands previously held by the Omaha, Ponca, Arikara, Kiowa, Cheyenne, and Crow. To secure this land and to keep control of it, they make war a way of life.

The Sioux culture was exposed to two powerful stimuli in the 18th century: the horse and the gun. Together they enabled the ambitious Sioux men to become great hunters and the world's most renowned mounted warriors.

The horse had been introduced to the New World by the Spaniards. By 1742 the Sioux had horses. Within fifty years the horse was fully integrated into the ultimate pattern of the Sioux culture. Not only was the highly trained horse an essential part of the hunter's skill and warrior's tactics, but it was a primary medium of exchange and a symbol of prestige. The Sioux people became more nomadic, wealthier in terms of goods derived from the environment, and more powerful militarily by fully exploiting the horse.[iii]

Some Sioux had muzzle-loaders by 1700. Soon they were using them as potent weapons in inter-tribal warfare. Firearms were of little value to Sioux horsemen in hunting, however, for the skittish buffalo stampeded at a musket's boom. The Sioux technique of hunting was to ride among the herd, killing effectively with the quiet bow and arrow and with the lance.

Stimulated by almost simultaneous acquisition of the gun and the horse, and located in the heart of the northern buffalo range, the Sioux way of life burst into a magnificence that lasted nearly a century. After 1750, the Sioux were a plains society whose existence depended on the buffalo. From its carcass they got food, from its bones they made tools, from its hide they made clothing and teepees. The vital importance of the buffalo caused the Sioux to consider him a symbol of the virtue Generosity. *Tatanka*, the buffalo, was a great provider and the basis of Sioux socio-economic existence.

Drastic changes occurred in Sioux society in the late 19th century. They came about through the unforeseeably and (for the Sioux) unbelievably powerful force of the white conqueror, who killed the buffalo in such great numbers that it disappeared almost entirely and who fenced in the land for farming or claimed it for mining. Finally, even the sacred soil of the Black Hills was torn up for gold. For the Lakota, the Black Hills were the dwelling place of the sacred spirits. The Treaty of 1868 had promised protection of the Holy Road—the road used by the Lakota to reach *Paha Sapa*, the sacred Black Hills—and of the hills themselves. The bloodiest Indian-white struggle was caused when whites violated this particular aspect of Red Cloud's treaty of 1868.

Then the white man came in overwhelming numbers and even the Lakota's most desperate defense was of no avail. With the buffalo's death, the Lakota way of life was drastically changed. With the military defeat, Lakota pride and self-assurance were undermined.

Character and Religion
The Old Way[iv]

The Sioux were and are a very religious people. One of the most important of the seven sacred ceremonies of the Oglalav was called the *Hanblecheya*, Crying Out for a Vision. An understanding of this ceremony can lead to some understanding of the Lakota religion.

The ceremony Hanblecheya is very old. The Oglala Holy Man Black Elk once remarked, "It is at the center of our religion, for from it we receive many good things." The brave Lakota boy must fast alone for four days in an isolated place without shelter or clothing, praying constantly in hope of receiving a sign of power from the spirits.

First, the boy who goes for a vision seeks the advice of an elder of the band, one trained in the ways of knowledge. This very honored man can teach the boy the ancient ways, the holy ways of the sacred powers who created the universe and all that is in it. The boy had probably already learned much from the elders of the band and from the warriors. On long winter nights he heard myths of the creation of the world, legends of heroes, and stories of mysterious, powerful spirits. From these narratives he has learned the manners and morals of his people. He has learned their history, both physical and spiritual.

Since he was a small child, the boy has also played rough games which have conditioned him for the hardships of plains life. He has been encouraged since boyhood to be brave at all times. He has endured many hardships to win the respect of his friends. He has begun to form close friendships; one friend in particular he will call *kola* (best friend), and will swear to sacrifice his life for that friend if he is in need.

From the warriors of the band, he has learned the skills of hunting and warfare. Under the observation of proven warriors, he has learned the skills of weaponry, not just the use of weapons, but the art of crafting his own from rough wood, flint, sinew, bone, and feathers so that his arrows will fly hard and straight. He has been trained to be hunter and a warrior: he will provide for his people, enrich them with horses, and protect them by warfare. He has hardened his body to pain and his emotions to fear. He is not yet fifteen years old.

At this crucial time, the boy who seeks a vision begins the spiritual journey of his Hanblecheya to pray to *Wakan Tanka*, the Great Mystery and all-pervasive force, for a vision and a sign. If he is given a vision and a sign, he will receive his secret name, a name determined by an old Holy Man, who will interpret the young man's vision. The most important sign will be in the form of an animal: an eagle, hawk, swallow, elk, deer, or buffalo. Each animal possesses a special power; each represents some particular spirit. Such a sign determines into which dream society the youth will be initiated. This society will greatly influence his development as a warrior and leader.

The Lakota world is peopled not only by men and animals, but by Wakan Tanka, and by the sixteen major and minor spirits who are his elements. Here is a diagram of these sixteen aspects of Wakan Tanka:

Wi	Skan	Maka	Inyan
Sun	*Sky*	*Earth*	*Rock*
Hanwi	Tate	Whope	Wakinyan
Moon	*Wind*	*Beautiful One*	*Thunderer*

Tatanka	Mahto	Tatetob	Yumni
Buffalo	*Bear*	*Four Winds*	*Whirlwind*
Nagi	Niya	Nagila	Sicun
Soul	*Conscience*	*Soul-Spirit*	*Charisma*

The major aspects of Wakan Tanka Himself are centered around the sacred number four. There are four superior, or higher aspects of Wakan Tanka: Wi, Skan, Maka, and Inyn. Inyan is the oldest, then Maka, then Skan, and then Wi. But in the order first given above, they can be seen as Chief (Wi), Spirit (Skan), Creator (Maka), and Director (Inyan). There is a secondary group of four which are the counterparts of the first group. Hanwi, Tate, Whope, and Wakinyan. The third group is Tatanka, Mahto, Tatetob, and Yumni. The final group is Nagi, Niya, Nagila, and Sicun. Wakan Tanka has four times four, or sixteen, primary aspects.

Each of these sixteen aspects represents the activities of Wakan Tanka as directed to distinct or specialized purposes. But we must never forget that they are only various aspects of Him. As the animating powers of the visible and invisible world, they form a single limited being or force: Wakan Tanka.[vi]

Many of the powers which are the elements of Wakan Tanka play important roles in Lakota literature. These characters will be discussed in more detail in the essay "Lakota Literature."

To understand the religion of the old way is difficult now, but vitally important. Art Raymond, in an attempt to clarify misinterpretations, offers these remarks:

"Our religion, before it was corrupted by the White Man's version of Christianity with hell and damnation, etc., held that the Great Spirit was everywhere and in everything. The Great Spirit is in you and in me; he is in the four-leggeds, and in the two-leggeds. To say less is to deny the infinity of the Great Spirit.

"Thus Wakan Tanka exists in the beautiful birth of a New Day. As the brilliant colors of dawn are splashed across the sky, THAT is the Great Spirit. A buffalo, or a rabbit; a certain mountain, or the song of a holy cottonwood tree IS the Great Spirit.

"The Great Spirit is in all things and in all persons. Thus it was that in our rituals and in our ceremonies we made our supplications of praise and of thanksgiving, of need and of sorrow, often conducting those rituals through or using the White Buffalo or a certain mountain or cottonwood tree. We did not then, nor do we now, believe that the buffalo, the dawn, the mountain, the wind or the whatever was God or a god. We did then and we do now believe that the Great Spirit is everywhere and in all things."[vii]

According to Lakota belief, a man must know and accept his place in the nature of things, the great circle of life, before he can receive understanding. A boy who would seek a vision would seek an understanding that involved knowledge of and an ability to interpret natural forces. The sign the boy seeks will unlock his ability to read nature's messages. He must learn to observe and analyze, but also interpret. Science (understanding how nature works) and religion (understanding nature's purposes) are not separate for the Lakota—they are one. Both lead to a fuller comprehension of the world in which the Lakota people live. This understanding begins with observation and ends in belief.

To illustrate, consider two extremely important figures in Lakota life: the Holy Man, *Wichasha Wakan*; and the Medicine Man, *Wichasha Wapiya*. Each is both priest and doctor. Each heals in various ways—according to his personal power. Their healing is both physical and spiritual.

Both these men are greatly honored and respected, and are very powerful in matters of governing. They serve as examples for others, especially the young, due to their high status and accomplishments. They are usually of high birth and respected family. This was true of the Hunkpapa Wishasha Wakan *Tatanka Yotanka*, better known as Sitting Bull. But high birth is not always required of those who rise to positions of honor. It was not required, for example, of the Oglala warrior and statesman Red Cloud.

Both Wakan and Wapiya Men are likely good hunters and brave warriors; both belong to a dream or warrior society (more is said of such societies in the third section of this essay); both have gone on successful Hanblecheyas; and both have danced the sacrificial Sun Dance to prove the spiritual strength of their commitment to their religion and to their people. Both men present and take part in sacred ceremonies to constantly prove their spiritual and physical strength to their people. All Lakota men aim at doing all of the above—few succeed.

The Wachasha Wapiya or Medicine Man has a practical and useful knowledge of roots and herbs, can cure many diseases and comfort many pains. He can set bones. His practical knowledge keeps many injured or sick people alive and healthy.

The Wakan or Holy Man is full of wisdom, is an excellent advisor, can deduce signs from natural occurrences, and can do many wonderful and supernatural things. The Wachasha Wakan can also accurately predict from visions, can interpret dreams. This is especially important, since the Lakota believe that power comes to a man in his visions as dreams. Once power is obtained, it becomes as much a part of the individual as his body or personality.[viii]

Both Men have a great power in common: the power to heal the spirit or soul, to drive away evil. Evil, for the Indian, is a lesser force than good, but both are parts of the Great Mystery, Wakan Tanka. Through their personal power to communicate with the spirits. Holy Men and Medicine Men are able to recognize and defeat evil. Communication with the spirits comes only to those men who understand the individual nature of all animals and things, and who sacrifice themselves in sacred ceremonies.

The Lakota believe all natural things contain spirit-like qualities: *nagi* or personality, *niya* or vitality, *nagila* or essence, and *sicun* or power (refer to the illustration of the sixteen aspects of Wakan Tanka, earlier in a part of this essay). All things have symbolic importance. When a creature, especially an animal or bird, appears in a dream or vision (a waking dream), it is considered an important sign which should be interpreted by an elder who understands the nature and power of Wakan Tanka.

A Wichasha Wakan knows the colors red, blue, green, and yellow signify the sun, the sky, the earth, and the rock. Black might represent evil or ignorance. A Holy Man knows that there are two great roads of direction, the Red Road and the Black Road, in the sacred circle of existence. The Red Road of good runs from south to north. It is the road to wisdom and purification. The Black Road runs away from the enlightenment of the east to the destructive darkness of the west. In the center of the circle, good and evil cross. It is the center of the circle that the mature Lakota seeks. In this center he has knowledge of both good and evil, but has the personal power derived from his vision to choose correctly to avoid or defeat evil.

Lakota rituals and ceremonies are patterned after the realities of the universe. They celebrate natural powers. The greatest ceremony is the Sun Dance, which is danced in a circle surrounding a cottonwood pole. The circular Sun Dance lodge surrounding the pole stands for the season and months. In this circle, the Sun Dance dancers dance while staring at the sun. Both the Sun Dance and Hanblecheya are designed to open the individual to the signs of spirit forces through visions. The Lakota religion is a moral system in which good clearly outweighs evil. It sets forth virtues to aim for and punishes their disregard. These virtues play an important role in determining an individual's status, since religion is fully integrated into the Lakota's total world.

The Conflict

The four great virtues of the Lakota existed in strict form long before conflict with the white man started, but they were put to new tests by the destructive wars following 1866. The four virtues were an important part of the Lakota man's existence, especially if he had ambition to be a leader of his people.

There was a very pronounced hierarchy, or sense of order and rules of leadership among the bands of the Sioux Nation, as there was a strict hierarchy concerning all social, political, religious, and military activity. The great leaders of the Sioux Nation met once a year to formulate national policy and to approve or disapprove actions taken by the leaders of individual bands during the year. These men were powerful because of their prestige and honor, and the respect such honor afforded from all men. Theoretically, these men were the ultimate authority for the Lakota.

In practice, however, each band of the nation functioned as an independent unit. Each band was under the authority of four leaders or "shirt-wearers." An individual could become shirt-wearer in his band only if he was of great personal merit and, usually, of good family. High birth afforded honor, but many specific factors determined greatness of merit: skill in hunting, fame as a warrior, presentation of ceremonies, and exhibition of generosity. The man who satisfied these requirements was respected by all members of the nation. Such a man's behavior was expected to reflect his people's way. Status had privilege, but entailed responsibility.

There were two kinds of men's societies that kept order in the various bands, and who governed them: societies that enforced Lakota law known as *Akichitas*, which were open to all eligible young men; and societies that were governing bodies, the *Nachas*, composed of elders.[ix] Akichitas kept order, punished law-breakers, and ensured that each person was adequately supplied with food. Nachas advised the younger warriors and hunters.

A man who had committed murder or adultery, the two greatest crimes to the Lakota people, was ineligible for membership in either kind of group. To be invited to join an Akichita group, a man must have been on at least one war party or have received his vision on Hanblecheya. If he was from an outstanding family, had counted coup (struck an enemy), or had already exhibited supernatural power, he might be admitted at an early age, sixteen to twenty years old. Two factors were considered in determining whether a man was worthy of membership in a Nacha: the accomplishments of youth and the wisdom of maturity.

Both societies held the four virtues as ideals. Generosity, bravery, fortitude, and wisdom were interdependent ideals. An understanding and practice of these virtues gave the warrior great power to control forces of evil by being one with all living things and by understanding their relations to the spirits. The virtues are associated with directions.

For example, the west is Wakinyan's direction, the direction of the "great" Thunder Spirit and of *Wakinyan*. It is the power of Wakinyan to create and to destroy. The west is the land of opposites and conflicts. Wakinyan

25

causes both cleansing rain and the damaging lightning and hail. He is the ruler of the winged kingdom: whirlwinds and the winged peoples are his messengers. Only a brave man dreams of Wakinyan, for such a dreamer must become a *heyoka*, one who acts in a manner contrary to normal all his life.[x]

Each animal is not only itself, but also a spirit that brings signs and messages. Before a Lakota hunter kills any animal, he says a prayer of thanks and asks forgiveness of the spirit of the animal he is about to kill, for he recognizes that all creatures are equal in the circle of existence. He knows that he himself will provide food for the animal in the ultimate pattern of the circle.

"It is better to die on the battlefield than to live to be old." This is an old maxim. Once the Lakota man could prove his bravery in war, other military activities, and hunting. This is today no longer possible, but he can still prove his fortitude through participation in the sacred ceremonies, principally the Hanblecheya and the Sun Dance. Both ceremonies involve self-inflicted pain and suffering: both demand tremendous strength and endurance.

The Lakota man is taught to be brave from earliest childhood with stories and games, but bravery is also a way of life—a reality. In early times, courting death was as important a part of war as achieving victory. Men who struck or touched an enemy were said to have "counted coup." Counting coup often substituted for killing the enemy. Just touching the enemy (whether or not he was ultimately killed) was a sign of great bravery. It was a dangerous maneuver in a deadly game. The Lakota warrior sang his death song, *Ich'ilowain*, his acceptance of the fate of the brave ones, before he entered the field of battle.

Although military encounters offered the Lakota man opportunity to demonstrate the virtue of bravery or valor, the opportunity for him to demonstrate fortitude was and is confined to the sacred ceremonies. Fortitude is exhibited in a willingness to withstand self-inflicted discomfort and pain without visible sign of emotional stress. Men on war or hunting missions were expected to suffer the pain of wounds soundlessly and to endure long periods of hunger and exposure without complaint. These are not, however, considered acts of fortitude.

The Lakota shows his fortitude when he voluntarily seeks and endures physical pain during sacred occasions such as the Sun Dance and the burial ceremony or during private fasts. During the mid-summer Sun Dance, a man has the opportunity to dance in concert with others around the great ceremonial pole to which he is tied with a sinew rope which passes under slits cut in his chest muscles. A dancer shows great fortitude who pulls so long and so hard on the rope that it tears loose. During a burial ceremony, a man may cut off the first joint of his little finger to show through fortitude his respect for the dead.

Fortitude, the virtue of the western direction, is the virtue needed for such feats of patience and endurance. Acts of fortitude present greater psychological challenge and require more control than acts of bravery because the individual has prior knowledge of the pain and discomfort certain to come.

These dramatic expressions of fortitude or endurance have day-to-day counterparts in a kind of quiet dignity and reserve. Personal relations are very low-key and to white men may seem noncommittal. Eyes are kept downcast because eye-to-eye glances, even among the closest of friends might be a source of embarrassment. White men may call this type of behavior stoical.

Proceeding in a clockwise direction, White is the color of the north and Wisdom is its virtue. The north also involves purification and cleansing. North is the direction of maturity and knowledge. The animal figure of the north may be White Buffalo. Wazi, the giant who creates snowstorms with his laughter also lives in the North. He loves to laugh at the mouse's stories.

The color of the east is usually the red of sunrise. East is the direction of creation and spiritual knowledge. There things are born and begin life's journey. The circle of tipis is always open to the east in tribal gatherings. East is also the source of light, enlightenment. The animal most associated with the East is the most sacred of all creatures, the Eagle. A single feather from this great spirit of the air carried enormous prestige.

Yellow or gold is the color normally identified with the south in Lakota culture. Generosity is the virtue of the south. The Elk Ceremony, a ritual celebration of fertility and abundance, is performed in the southerly direction. Generosity and sharing are insisted on in Lakota culture. The Lakota frequently stated: "A man must help others as much as possible, no matter who, by giving them horses, food, or clothing." To accumulate property for its own sake is disgraceful. The more one gives, the greater his prestige and honor. This way of thinking meant that no member of the band had to go without. Giving is of two types: spontaneous gift-giving, to those in need; and the formal, dramatic "giveaway." The south is the land of Generosity, reproduction and gentleness.

More History

The old way was almost destroyed by white men. An examination of the events leading to the Sioux surrender and confinement on reservations is necessary for anyone who wishes to be aware of the white man's largely successful attempt to suppress the Sioux Nation's religion and to eradicate its way of life.

In 1866, two years after the massacre of five hundred Cheyenne at Sand Creek by Colorado volunteers, the Oglala Chief Red Cloud began his war on white men. Red Cloud's forces fought well enough that by 1868 United States officials in Washington, D.C., wanted peace. The treaty Red Cloud signed promised the Lakota a reservation that included all of what would become South Dakota west of the Missouri River. This territory included the Black Hills, the sacred Paha Sapa, dwelling place of the sacred spirits. The Lakota had won their first and also their last war against the United States.

In 1874 and 1875, General George A. Custer, presumably acting on orders from his superiors, violated the terms of the Treaty of 1868 by leading a geological and surveying expedition into the Black Hills. In ensuing years, Custer and his army supported the settlers who violated the treaty's terms in seeking gold and possession of the rich reservation land. The Lakota resisted such settlements with armed force.

Generals Crook and Custer met the widespread Plains Indian uprising with a large expeditionary force. General Crook was met by superior Native American forces under the command of the Oglala war leader and visionary Crazy Horse on the banks of the Rosebud River and was soundly defeated. Custer's immediate command was destroyed at Little Big Horn by the combined forces of the Sioux, Cheyenne, and warriors from other tribes under the spiritual leadership of Sitting Bull, Tatanka Yotanka.

After Custer's annihilation, which occurred a few days before the Fourth of July 1876, the Plains Indians knew that whites would seek revenge. They scattered to the north and west like oak leaves in autumn. Crazy Horse was captured and murdered. Fourteen long years of wandering in hunger and despair followed. Forced submission to reservation confinement facilitated the destruction of new religious hope under white military rule, and allowed revenge for Custer's death to take open, violent form at Wounded Knee, South Dakota.

In these fourteen years of pursuit and confinement, a great demoralization occurred. The cruel betrayal and subsequent murder of several Sioux military and religious leaders was one factor which led directly to the tragedy of Wounded knee. The murder of Tatanka Yotanka, Sitting Bull, whose death must be attributed to the religious and military crises precipitated by the phenomenon of the Ghost Dance, was the most important single event.

The Ghost Dance was the central image and ceremony of a new religious movement which had gained much force among the Plains Indians in the late 1880's. This religion had its origin in a Paiute prophet, Wovoka. It prophesied the return of religious and military power to the Indian Nations and the obliteration of white civilization. The Ghost Dance doctrine preached nonviolence and brotherly love. It called for no action except dancing and singing. The Messiah would bring about the resurrection. The buffalo would return. The white military complex feared that the promise of the Ghost Dance religion would result in open rebellion on the reservation. These fears, similar to those which led to the capture and murder of the military leader Crazy Horse on September 5, 1877, gathered with seemingly inevitable and tragic force around the great Hunkpapa Holy Man, Sitting Bull.

All Ghost Dancing had been forbidden under martial law in the autumn of 1890. Yet it was rumored that Sitting Bull would lead his people in a great Ghost Dance. This rumor brought more troops to the reservation to put down the uprising which might result from Sitting Bull's decision to dance. In such a dance, those who wore Ghost Dance shirts would become invincible to white man's bullets. It was Sitting Bull who had designed the Battle of Little Big Horn. His decision to dance would have great effect.

On December 15, 1890, the great chief was taken from his house at Standing Rock, where, after a series of confusing episodes, he was shot in the head and killed. Soon after this useless and disgraceful murder, Big Foot, a clan leader and ghost dancer, led his band northwest. (Several bands had resisted federal government orders demanding settlement on reservations, until starvation and disease forced them finally to comply. It was this spirit of resistance and fear of outright murder by soldiers that prompted Big Foot to flee after Sitting Bull's Death.) Two weeks later, on December 29, 1890, in dead of winter, this band was forced by soldiers under Major Samuel Whiteside to camp at Wounded Knee Creek. Emaciated, demoralized and bitter, they set up camp and were surrounded by army forces. The situation was a tinderbox of anguish and tension.

A shot fired while soldiers were disarming the warriors set off a massacre which left over three hundred Indian people dead. Although no military justification was given, Sioux men, women, and children were killed indiscriminately. Twenty-five soldiers were killed and thirty-nine wounded, most of them struck by their own forces' bullets or shrapnel.

Black Elk, the Oglala Wishasha Wakan, remembered the day of Wounded Knee and what it meant to the Lakota people:

"And so it was all over.

I did not know then how much was ended. When I look back now from this high hill of my old age, I can still see the butchered women and children lying heaped and scattered all along the crooked gulch as plain as when I saw them with eyes still young. And I can see that something else died there in the bloody mud, and was buried in the blizzard. A people's dream died there. It was a beautiful dream.

And I, to whom so great a vision was given in my youth,—you see me now a pitiful old man who has done nothing, for the nation's hoop is broken and scattered. There is no center any longer, and the sacred tree is dead."[xi]

The Hungry Present

As we have mentioned, the color of the east is yellow or red, i.e. the morning star or rising sun. Wisdom is the quality of the east, and the fourth great virtue. It is the virtue hardest to describe. Generosity, bravery, and fortitude can be displayed, but wisdom for the Lakota implies far more than just intelligence. It implies power from the supernatural. We have seen this in the case of the Wichasha Wakan, who receives powerful insight from the supernatural. Wisdom involves the ability to get along with others, to arbitrate disputes, to instill confidence as a leader of war parties or as an advisor of young men. Those who are truly wise perform the sacred ceremonies. They are thought to have the power of helping others and their word comes as if from the spirits. Few members of the band are considered truly wise.

Sitting Bull was considered a man of wisdom and was greatly respected as a holy man of the Sioux Nation. He was a strong leader among his people. During his lifetime, the Sioux both reached their zenith and were driven to the depths. In 1860 they were rulers of the plains; but by 1890 they were prisoners of war, confined to reservations. Sitting Bull, unlike Black Elk, saw only the beginning of the destruction of his people. Perhaps death was kind because it did not allow him to see the continuing phenomenon of the destruction of his people's culture.

The destruction began with the slaughter of the buffalo herds, which provided the Lakota with so much essential to their way of life. The source of the customary food, clothing, shelter, and tools was destroyed seemingly overnight. With the buffalo went opportunities to exhibit wisdom in planning hunts, bravery in hunts, and generosity in sharing the kill with less fortunate members of the band. Part of the Lakota religion also died with the buffalo. His Indian name, Tatanka, has many sacred connotations. The buffalo's great meaning is generosity. His near-extinction caused much of Lakota culture irreparable damage.

The destruction of the great Sioux Nation continued as the nature of war changed for the Indian. War had been an important part of the Lakota way of life before the white man came, but it became the sole means of survival during the Indian-white wars. The sport and ceremony of war disappeared; stark strength and stamina became necessary to survive. The nomadic pattern of existence, once dictated by the movements of great herds of Tatanka, was disrupted by the gathering clouds of white settlers and soldiers who made an almost constant change of campsite necessary to avoid destruction by the military. Soon the buffalo was gone and, no matter where the Lakota camped, they confronted endlessly the reality of cold, hunger, and disease. The specter of the buffalo could not clothe them or make them well.

For the Lakota male, war was best way to demonstrate the virtue of bravery. It was all important for the young man to prove himself a brave warrior. It brought him honor in the eyes of his people. Participation in war or raiding parties gave the young victor opportunity to prove himself generous, as well.

Red Cloud recognized very early the futility of the Lakota struggle against whites. He had toured the eastern United States and counted the endless numbers of *washichu*, white men. Other leaders, Sitting Bull, Spotted Tail, and Crazy Horse, came to this realization much later. Pride in their way of life would not let them change their ways as quickly as Red Cloud suggested.

Within one generation, the rapid and awesome physical destruction of their people—now without the buffalo or stable campsites—made surrender necessary. The purpose of all men's societies and the general social structure of the nation was made obsolete by surrender to a more powerful nation of white men. The traditional meaning of wisdom was drastically changed by confinement to reservations. Most sacred ceremonies of importance were forbidden, principally the all-important Sun Dance. The environment itself was violated: the earth was torn for yellow metal; the animal nations were ruthlessly killed for their skins, or merely for sport.

As the outer world was destroyed, the inner world of the Lakota was violently changed. Without sacred ceremonies to establish contact with the spirits or without wildlife to bring signs and messages from the spirits, how were the Lakota to contact the supernatural and gain wisdom to advise and instruct others? Personal power became very hard to define. It is no wonder that the Lakota came to consider the white man as Iktomi incarnate, an ambivalent, evil representative of the dark side of humanity.

Before his death, Sitting Bull envisioned a new wisdom for his people. It was based on gaining an understanding of the ways of the white nation, taking only the good of these ways (for there is much that is bad in any nation of men), and molding a new existence from the best of both Indian and white ways. Sitting Bull saw this as a necessity and a solution which would allow his people to survive in a white man's world. From the despair of defeat and the destruction of the old way, he found a constructive alternative in which his people might place hope for a better tomorrow—or at least hope for survival.

Sitting Bull was seeking a new way to state for his people the old maxim, "The past is dead, you cannot go back." At the same time he was drawing on the traditional wisdom of his people in finding new solutions. As a wise Holy Man—Wachasha Wakan—and leader of his people, Sitting Bull knew this very well.

NOTES

[i] Refer to the Appendix for a chronological listing of important events in the history of the Sioux Nation.

[ii] There are several descriptions of the Sun Dance. J.R. Walker's paper entitled "The Sun Dance and Other Ceremonies of the Oglala Division of the Teton Dakota," (American Museum of Natural History, *Anthropological Papers*, Vol. XVI, Pt. 2, 1917) is the definitive study.

[iii] For a fuller understanding of the function of the horse in Sioux society, see Thomas E. Mails' profusely illustrated volume, *The Mystic Warriors of the Plains* (Garden City: Doubleday, 1972). This book is good for general knowledge of Plains Indian culture.

[iv] Royal B. Hassrick's ambitious *The Sioux: Life and Customs of a Warrior Society* (Norman, Oklahoma: University of Oklahoma Press, 1964), covers many facets of Sioux culture, concentrating on the period 1830-1870. Other references will be made, but Hassrick is basic to any study of Sioux culture.

[v] For a full account of the seven sacred ceremonies, read *The Sacred Pipe: Black Elk's Account of the Seven Rites of the Oglala Sioux*, edited by J.E. Brown (New York: Penguin Books, 1972).

[vi] This explanation of the sixteen aspects of Wakan Tanka is modified slightly from one which appeared in the *United Sioux Tribes Newsletter* (Pierre, South Dakota, 1972).

[vii] Letter from Art Raymond to Richard Moore, 19 November 1975.

[viii] The greatest written record we have of the life of a Wakan Man is John G. Neihardt's biography *Black Elk Speaks* (Lincoln: University of Nebraska Press, 1961). For a complete, personal view of a Holy Man's life, this book is unexcelled.

[ix] Thomas E. Mails gives a history and record of such societies in his book *Dog Soldiers, Bear Men and Buffalo Woman: A Study of the Societies and Cults of the Plains Indians* (New York: Prentice-Hall, 1973)

[x] Read more on the subject of *heyoka* in Mails' book *Dog Soldiers, Bear Men, and Buffalo Women*.

[xi] Neihardt, *Black Elk Speaks*, p. 276.

LAKOTA LITERATURE

Native American literature of the Great Plains is an oral literature of myths, legends and stories. Oral literary traditions exist in all countries of the world. Many modern folk singers are direct descendants of this tradition; for example, Pete Seeger or Buffy Saint-Marie. Many of Western man's great epics, such as *The Odyssey* and *Beowulf*, are products of strong oral traditions.

Lakota literature began to be recorded in the white man's way in writing, in books only after reservation life placed interested white scholars and Lakota storytellers and singers side by side. This began during the last half of the 19th century. Recently there has been a growing interest in Native American literature and music, as well as in the arts of many other ethnic groups.

The purpose of Lakota literature was and is to delight and instruct. In the old days, it was good entertainment during the long winter months of confinement when snow made travel and hunting impossible. Elders of the Lakota people were revered and honored by children as storytellers and teachers. Even warriors were instructors as well as brave protectors and providers.

The Lakota and white cultures differ in what they assume the purpose of literature to be. For the Lakota storyteller, literature's purpose is rarely self-expression. He seeks in his songs, ceremonies, myths, legends, and stories to bring himself in to harmony with his people and nature. Through his words he expresses his fundamental belief: that all life is a circle of being and that all things belong in that circle. He seeks harmony with the forces of nature so that he might become one with them, one with the Great Mystery, which is in all things. The Lakota people celebrate with the storyteller or singer as he practices his art.

Customs and laws are the subject of many Lakota stories. These stories represent almost the only historical records kept by the Lakota people. Traditions are maintained through them. The great virtues of the warrior (generosity, bravery, fortitude, and wisdom) and of the women (bravery, fortitude, truthfulness, and childbearing) are an important part of the stories and legends. This oral literature is part of *lakol wishohan*, the Lakota perspective on life, the ways and beliefs of the Lakota.

This short study will give examples of three major types of Lakota Literature: myth, legend, and story. A fourth type, song lyric, will be discussed briefly in the final essay, "Lakota Music." Oratory is a fifth type of Lakota literature, and the great speeches by the old Lakota chiefs are many.

Myths: *echanni woyake*

Ehanni woyake are traditional Lakota narratives of unknown origin, dealing with the following: the creation or beginning of the world; the creation of life and natural objects on the earth; the origin of the Lakota spirits; the origin of the people; and the creation of particular ideas as varied as the circle, the four seasons, the weather, the heavenly bodies, and early religious celebrations. These narratives are generally told in the evening. They are considered to be true. They emphasize tradition, and help the young Lakota understand his universe.

The Blood Was Blue

At the beginning of everything, before there was anything else, there was Inyan whose spirit was Wakan Tanka. Hanhepi was then no more than the blackness of the dark, and there was nothing else. And Inyan was without hardness or fixed shape; and yet he had all of the powers in him, in his blood. And yet powers without something for power to work on are useless. And Inyan wished to have some other thing or creature over which he could work his powers. And to create that other thing or person, he had to create it out of himself, giving it of his spirit and his blood, giving to that other thing as much of his power as he gave of his blood. And Inyan determined to create another who would be part of himself, and he created Maka from his own veins, allowing the blood to flow from himself into a great disk which he had created from himself. And the blood flowed into a disk which became water, and the powers in the water could not stay in the <u>water</u> disk, and so they in turn separated from the water disk and formed the great blue dome which is the sky and the spirit Mahpiyato. And then Inyan, the first thing, now became a hard and powerless rock at the center of things. There was now also the disk of Maka, the earth, and the circle of the waters, and the great dome of the sky, Mahpiyato, the final judge. And Maka scolded Inyan for creating her a part of him and leaving her in Hanhepi's darkness. And Mahpiyato heard Maka's complaint and Inyan's appeal that Maka should be appeased; and he ruled that Inyan should remain attached to Maka and Maka to Inyan but that Anpetu, the dawn light and redness, should be created. And Anpetu, the dawn light was created. And when Maka shuddered in the cold and complained to Mahpiyato, he created beyond the dawn light, Wi, the sun, and gave it a spirit. He placed it in his blue dome and mandated that Wi should give full heat and light to Maka's world. And Maka in the sheer glare of Wi's brilliance asked once more for the shadows of Hanhepi. And Mahpiyato heard and commanded Anpetu and Hanhepi to follow each other successively into the world and under the world and the powers of the sky, of the day and the night. Wi and Hanhepi obeyed. And what was commanded was done.

In scope, in completeness, and in beauty, the entire body of Lakota creation accounts compares favorably to that found in Genesis of *The Bible* or in Greek myth. The preceding passage concerns the creation of the universe; the beginning of the world; the natural functions of the elements such as darkness and light, day and night, cold and heat; and the origin of color in water and sky.

The Bible says that God created the earth and all that is in it in six days; on the seventh day He rested. The Lakota accounts of creation give a sense of before and after, but do not place the creation in so exact a time frame. This points to an important difference between Lakota and Western cultures. People of Western cultures are very time-conscious; most of their activities are built around exact time schedules in small units of hours, minutes, and even seconds. The Lakota did not, and to a great extent still do not, live by the clock. Their activities and events—whether economic, social, or religious—occur in harmony with natural changes in the environment. For example, the Lakota people name the months after natural phenomena:

January	*Moon of Frost on the Teepee*
February	*Moon of the Popping Trees*
March	*Moon of the Snowblind*
April	*Moon of the Red Grass Appearing*
May	*Moon When the Ponies Shed*
June	*Moon of Making Fat*
July	*Moon of the Red Cherries*
August	*Moon When Chokecherries Turn Black*
September	*Moon When Leaves Turn Brown*
October	*Moon of the Falling Leaves*
November	*Moon of the First Snowfall*
December	*Moon When Deer Shed Their Horns*

Likewise, ideas of land ownership differ between Lakota and Western cultures. For the Plains Indian land could not be "owned." Mari Sandoz puts it this way in *These Were the Sioux*:

> *To the Sioux, land, the earth, was revered as the mother force [Maka] in the Great Powers [Inyan, Wi, and the other spoken of above] from whom all things came. Plainly nothing could ever be done to diminish this land, nothing to make it less for all those whose tracks were still to come.*[1]

In contrast, a centuries-old tradition of ownership made possession of land a great social and symbolic importance to the white man. Such basic differences in values caused much pain and suffering for both peoples as the Great Plains were settled by the white man. This particular difference played a major role in the destruction of Lakota culture.

The white man sought to control his environment, using it for personal gain. The Lakota sought to be in harmony with his natural environment, taking only what was needed to survive. He was grateful for what his environment gave him and his people.

Many minor spirits appear in Lakota story and play very important roles: Wakinyan, the Thunder Spirit; Hu Nunpa, the Bear, a Spirit of Wisdom and protector of Holy Men; Whope, who appeared to the first people as White Buffalo Calf Woman and brought them sacred gifts and food; and certainly the greedy, selfish Iktomi, formerly a Spirit of Wisdom but now one who tricks and betrays all animals and mankind.

Iktomi deserves special mention. His name literally means "spider" in Lakota. According to some legends, the Spider Nation once helped mankind by chipping flint for arrowheads. But they could also shoot very tiny and deadly arrows at anyone who bothered them. Iktomi rarely appears with a spider's characteristics in Lakota literature. Even so, some Lakota people today still consider the sign of the spider very powerful.

In the oral tradition, Iktomi appears often. He is "always up to no good." Although a lesson may result from meeting him, any good which comes from him is an accident. So old Iktomi is both bad and good because his evil intentions usually backfire, accidentally resulting in learning, which is good. He generally appears in human form in Lakota narratives, but frequently assumes animal characteristics.

The circle is all-important in the Lakota culture. All good and natural things are circular in form. In the center of the circle, man will have a balanced knowledge of the good and evil which are everpresent in the world. His personal strength as a warrior who exercises generosity, bravery, fortitude, and wisdom for the good of his people will give him power to resist bad and do good. His purpose will be not to destroy the evil or bad, for this is not possible, but to make evil ineffective through his personal knowledge— power. Iktomi is banished from the circle of the natural.

We call the Lakota trickster or evil figure Iktomi, but Iktomi came among the first people on earth as the spirit Gnaski. Instead of helping them with his knowledge, he tricked both men and spirits into making fools of themselves. For this Mahpiyato, the Sky-Judge, banished him from both spirits and men. Ikotomi didn't lose all his magical, evil powers in banishment. Iktomi is so mean and so bad that he doesn't seem to mind his punishment—he is too busy making trouble for others.[ii] Most stories about Iktomi are not *ehanni woyake* but *ohunkakan woyake*, the third type of story.

Banishment, or exclusion from the band, was considered by the Lakota people to be a fate worse than death. Only grave social or religious offenses were punished in this way. It meant not only loneliness, exposure, and hunger for the offender, but probable death at the hands of the enemy. Such a person was excluded from both the social and the spiritual communities. This Lakota practice is in some ways parallel to certain Judeo-Christian practices. Under Hebraic law, children who marry "outside the faith" are considered to be spiritually and even physically "dead" by the parents. Under Catholic law, persons judged guilty of certain offenses are excommunicated, or are not allowed to participate fully in religious services. All these situations are similar in that punishment involves isolating the "sinner" from the socio-spiritual community.

Some of the powers bring men together. Long ago, according to the White Buffalo Calf Woman story, the first people were hungry and scattered over the plains. Whope, the White Buffalo Calf Woman, came bringing the sacred peace pipe, the sacred medicine bundle, and food. Because Whope appeared in the form of a white buffalo calf (white animals are considered *Wakan*, sacred), the Buffalo Nation was and is considered most sacred of animal nations.

Whope is the only spirit who came to earth to help man. She sacrificed greatly for mankind. In one account, she was tricked by Iktomi into digging into the earth with her hands to save a friend buried alive. She dug until her hands bled. According to *ehanni woyake*, Whope married a mortal. His name is Okaga, and he was the fourth son of Tate. Okaga, according to Lakota myth, travelled with his three brothers in a great circle around their father's camp to set the four directions and the four winds in order. Once he had set his direction, the south, he was allowed to marry Whope as a reward for his generosity, bravery, fortitude, and wisdom.

Legends: *ehanni wico oyake*

Ehanni wicooyake are historical narratives of events of relatively recent times. Like myths, which are concerned with ancient times, they are considered to be true. They include accounts of the origins of various bands, the deeds of still-remembered leaders of these bands, the origin of place names, and other occurrences of the last few generations. Because legends are, by their very nature, an oral form, few authentic accounts are available in written form. The interpretations of these legendary figures and their lives that have been written by well-meaning white people tend to be inaccurate and biased. These distortions have help destroy the Lakota's own view of these leaders and events, and have discouraged the continuity of their oral literary forms.

Crazy Horse was a war leader of the Oglala band. According to legend, he could not be wounded in battle. He proved this many times, never more clearly than in his brilliant leadership of Sioux and Cheyenne forces against General Crook on the bands of the Rosebud River on the morning of June 17, 1876. When these near-equal forces met, the whites were soundly defeated. Crook recorded that Rosebud action as one of the fiercest in his long military career. By several accounts, Crazy Horse was seen wherever the battle was most fierce, armed only with a coup stick. He was not even wounded that day. Little wonder that this man became a legend in his lifetime.

Crazy Horse came from an outstanding family. In the first essay, "Lakota History and Culture," we have stressed the importance placed upon inherited qualities in Lakota culture. Crazy Horse's father was a Holy Man. The greatest Lakota-white conflicts resulted from white repossession and settlement of the Black Hills in violation of the treaty of 1868. The white men went into Paha Sapa seeking gold and farmland. To the Lakota this land was sacred, the home of many good spirits. The Lakota feared the spiritual death of the Black Hills, and through this, of themselves. Paha Sapa, the Black Hills, were not to be "possessed" by anyone in the Lakota way of thinking. They were more than land; the hills were spirit. And they were defended by the Lakota with all the strength of the physical and spiritual combined. Crazy Horse's Rosebud victory and the victory at Little Big Horn were the results.

Despite the brilliant military victories at Rosebud and Little Big Horn, the victors were pursued unmercifully and then forced onto reservations. From this time of defeat and humiliation come the massacre of Chief Big Foot's band of Mineconjous and Wounded Knee, and the mystic ceremonies of the Ghost Dance which the U.S. army violently suppressed when they mistook this nonviolent religious movement for a military uprising.

At almost the same time, white hunters such as Buffalo Bill destroyed the last of the buffalo herds. The buffalo was not merely a symbol of majesty and power. The Buffalo, *Tatanka*, was considered the greatest of the minor spirits, and was literally the major source of life for the Lakota. Every part of his body was used in the old way, even his bones. Other animals were hunted, but none compared in importance to him. With the slaughter of the Buffalo Nation, the Lakota culture entered an age of trial and tribulation.

Stories That Teach: *ohunkakan woyake*

Ohunkakan Woyake are Lakota narratives designed to teach proper behavior, to present a lesson. They may involve a mixture of mythic characters, animals, and men. The incidents they describe occurred in the vague past, in no specific place. Many such narratives are about the adventures of Iktimi. These stories also entertain. They are evening stories.

Coyote is the most important of these lesser characters. Iktomi usually appears in the form of Coyote in the tales where he comes into contact with other animals. When Iktomi deals with men, he appears in human form. He is something of a shape-shifter in these stories. Ella Deloria has made the following free translation of "Iktomi in a Skull." It involves Coyote and kind-hearted Mouse.

1. Iktomi was off on a trip when he heard singing and shouting and dancing nearby. He stopped to listen. 2. Immediately he wished to dance too, so much so that his soles itched; and he tried hard to locate the source of the sounds. 3. While he listened, it seemed as though the dancing and shouting grew louder and louder; and at last he knew that it came from a dry buffalo skull lying near his path. 4. He saw that the interior was all cheerfully lighted up, and inside was great jollity. 5. When he peeped in through one of the eye socket openings, he saw that the mice were staging a great dance. 6. So Iktomi knocked on the door and said, "My little brothers, take pity on me and let me enter. I want to dance too." 7. "Aw, let's open for big brother!" they said, and opened the back door for him. He thrust his head in and could go no further. 8. Then someone said, "Look out! It is Iktomi!" and soon they disappeared into the darkness. 9. Iktomi sat down with the skull on is head and began to weep. 10. He sat by the road and whenever he heard someone going by, he wept loudly, and when they went on past, then we wept in a low voice. That is all. [iii]

That's Iktomi, just "going along" and making trouble for everyone. Notice that the mice are portrayed as a band, part of a nation, holding a dance in Buffalo's skull. Once there was a very great and generous Buffalo Nation—now there is little left but bones and skulls of these people.

In addition to just "going along," Iktomi is just "up to no good," no matter what form he assumes. In many stories he tricks other animals into helping him kill game—usually Buffalo—then tricks them (or is sometimes tricked himself) out of the meat. Iktomi is always up to such tricks.

NOTES

[i] Mari Sandoz, *These Were the Sioux* (New York: Dell, 1961), p. 105, inserts added.

[ii] For a very complete study of the Winnebago Indian Tribe's Iktomi, see Paul Radin's *The Trickster: A Study in American Indian Mythology* (New York: Schocken Books, 1956)

[iii] Ella Deloria, *Dakota Tests*, Publication of the American Ethnological Society, Vol XIV, ed. By Franz Boas (New York: G.E. Stechert & Company, 1932), pp 45-46.

LAKOTA MUSIC

Music is one of the central art forms of the Lakota culture. This essay describes the role music plays in Lakota life, lists the types of Lakota songs and briefly analyzes the elements of some of these songs, indicates the instruments commonly used, and presents the standards by which the Lakota evaluate the quality of a composition and its performance.

Music has always played a major role in virtually every aspect of Lakota life, and is not separated from the ordinary world. The Lakota has songs for his religious ceremonies; to express his beliefs and virtues; to recount his hunts among animal nations, his nights on the town, or any other activity in which he participates or has an interest. In no other culture is music more loved and more integrated into social activity.

In the old days the Lakota passed their songs, like their literature, from generation to generation through a strict tradition of oral learning and recitation. Both music and literature are still preserved in this traditional manner, although some contemporary Lakota also learn the old songs with the help of written and especially recorded music.

Much of the history of the Lakota is contained in their music and literature. Lakota music reflects the cultural patterns of the Lakota Nation at the time it was composed. Lakota music can be fully appreciated only when heard in live performance. Because the performers should be seen as well as heard, recordings present a limited perspective. Music unifies by dance and intense involvement all who attend Lakota social events.

Lakota men are generally the composers and performers of songs which make up ninety-five per cent of Lakota music. Women, however, may also compose and sing songs, while children readily join in the dancing at social occasions. Most contemporary Lakota treat composition as a craft; they consciously and actively create songs. But a hundred years ago most composers saw themselves as a tool of mystic powers and received inspiration for their songs from dreams and visions. In this respect Lakota music still reflects old values: even though it is performed at social gatherings, it is composed and performed more for self than for the audience. Judgments may be made, however, by the audience about the quality of the song and the skill of the performers.

Lakota music reflects values and purposes different from those of western music generally. Although many songs are entertaining and beautiful, most Lakota music serves a particular purpose. Lakota people value a song according to how well it accomplishes some purpose, not according to its beauty. A song is good when it results in a cure; when it secures game; when it helps a person be brave, find peace in his heart, or express joy.

Types of Lakota Songs

To understand the importance of music to the Lakota and the complexity of the art, one should examine the many types of songs and be aware of the great number of songs in each type. We have grouped them roughly into five categories:

I.   SACRED MUSIC: songs having a supernatural source which are used in ceremonial settings.

Healing songs	Inipi songs
Yuwipi songs	Hanblecheya songs
Songs of the Sacred Stones	Soul-releasing songs
Sun Dance songs	Marriage songs
Kettle Dance Songs	Initiation songs (women)
Alowanpi (Hunka) songs	Native American Church songs

Tokala Songs

II. SOCIETY SONGS: songs not strictly religious, but having a super natural source, which are performed in formal settings.

Akicita Society	Dream Society
	Omaha Society Songs

III. SOCIAL DANCING MUSIC.

Grass Dance songs	Doorway (Begging songs)
Round Dance songs	Charging songs
Rabbit Dance songs	"49" songs
Sneak-up songs	Flag songs
Victory Dance songs	Sioux National Anthem

Honor songs:
Memorial songs
Mazasha (Penny Dance) Name-giving songs
Shunka songs
Chief songs
Not-dressed-to-dance songs
Veteran songs

IV. SHOW MUSIC: songs mainly intended for the enjoyment of the audience and used for competitive dancing.

Gourd Dance songs	Bustle Dance songs

Contest songs:
Fast War Dance songs
Slow War Dance songs
Trick songs
Stomp Dance songs

V.   OCCASIONAL AND PRIVATE SONGS AND MUSIC: songs
sung spontaneously and not danced to.

Game songs:	Lullabies
Moccasin Game songs	Love songs
Stick game songs	Ich'ilowan songs

Lakota music plays a prominent role in religious ceremony. Sacred music is generally received through visions sought during Hanblecheya or the Sun Dance. On these occasions the individual pursues the mysterious power pervading all nature, seeking a sacred song. Once the seeker receives a song in vision or dream, he may then make it an integral part of other activities, such as hunting.[i] Songs received on Hanblecheya remain private, while songs received during the Sun Dance may be shared with the entire community and become a standard part of public ceremony. Generally, every aspect of a religious ceremony is accompanied by song. The Sun Dance is the primary example.[ii]

Because sacred music is so vitally important to an understanding of the Lakota way, we will discuss it in more detail than the other four categories. Many Lakota songs climax in an invocation to Wakan Tanka, the Great Mystery within all things—in every living creature and in all of nature. In this sense, song links the individual with the spiritual, allowing him to communicate with mysterious forces. A sacred song is considered a gift from the spirits, a gift to be used with reverence, with purpose. Religious songs have always been sung in every undertaking which the individual feels is beyond his personal power to accomplish. They are used in healing, for example.

During reservation confinement, the Lakota were for a time forbidden to hold ceremonies of the old religion in which music figures so prominently. They were forbidden to Sun Dance. In maintaining an oral tradition of music, continuity is essential. When songs cannot be sung, they may fade from memory. Many of the sacred Sun Dance songs are lost now. Yet, at one time over three hundred songs were employed in this ceremony to describe every event of its two to four-day duration.

The older sacred songs are many times personal stories, composed during dramatic circumstance, when an individual creates a need to express emotion beyond the power of words alone. These songs are powerful or good because they have a supernatural source. When curing, a healer re-enacts the occasion when he or she first received healing power. Black Elk has given us the following account of a vision and song he received while still a boy:

Then I looked up at the clouds, and two men were coming there, head-first like arrows slanting down; and as they came, they sang a sacred song

*and the thunder was like drumming. I will sing it for you. The song and the
drumming were like this:*

> *"Behold a sacred voice is calling you;*
> *All over the sky a sacred voice is calling."*[iii]

In the particular case of Black Elk's great vision, which was received
later in his life than the one described here, the Holy Man who interprets
this young warrior's vision arranges for the whole band to re-enact the events
that occurred in it.

The second category of Lakota music is the society song. There are
three types of society songs. These songs may be sung with or without words
and are generally shorter than religious songs. A Fox Society song will be
discussed later in this essay.

The third prevalent use of music by the Lakota is in non-religious,
social dances, called celebrations or Pow-wows. Often these events are the
occasion for the public side of naming or honoring ceremonies, which
involve Give-away. Nowadays contests in which dancers compete for cash
prized are part of these events. More and more, the purpose of singing is to
accompany social dancing.

Many songs focus on the art of warfare. Just as there are songs for
every aspect of ceremony, there are songs for every aspect of war: songs sung
to create courage before battle, songs sung by women to returning warriors,
and songs sung in celebration following victories. In victory celebrations
and related events, music frequently played a role in the narration and re-
enactment of experience. In order to prove their personal power, individuals
would dramatize in song, dance, and story an act of bravery or the event of
receiving their power from spirits. Sneak-up songs, for example, are
accounts of past war adventures. Re-enactments of visions might involve the
song the individual received when his power came to him. In some cases, it
is believed that acting out an incident which might happen, will prevent it.

One type of personal song (the fifth category) is the *Ich'ilowan*, usually sung when alone, for one's self, and many times mournfully, from the
heart. There are fewer of these songs nowadays. The destruction of the old
way of life—with its ceremonies, conflicts, and hunts—has contributed to
the decline of the traditional solo song. When an individual sings solo at a
gathering, it is not because he has a good voice, but because the song
belongs to him through his gift of interpretation or style, by inheritance, or
through "gift of spirit." A healer (Wichasha Wapiya) may sing alone when
treating the sick, but he may also desire the family or friends of the sick person to join him.

Melody and the Voice

Melody in the voice and rhythm in percussion are the two major elements of Lakota music. The melody is analyzed according to three factors: 1) its rhythm; 2) its movement, or contour; and 3) the intervals, or distance between notes which form the contour.

There are three basic rhythm structures in Lakota melodies. Some song melodies are iso-rhythmic: their structure is determined by the repetition of a few rhythmic phrases, regardless of pitch changes. Thirdly, more complex song melodies may have two, three, or more different rhythmic phrases which are repeated in an interesting arrangement. The great variety of rhythmic structure of Lakota song melody is only hinted at in available examples.

The melodies of many Lakota songs have a cascading type of melodic contour sometimes called "tile" or "terrace" movement. The graphic transcription of a Wolf Song reveals clearly why "terrace" is an apt metaphor for songs with a cascading melodic contour. The melodies begin quite high in the vocal range and work downward in descending phrases. Each phrase begins on a tone the same as or slightly higher than the last tone of the preceding phrase. "Terrace" melody contours are lilting, and the sameness of rhythm patterns with pitch variation gives the melody of many songs an interlocking quality.

The intervals (that is, the distance between notes) within Lakota melodies vary as widely as they do in western melodies. Major sevenths, minor seconds, and tritones, can be found with some regularity; the most common intervals, however, are the perfect fourth, perfect fifth, major and minor thirds, and major seconds. There is also a tendency in most melodies to hold on a long note after extensive movement from note to note. The Lakota melody is similar to early Gregorian chant in its uncanny knack for simple melodic movement, for unexpected, cadencing and contour, and for variety of rhythmic patterns which sound natural and uncontrived. Melodies are written in either major or minor key (mode), but there seems to be little connection between mode and the intent or mode of a song.

Some melody lines imitate animal calls or howls. In tapes of some love songs, you will hear, along with a Lakota soloist, animal sounds made by the group to embellish the melody line. Songs such as a lullaby establish a mood. This echoing of natural sounds in song melody shows the great respect the Lakota has for natural phenomena, and his wish to be one with nature, to exist in harmony with the whole circle of existence.

Within Lakota song, the rhythm patterns of the melodic lines themselves are greatly varied. The time signature within the melodic line of a single song may also change frequently. This variety indicates the primary importance of melody in Lakota music. In comparison, the rhythmic units of instruments and the song lyrics are repeated in patterns dictated largely by desired melodic contours.[iv] The drum rhythms are very regular and constant, except for increases in tempo. In Lakota song lyrics, rhyme is sometimes present, but not essential, and regular meter is absent. Words that express the thought are chosen by the composer to fit the melody. In many cases only vocables (syllables, not words) are used.

The manner of classic Lakota tone production (singing) is quite different from the western classic style of singing. The vocal tones that the Lakota singer produces are very loud, and tend to be nasal and full of throat vibrato. These qualities result from the open but set jaw and throat position. The particular carrying power of the Lakota singing voice also results partially from this characteristic jaw and throat position. Since the Lakota sings almost all of his songs out-of-doors, volume and audibility are very important.

The *bel canto* ("beautiful singing") tradition of western culture differs in several ways from Lakota singing tradition. *Bel canto* requires a controlled, focused tone. Such tone is produced by breath support, an open throat, flexible jaw and lip movement, and a balance of throat and nasal resonance which allows control and therefore variation of volume, color, and texture. This is the western idea of classic singing, and to the western listener it may come closer to sounding beautiful on first hearing than classic Lakota singing.

While everyone in the Lakota Nation may sing, the Lakota have standards of excellence by which they distinguish good singers from lesser singers. They admire the singer able to sustain the pitch of a tone, and even more, the singer able to recreate a song with exactly the same notes and rhythm when he has not sung it for several years. A pronounced vibrato (pulsating quality of the voice), a loud falsetto (the range an octave above the singer's natural singing tone), a very broad vocal range, and smoothness and projection of voice are also considered attributes of the good Lakota singer, male or female.

Finally, the Lakota listener judges the emotional and intellectual interpretation which the singer brings to a song. Naturally, the personality of the singer has much to do with the success of his interpretation. As interpreter, the Lakota singer makes aesthetic decisions, such as whether or not to use a nasal quality in love songs, to wail in songs of illness or death, or to croon in lullabies. The good Lakota singer must be possessed by his song, presenting self and song with confidence and authority.

The Instrument and Rhythm

Rhythm is an important element in Lakota music. The Lakota create rhythm with flutes, whistles, gourds, rattles, bells, and drums. Flutes are played by men and only for love songs. Eagle wing-bone whistles are used primarily in the Sun Dance and by Wichasha Wakan and Wichasha Wapiya in healing ceremonies.

Gourds are used in religious ceremonies, most commonly in the Yuwipi ceremony. To make these gourds, four hundred tiny stones are taken from the mound of an ant colony. These stones are *wakan*, very sacred, for Ant is a very important example to man. The Wakan stones from Ant's home provide the healing rhythms of the sacred gourds, by whose sound the spirits are summoned. The stones represent the spirits and become them in the ceremony. Gourds are considered sacred objects, and are used only in religious and social rituals.

Bells, on the contrary, are used in social dancing. They are worn by male dancers and create a lively accent to the strong body movements of the performers. The bell sound must be skillfully controlled to create rhythms complementary to the drums, which accompany social dancing.

Drums are the heartbeat of Lakota culture and its vision of the universe. The drum is circular and draws power in tone from its sacred form and shape. The large ceremonial drum sits on Maka, the earth, and draws resonance from her forces. The ceremonial drum is considered to be alive, a living thing with *nagi*, a spirit that can speak in songs the group performs. The drum rhythm sets the mood of each musical composition and reflects its purpose. Rhythm is associated with the supernatural in many ways.

There are three types of drums: ceremonial drums, water drums, and small hand drums. The frame for a large, ceremonial drum was originally made from a large, hollow log, burnt and chipped out. Then a buffalo or deer hide was wet, stretched over the frame, and laced or pegged to it with rawhide. After it dried, the taut hide made a resonant sound when struck. The pitch and resonance of these drums vary with the temperature and humidity. Several men sit around this drum, pounding it and singing in unison. (In the traditional Lakota way, drums are played only by men.) Water drums are used by the Lakota in ceremonies of the Native American Church, a peyote-inspired religion. Hand drums are commonly used by solo singers, performing in public or in private.

In many older songs, there is greater freedom between the tempo of the singers and that of the drumbeat. This accounts for the effect called cross-rhythm, in which stress, or accent values of voice and rhythm patterns of drums do not often coincide. This is common in most Lakota contest music and especially in modern Omaha or Fast War Dance songs. The interplay is complicated by the fact that tempos may increase within a single song, and fluctuating note values may result from the various interpretations of the singers. The performer who can sing and play the drum simultane-ously with accuracy, while performing such complex cross-rhythms, demands respect in any culture.

Song Form

Despite, or perhaps because of the tension created by the interplay of vocal and drum rhythmic patterns, the Lakota song is a very exciting event when performed by an accomplished group like the Porcupine Singers. The best Lakota social music is marked by an intensity of the indi-vidual's concern for communication with the spirits of the universe or with his fellow man—communication that is accomplished only in live perform-ance before an audience.

In group presentation of songs, participation follows a specific pat-tern. In the Fast War Dance and other songs, the group leader for a particu-lar song introduces the melody very high in his vocal range. This first, or lead, phrase indicates which song is to be sung and establishes the volume, mood, and pitch. The leader's voice must be clear and strong. The introduc-tion is a crucial point in the song.

Immediately following this introductory phrase and generally before it ends, a second singer (or in some cases the rest of the group) will repeat the lead phrase entirely. Then the entire group, or chorus, sings the main phrase and the first ending. The first ending signals the halfway point in the song. The main phrase is then repeated by the group. In Lakota music the final ending is signaled by the repetition of the first ending with the substi-tution of "o" for "hoi." If the song is to be repeated, the leader will re-intro-duce the lead phrase before the final phrase is completed. At the conclusion of the song, there is often a pause, and the final half of the song or the last phrase is repeated one last time. This is often called a "tag."

Honor Dance songs, Penny (Mazasha) songs, and several other types have a short introduction (common to most songs), two main sections with identical melody, and a tag ending. The main section is generally sung the second time at a faster tempo. The Omaha Dance song can be distinguished by strong accent beats on the drum when the main section is repeated. (In referring to Grass Dance and War Dance songs as "Omaha Songs," the Lakota mean a type of Lakota song, and not songs of the Omaha Nation.)

Sneak-up, Tokala, and some Yuwipi songs are introduced by drum rolls and are interrupted by sharp accents. The last half of the Sneak-up song is sung at a faster tempo, as in a War Dance song, but without final ending.

Song form extends beyond the single verse or cycle of a melody, how-ever. In repetitions of the melody, the singers often increase or double the tempo, as in the Penny song and the Sioux National Anthem. Further, the group, at the direction of the lead singer, may intentionally raise or lower the pitch of the repetition, as is often done in western composition.

Guidelines for group presentation of music may also extend beyond a single composition. Several songs may have to be sung as a group, as in the case of the Victory songs. Other songs may be arbitrarily arranged by singers in a program. The numerous types of song form, the differences between songs of a particular type, and the innumerable variations upon and exceptions to the generalizations prevent us from extensively covering song form within this essay.

NOTES

[i] Frances Densmore in her definitive *Teton Sioux Music* (New York; Da Capo, 1972) gives the following examples: "The songs of those who went to look for a suitable pole for the Sun Dance were also used by those who went to look for buffalo or for the enemy. Songs in honor of a warrior could be sung when begging for food before his lodge, as well as at the victory dances and at meetings of societies" (p. 11).

[ii] See J.R. Walker's paper, "The Sun Dance and other Ceremonies of the Oglala Division of the Teton Dakota" (American Museum of Natural History, *Anthropological Papers*, Vol Xvi, Pt. 2, 1917) with regard to the role of music in the Sun Dance ceremony. Other books that deal with this subject are Olive Fletcher's *Indian Story and Song in North America* (Boston: 1900), Natalie Curtis' *The Indian Book* (N.Y. & London: Harper and Bros., 1907), and Luther Standing Bear's *My People the Sioux* (Lincoln: University of Nebraska Press, 1975).

[iii] John Neihardt, *Black Elk Speaks* (Lincoln: University of Nebraska Press, 1961), p. 19.

[iv] For a discussion of the three elements in detail, see Densmore's *Teton Sioux Music*. Olive Fletcher's *Indian Story and Song in North America* explores the relationship between Indian languages and music.

3

ON CONVERSION TO JUDAISM

ON CONVERSION TO JUDAISM

1

Let me begin by saying that I think in every discussion of a topic such as conversion, which is essentially involved with things unseen and unknowable, it is of great value to ask concrete questions. In such matters of the heart and soul, it is the questions that are permanent, and the answers which vacillate endlessly. How did I come to believe in God? Why did I choose Judaism? Where am I now in my belief? Each of these questions is dangerous because each requires that I deal openly with the anguish of spiritual insecurity—I admit I wrestle with it constantly—and with apprehending the presence of God in the world. (Certainly, my study of Judaism and the history of the Jewish People has led me to question the presence of God in the world. Yet, it is very clear to me that I believe in a transcendental God of grace and infinite power.) My motivation for asking such questions is to find at least partial answers to my questions concerning my own conversion and to share these answers with others.

Clearly, part of the challenge of working with conversion as a concept has to do with the nature of belief in God. This belief seems to me to consist of a series of transitional states, never static enough to be defined in rational terms. Clearly, however, such belief is based securely on something extraordinary, something we never expect to find: the discovery at the hidden heart of every religion—namely an encounter with God, an encounter which transcends secular specificity. So, my purpose here is to give you the discrete events that precipitated my encounter with God and my attraction to Judaism as a way of life, which in turn prompted my decision to convert to Judaism, dignified my conversion, and continues to direct my life as a Jew.

To explain or justify belief in a transcendent God to others may be impossible, but I want to attempt it, for my own sake and also for the sake of my children, who will at one time or another face a crisis of faith in their own lives. I do not mean to imply that their merit will in any way come from me; I mean no *tsukat avot*, but I want them to know about that part of my wrestling that I can approximate in words. I also want them to know the circumstances of my conversion experience. Essential to my motivation for writing this essay is the desire to share with my wife and my children my spiritual journey to the ever-changing present that is our life together.

Among the challenges facing the convert are some that are quite subtle. One is in general surrounded by doubt in the contemporary world. It is difficult not to internalize this skepticism. A playful side of the skeptic inside me might compare religious belief to listening to classical music. As I listen, I sense that this music implies an unseen form, which in turn may imply that existence itself has an unseen order. Isn't this implied unseen order similar to that which serves as the basis for religion? And some people do feel more comfortable worshipping music than God. Then there is also the figure I have internalized since entering secular Jewish circles. He is a kind of *golem*. The breath that gives him life is the breath of doubt, sarcasm and, sometimes, self-hatred. This is the loud bitter voice of the wounded, the scarred, of those unable to forgive. And our hearts—all our hearts—must go out to this voice, for it is the voice of broken mirrors, of a soul driven to the sharp edge of despair by the destruction humanity has wrought on Judaism in the darkest of centuries, the 20th century.

My conversion was not an apology or expiation for Christian sin against the Jews; it grew from a desire to express my love of God in the way I found most acceptable to me as a thinking being living in this world; it became the gateway to a new way of life, a way that embraces Torah and its *mitzvoth* (laws), *tsedakah* (righteousness; charity), and *tikkun olam* (healing the world) as a way to live a righteous life and to insure the existence of a decent world to pass on to our children. It may well be that guilt does play a role in the conversion of some converts, but it is most likely a turning *away* from guilt that motivates the belief of the sincere convert. Judaism has survived Shoah; it will survive anything this world has to offer. My conversion was, in part, an expression of my personal need to leave the guilt evoked by original sin on the scrap heap of history. Judaism allows me that, although Judaism, in all its complexity and divisiveness, gives many other challenges to the convert. Any religious way of life does that.

2

Conversion has always been practiced by Judaism for highly diverse reasons, always rooted in advantage, sometimes in survival. In our time perhaps the chief motivation to proselytize is to replace the six million *shoah* victims, the loss of the children of intermarriage and the ever-larger numbers of Jews who are becoming emotionally and intellectually estranged from Judaism. My personal belief is that converts to Judaism will constitute one of the great forces in Judaism of the early 21st Century. Converts are essential to Judaism's health.

In the Biblical Period conversion was widely practiced but not formally articulated. Canaan and its inhabitants together offered unique challenges to the twelve tribes who began to settle there in 1200 B.C.E. There was probably no "national conquest" but a gradual integration of less organized people into the Israelite Nation.

The ideological underpinning for conversion is clearly outlined in Isaiah 56: 3, 6-8:

Neither let the stranger, that hath joined himself to the Lord, speak, saying: "The Lord will surely separate me from his people;" ... Also the strangers, that join themselves to the Lord, to minister unto Him, and to love the name of the Lord, to be his servants, every one that keepeth the Sabbath from profaning it, and holdest fast to My covenant, even them will I bring to My holy mountain, and make them joyful in My House of prayer. Their burnt offerings and sacrifices shall be accepted upon My altar: for My house shall be called a house of prayer for all peoples. The Lord God, which gathereth the outcasts of Israel, saith: "Yet I gather others to him, beside his own that are gathered."

"The tension between desiring the integration of gentiles through conversion and maintaining aloofness from others has remained a part of the Jewish ethos since antiquity."[i]

The Rabbinic Period stretches from the 2nd Century B.C.E. to the rise of Islam in the 7th Century C.E. Beginning with the destruction of the temple in 586 B.C.E., religious policy became part of a pattern of survival, and conversion of non-Jews became a part of the pattern. During this period, the Rabbis began to see Abraham as the first convert and conversion as a social device through which Judaism was to become "a light unto the nations." Yet clearly under Ezra, tribal purity was to be strived for. Mass conversions were probably common in Palestine in the biblical period. As we approach Diaspora the convert is held in suspicion by the priestly classes and limited in social and political possibilities. The process of conversion and the converts' status were formalized at this time. Ironically, Judaism, which served in most respects as a model for both Christianity and Islam (which were to take that part of the model that concerned conversion and develop it much further than Judaism), was itself to suffer under the proselytizing doctrines of both her sister religions.

In historical overview, the Medieval Period found the Jew embattled and expulsed. Where Jews were allowed to remain, they were forced unto themselves, into ghettos, later into shtetls. Jews generally withdrew from Muslim lands during this period. There was extremely little conversion between Jews and Muslims. The opposite is true of Christianity, whose late medieval attempts to forcibly convert Jews are infamous. The Jewish reaction to outside pressures on Judaism caused a change in Jewish restrictions on conversion. Judah Halevy relegated to the convert a new soul not quite as high in quality as the soul of a born Jew. But conversion to Judaism continued, as it always had.

During the Renaissance, nationalism, loyalty to a state rather than a religion, replaced religion as a means of organizing people. Jews fared better in this period. After the French Revolution, German Jews saw in nationalism the opportunity to not only fulfill themselves in their own unique culture, but to cease being a vulnerable minority. During this period, the *Haskalah* (Enlightenment), the German Jewish Enlightenment, became a powerful intellectual-social force in Germany and quickly spread through the *maskalim* (proselytizers) to central Europe where it played a central role in the development of Yiddish Literature. One effect of the *Haskalah* was to encourage cultural and social assimilation. (Another, indirect effect was to help develop Yiddish Literature.) German Jews intermarried in great numbers and conversion could not replace these losses among the Ashkenazim.

Yet the terrors of separateness and anti-semitism also flourished in the new freedoms of Europe, and this psychotic hatred reached its dreadful climax in the ovens of Auschwitz. I believe that anti-semitism and *shoah* are powerful facts in the hearts and minds of most converts, as it is in anyone who studies modern history. When my wife, Leslie, and I consciously chose to have at least three children and to raise them Jewish, in the back of our minds was the horrid losses of Judaism to *shoah* and our fond duty to replace those lost. As if to reinforce our thoughts, God gave us in our third pregnancy not one, but two beautiful daughters to replace those lost in the fetid machinery of contemporary European history.

3

The standard definitions of conversion are straightforward in nature. There are four. *First*, a turning from sin to God in faith and repentance. In this sense, each Jew is instructed to "convert" during the high holy days each year. *Second*, a drawing close to God from a routine, insensitive life to a more intense way of living a religious life. This also implies that each of us is in a constant state of conversion, even if we have never altered our religious affiliation. *Third*, a change from non-belief—one may be an atheist, an agnostic, or belong to another religion—to a belief in God. *Fourth*, the change from one religion to another. The third definition best describes my conversion: although I had been raised in the Anglican Church, I converted to Judaism from a state of non-affiliation, if not non-belief. The other three definitions also apply to me as a convert to Judaism and are important, if not essential to every believer in every religion. Conversion is a universal phenomenon, timeless and full of challenges and turmoil.

The event of my embracing the Jewish faith 25 years after leaving the faith in which I had been raised, the Church of England, was preceded by a "turning to God in faith and repentance" and "embracing a more intense ... religious life." Had I known the costs of conversion to Judaism—the estrangement from parts of my mother's and father's families, the lack of acceptance by many Jews, the necessity of facing feelings of failure and betrayal in myself—I would still, I am sure in my heart, start down the same road again.

Each deeply felt conversion is unique, yet all conversions share certain essential characteristics We can ask each sincere convert the same questions and elicit a whirlwind of highly individual answers. This seems to me natural. Nothing is more stultifying to one who has been through the soul-searching of sincere conversion than to be conveniently stuck into a pigeon hole: "Did you marry a Jew?" "Yes." "Well, then this is a 'conversion because of Marriage.'" To the sincere convert, such an assumption is dismissive; it discounts spiritual and intellectual struggle and honesty of intention. Categorization may be necessity to "create" statistics, but it is often dehumanizing. In the words of my colleague Zev Garber, "From the path of Torah the Jew is told to walk with dignity. But dignity is not merely an inheritance of genes or a product of the environment. It is more likely the result of individual assertion. That kind of dignity rests on the individual's relation to one's conscience, universe, God. It reaches from person to person and embraces different nations and groups."[ii] So, in Professor Garber's terms, my words here are an "individual assertion."

First and foremost, my conversion to Judaism was based on a rediscovery of God's presence in my life, my whole life, from my first conscious recognition of it in nature, in music and in those around me to my present work with these words in the present, the here-and-now. I will attempt to describe the events of my life in such a way as to place my individual life honestly before the reader. I often think of life as a *peregrinatio*, a spiritual wandering in search of the creative forces that shaped me. A part of every conversion is the life and truth of the convert's autobiography. Is it important enough to write about? I believe so. Or perhaps I see it as necessary simply because God has made it possible.

My conversion was the climax of an active, decade-long, studious search for God in sacred and temporal literature, in philosophy, in history— in the phenomenon of language itself. The search also involved an intense search of my personal past, as well as my personal and professional activities. In short, my conversion involved an intense examination of my whole life as a performer, teacher and writer—my self. My study of religion and Judaism often occurred in the company of others, but searching for the answers to all the hard questions were essentially lonely acts. Ultimately, I converted to Judaism on July 8, 1988 in the intimate surrounding of my Rabbi's rose garden.

My conversion was voluntary and gradual. In such a willed conversion, the joys are subtle, the doubts and losses sometimes great. I would like to read you a passage from a letter Peter Marin sent me July 18th of this year in which he addresses the process of the profound "sea change" of the willed convert, as opposed to the convert transformed by ecstatic experience:

> But what is it like to <u>will</u> a change in how things are seen and felt, and to study towards it manfully, dutifully and consciously, that is, to seek God out, or to resolve to seek him out, rather than being found and thereby transformed. In sudden conversion no loss is felt, all that is given up apparently seems as dross, as straw— ... but where choice is all, and yearning consciousness, what else enters in?

In the words that follow, I will try to answer Peter's question. I want to say, also, that I am no stranger to revelation, at least to revelation as I understand it. In the passages that follow, I will describe certain essential elements of my life that were very important in forming the person I was in 1988, the person who chose to become a Jew. I will be as honest and as factual in these accounts as memory will allow.

I remember one very important event in the life of my belief. I was a student in Europe in 1979, at the Conservatory for Music and Dramatic Arts in Hanover, West Germany. A Jewish friend and I took the train to Amsterdam and wandered one night into the Anne Frank House on *Prinsengracht*. I was suddenly overwhelmed by emotion on the narrow stairs that allowed us to ascend to the small rooms of the third floor and the attic where Anne and her family lived those long years, months, days, hours, minutes before being betrayed—as so many million were betrayed. I believe it is the absence of such concrete evidence of the sufferings of the Jewish people that has lead so many young Jews to consider the crown of their Jewishness so lightly. Of course, the crown also carries the weight of pain with it. As I climbed those stairs in the Anne Frank House, I became not only Anne and her parents; I was the neighbors who hid them; I was also the arresting officer. The entire drama of the Jewish people's survival from Esther to Anne Frank became a very real part of my emotional life.

In 1980, less than a year after leaving Hanover, a city less infected than some with the anti-Semitism I found to be still universal in Germany, I met my wife to be, a native of Los Angeles named Leslie Horn, a Jew, in a small town in northeast Bavaria where we were both engaged as performers, and we began to plan the remainder of our life together.

4

The following were the most important steps that immediately preceded my conversion. All of this was preceded by years of personal spiritual and intellectual questioning. It was made possible by hundreds of conversations, thousands of hours reading and a million doubts and questions.

First, we joined a temple, and I began there to find a home for that part of myself that wanted to dedicate itself to Jewish Studies. *Schul*, or Torah Study was very important in this regard. When we parted after our *Shabbos* hour together, we often broke into groups that continued indefinitely. And we parted with the promise to see each other next week.

Second, the availability of the rabbinical staff for consultation was important. Although I found—and still find, occasionally—that Rabbis generally lean toward Judah Halevy's valuing of the convert's soul, being able to ask questions of the living word is very important. As often as I have been given a pat answer—for example the one that begins with (for me the discomforting, phrase) "Yes, I've dealt with that very same problem many times before, and can tell you exactly what you need to know"—I have found a learned Rabbi who was willing to take the time to consider me an individual worthy of his time and consideration.

Third, my wife Leslie's family was itself a welcoming experience. They were warm and supporting in every way. The question of conversion did not come up with Leslie's parents. It did, however, with Leslie's grandparents.

Fourth and most important, our first child was born and my unassailable belief in the small and great miracles indicating God's presence in the world was reawakened and solidified.

Avram of Haran was the first convert to Judaism, Avram the son of Terah the idol maker from Ur of the Chaldeans. Abraham's father Terah began the journey to Canaan, but settled and died in Haran. Then the Lord said to Avram, *Lech-lecha*:

> *Go forth from your native land...*
> *And I will make of you a great nation,*
> *And I will bless you,*
> *And curse him who curses you;*
> *And all the families of the earth*
> *Shall bless themselves by you.*

All serious converts to Judaism treasure this passage because we are all "bar" or "bat Abraham." For example, my name is Ze'ev Asher ben Abraham. I am a "son of Abraham," the first convert to Judaism. The very words *Lech-lecha* contain a "High Test," for the Lord tests or tries the righteous. Abraham's high test was the sacrifice of his only son Isaac.

Like Avram, I left my safe land, my Haran, my godlessness and worship of idols and the works of my hands, and began my long journey toward my Canaan, my promised land. Los Angeles was and is my Sechem. I have pitched my tent here, with the high desert to the east and north and the Pacific rim to the west. There is no place to run.

Here my wife Leslie and I have become a part of the great nation that descended from Abraham. God has blessed us with a family, with two sons, Asher David and Joshua Ari, and twin daughters, Rachel Dorit and Zara Ilana. My wife, having been born a Jew and a child of Sarah, chose God in her youth, and she was essential in my rediscovery of God and of Judaism. Just as the Jewish friends I knew and loved long before my conversion collectively prepared me to understand Judaism, so my wife in her patience and quiet forbearance allowed me the opportunity and encouragement needed to begin my own discovery of need to return to a belief in God—because my conversion to Judaism was preceded by a return to belief in God.

My wife accepted me as I was, with few conditions. I think that for every convert there must be a crucial figure like my Leslie, a Jew to help the convert deal with the serious questions and self-doubt—above all, the re-creation of self, the sea change of feelings and thoughts that the sincere convert experiences. Leslie was this person for me. Our engagement was preceded by the agreement that our children would be raised Jewish. Behind the trellis of this tacit agreement grew the tender vine of the Diaspora restored. Every Jewish child replaces a victim of Shoah; every Jewish parent draws ashes from the air and shapes them into new life—the essence of the future. When my wife now talks about my conversion, she says, "You always had a Jewish soul."

Asher, our first-born, is my Isaac. I will never bind him to my will, but my wife and I have determined to bind him to God's will in that it is within our power. His birth was a spiritual cataclysm for me, a revelation. I saw my son's birth, not as a rebirth of myself, but as a miracle indicative of God's presence in the common-yet-magnificent miracles that surround us every waking moment. As the poem "Asher's Moment" expresses, I saw in Asher's birth nothing less than the re-creation of the world.

> Your first breath seemed
> to me the breath of God—
> pale and pure, it flooded
> the surface of my face.
>
> As you hesitated a moment,
> head turning up, body buried
> in your mother's flesh,
> the land of my heart formed.
>
> Your eyes opened—skies appeared.
> Restless, to taunt the spirit,
> your shoulder lifted within—
> and a whole, perfect image

slipped from sea to air.
Then all things formed about you,
little fish writhing in first light,
little angel of my heart.

And indeed the world is created again in our first child, Asher, for he will see the world with new eyes. It is recreated in each of our children, and in every child. The universe will be recreated though the magnificent acts of comprehension and consciousness of our children, and of all children.

As Abraham is my personal ancestor, my father, my eternal brother and friend, the singular event of Asher's birth gave me great courage to believe strongly in God again. Because of this I included Asher's name in my own Hebrew name: Ze'ev Asher ben Abraham. So my Hebrew name ties me to my spiritual model, Abraham, and our first child (representing each of our children), Asher. We all know the importance of names and this is the story of mine. It expands to both the far past and near future.

Once Asher's birth had shown me the breath of God in the world, I began my real wrestling, like Jacob. Having felt the breath of God, I longed for the face of God. I longed to make Los Angeles my *Peni-el*, the sacred place where I wrestled with the messenger of God and received a name that would represent my new state. So I began a more intensive study than ever before. I knew from the beginning that this course of study would last a lifetime and I quickly sensed that the struggle would yield at best a few blessings.

5

My conversion occurred in July, 1988 in the garden of Rabbi Harvey Fields. After a brief ceremony of prayers, we went to the pool where I was to submerge myself three times in accordance with the conversion ceremony's form. With each submersion, I rose a more complete and richer person. Before the first submersion, I was acutely aware that I was surrounded by loved ones. Then I submerged myself and I was suddenly surrounded by the sunny, cool silence of the pool's water. When I rose the first time from that water and it ran down my body like liquid fire, I felt a deeper circle about me, one of love and spirit. This was the circle of love I had always longed for. Suddenly, I was standing by the pool of my boyhood with the smell of wild flowers in the air and the peace of nature enclosing me. The impulses I first felt in childhood were being fulfilled. Each person around me seemed a flower of sweetness and beauty.

Then I heard the words of the Rabbi and found myself in his rose garden again, where each bloom and each petal of each of his carefully cultivated roses stood out in its particularity and special qualities, reflecting in its clarity and complexity the miracle of creation.

As the water slipped over me for the second time, I sensed the presence of my mother. I curled myself into fetal position and lingered a moment in the special quietude and light of the submersion, and in the moment before rebirth. Never had I felt greater gratitude or love for her, for her guidance, compassion and concern. There, beneath the surface of worldly things, I revived my oldest connections with nature and family.

As I emerged from the water the second time, I was blinded by the sun, the eye of God's sky. The idea of rebirth, of redemption began to form in my mind. I might be born again, be burned clean by holy fire. The words of the Rabbi seared my mind.

As I submerged myself a third time, an image formed from the black and crimson shields of my vision. It was a face, and on that face was etched longing and a great desire to be loved. It was my father's face, and I slowly recognized my own face, and then the face of my sweet son Asher. In that ecstatic moment I knew my father as my self. It was revelation, a pure gift of God.

When I emerged from the pool and put on my robe, I was strangely calm externally, but inside I was inundated by impressions and emotions. As we shared food and drink, I was filled with overwhelming feelings of love for those present. I had taken an oath, and every thought now seemed a prayer, every image a poem. The roses, the water and the sun were now within me, illuminating my personal history, fulfilling the vague longings which I now saw as the qualities of nature God granted me as a visionary child in my conversion ceremony.

6

Is it enough to follow the laws given us in Torah? It is essential that each Jew tries to do this, but—given the sincere effort to obey the laws—it is not enough. If acts are performed devoid of an understanding of the reason why they are performed, they are not enough— although I know Jews who argue the opposite. I believe that if the external acts of a Jew, or any believer is devoid of adherence to internal life and an understanding of Torah, then the acts alone are not evidence of moral involvement. We must understand *why* we do what we do. We must study Torah diligently and consciously seek to obey God's law—a doctrine of righteousness.

We converts have to hunker down and go on. Each of us works toward conversion as best we can. The blows are few and the joys many. It seems to me that the convert often develops a pride in having attained a certain kind of spiritual autonomy amounting to *aloneness*. (It is important to distinguish this state from *loneliness*.) I mean by this a certain stalwart security of belief that does not depend upon the approval of others—not even religious authorities. If this sense of being alone becomes painful and leads to despair, then serious mistakes have been made. But if the aloneness leads to contemplation of the nature of individual belief in God, it may be a necessary blessing, a mitzvah. Conversion can be a lonely experience; because, in the long run, not only God tests the true believer—everyone does, including the convert himself. That may be for the best.

The convert begins to share the hostility surrounding the Jewish world. In Europe, this hostility was often open. In America, it is more subtle. (I think of Gregory Peck's role in the great film *Gentlemen's Agreement*. You will remember that he portrays a reporter who poses as a Jew in the American Gentile society characterized by an unspoken anti-Semitism, a "gentlemen's agreement.") A very painful part of this aspect of conversion can be dealing with one's own immediate family, especially siblings. In the years since my conversion, my three sisters have quietly adjusted to the profound spiritual changes in my life, and I love them even more for their patience and acceptance.

There is—and this may become a profoundly personal matter—the daunting challenge of becoming a part of the Hebrew language tradition and the Jewish intellectual tradition. For those of us who are not gifted in languages and who spend almost every waking moment trying to make a living, sometimes even biblical Hebrew seems an insurmountable challenge, which we chip away at as often as possible. Yet, clearly, this endless intellectual and spiritual wealth contained within Torah, Jewish Studies and the History of the Jewish People is one of the great joys and motivating forces for the true convert.

By the terebinths, the oak trees of Mamre, Abraham welcomes three men, whom he does not know, bathes their feet, insists that they recline in the shade of the oak trees before they continue down the dusty road to Sodom and Ghemorrah, and serves them food. How can we do any less for the convert than we are instructed to do for the *stranger* in the Torah? Dare we be as inhospitable as the inhabitants of Sodom and Ghemorrah? Should not we strive to be more like Abraham? Then how much more should we welcome the sincere convert.

It may be in some ways natural to question the motivations of the convert. Who would choose a way of questioning and wrestling, when an easier way exists? I believe that, in every way that matters, the sincere convert does not choose, but is *chosen*. The sincere convert, like Abraham, hears a voice saying *Lech-lecha*.

7

Every discussion of a topic such as conversion, which essentially involves things unseen and unknowable in the concrete sense, it is of great value to ask questions. As I stated earlier, the questions in such processes are permanent and the answers vacillatory. Religious belief may appear to be a series of transitional states, but belief is—in its essence—based securely on something extraordinary, unexpected—an encounter with God. I have tried to capture in what follows the essential characteristics of my life, my self, my belief in God, and my Jewishness. I rediscovered my belief in the context of Judaism. I know my children will be better accepted by the Jewish world than I have been, and I rejoice in that, because if they experience half the joy and love I have experienced as a Jew since my conversion, they will live and love with full hearts. Ultimately and immediately, my concern is with *them* and their lives rather than with my self. They are the essence of my Judaism, my wife's and my future hopes, and, it seems to me, God's chosen.

Where am I now? That is a question I will be asking myself the rest of my life. How will I answer it? By gazing lovingly into the mirror of the Torah. Why believe in God? Why breathe the air? God is a part of life and life is to be lived fully. One evening, when Asher was two, I walked west on Wilshire Boulevard past the Tar Pits, *la brea*. It was a magnificent, wind-swept evening. I wrote these words:

> O God, how majestic is your evening sky,
> The gold and crimson weave of Your aery mantel
> Above the cloud-brushed, western expanse.
> The dome of darkening blue is awash
> With purple fleece and thunder song.
> The wind's great wing sweeps eastward toward morning.
> Beneath this star-pierced map of an exploding,
>   collapsing universe,
> Under this great layered growth of time and matter
> Only sketched for the earthbound
> In the cold words of science,
> But veiled in the shroud of cosmic distance—
> I seek you everywhere,
> Architect of eternity's arch.
>
> Far beneath You I dream,
> As my eyes strain to fix in the vast swirl
> A sign among the numberless movements
> Above the clouds
> As stars emerge—
> The flickering signature of your first fire.

Cool wind sweeps down now
From the mountains to the north,
And from Your interstellar castle
Of pure line and point.

Lord of river slide, sea shift,
And the earth's ride about the darkening sun,
Accept my restless soul
Into the vast ocean of your burning night—
This eternal distance hovering
Between thought and action.

Why choose Judaism? Because I know that—burning in my mind, filling the pure space between the Torah's text and the eye that lovingly and critically examines each sign of each word—there exists a divine presence which both my intellect and my soul were created to understand.

Who is honored in your presence more,
One who accepts, or questions?
Are my doubts anathema?
Am I wrong to see a new wilderness
In this land of unbearable riches?

Lord beyond space and time, bring peace
To the forked creatures of your earth
That we may write Your name with our flights
Into the cold heavens we know and study
As airy fire and artless flow.

Who can blame our longing for a sign?
Would one more proof
For the blind and foolish
Beast struggling below,
Separated by so many generations
From Your cleansing fire,
Shame Your greatness?

Yet my heart echoes still within
For I know that just as my soul
Is suffused throughout my flesh,
You are here about me, everywhere,
In all things—in me, in my questions,
Even in my doubts.

I hope that my brief history may offer the convert some peace, if only as a mirror for their own struggle. I hope that the Jewish reader will come to a deeper appreciation of the sincere convert through my words. I hope that Christians will gain from my words a better understanding of the essential beauties of Judaism. We had best all work together in healing the world, celebrating our likenesses and underplaying our differences. Otherwise, a great loss may result. Our children cannot afford such a loss.

My doubts are the doubts of a believer who lives in a world that can become cruel with stunning quickness. The world's cruelty is temporary, however, and the joys of belief eternal in the everyday series of revelations that make up a day in the life of the true believer. I wish the joys I have known for each convert to Judaism—to each Jew, I mean to say. I know in my heart that we are one and the same. If I could make a single, well meaning wish for human kind, it would be that the nature of conversion—in its deepest and broadest sense—be considered by every person. I want to thank my wife-and-helpmate Leslie, Joshua Heschel, Peter Marin and Harvey Fields for helping me learn what a convert truly is: one who turns to God from lesser things, one who questions everything before the face of God, one who speaks out of God's shadow, *b'zal el.*

NOTES

[i] J. R. Rosenbloom, *Conversion to Judaism*, Hebrew Union Press, 1978, p. 15

[ii] *Pondering the Imponderable: Thoughts on Anti-Semitism and Shoah. A Personal Memoir*, [1995] p. 5, unpublished version.

YOU DON'T WANT TO KNOW

1

I have no distinct memory of meeting Dora, my wife's grandmother, for the first time. She simply appeared on the sofa wherever there was a family gathering and I would be attracted to her settled, easygoing qualities. She carried her own sense of place, and Dora's place was comfortable for me. We never spoke a great deal after I settled near her; it seemed enough to us that we were there, simply together. Sometimes she would hold my hand, not clinging or anxiously; and she surrendered me without a fuss to practically anyone. Whatever she saw in me, she could share with others. We came, in time, to kiss on the lips. Her kisses were dry and gentle, without a trace of blunt need of attention, simply representing an unspoken intimacy, a gift experience had left her to bestow on those she chose.

In the later years, she felt even less like talking, or perhaps felt defeated by memory. During our decade together, I attempted to record her version of family history, and she refused to say much. I would mention the name of the town where she was raised. She would look at me curiously, as if to say, *You know this, and you're asking me?* Yes, they had owned land. No, she could not attend school. No, it was not pleasant. She did not react at all to key words: discrimination, pogrom, shoah. Finally, during the second attempt, I gave up and turned the tape recorder off. There was little on it really, but an often repeated phrase, *You don't want to know.*

In the year before she died, we communicated very little. I was rushing from one project to the next. Sometimes I would simply settle into a chair near her at gatherings and touch her arm hello. Occasionally, it fell to me to fetch her for gatherings. She always called me *Schweetheart* when I did this. I wish I'd done it more. She was saving her energy during this time, energy needed to deal with weakened limbs, the slight overweight her healthy appetite produced, and the inevitably increasing bouts of tiredness. Still, her eyes brightened and deepened when she saw her great-grandchildren, those who would replace her.

This past Thanksgiving, I glanced into the Horn's kitchen looking for Asher, who was hiding in another room as it turned out, and I saw an ashen presence, a shrunken waif huddled down in a great chair that had been pushed up close to the table. Even in her frailty, I had a strong sense of Dora's stubborn substantiality. Her sense of place was still intact. She did not see me; it was as if she were asleep with her eyes open. She was a sad and still center in the whirling atmosphere of our house.

This was three months before her death. The next month, she came to our house for Hanukkah, and almost fell as she negotiated the curb of

Stanley Avenue. A vast space had appeared between the car and our house. Once inside, she settled into our playroom, which is pretty much the center of activity in our house and did not move from there. Later, I observed a flushed but grim expression on her face, and went over and kissed her. She looked away from me with no recognition in her eyes. The days of recognition were past.

Gradually, it all became a burden, and she no longer left her bed. When we left for Utah on January ninth, she was taking in little but beer. Fluid leaked from her knees and ankles. We stopped by when we returned ten days later and she recognized us individually and seemed delighted that we were there. Her companions—her international community of friends: Yawapah from Thailand, Rosa from Mexico—took good care of her. All of this was arranged by her daughter-in-law, Rita, of whom Dora once said to me, *She is as good to me as a daughter.*

Then, close to midnight on Friday, Jan. 22, my wife Les was awakened by a phone call from her brother Michael. Dora had been gathered in as she slept. Hadn't we all said to ourselves, it would be a blessing if she could go peacefully? Les called her brother Brian, with whom she had planned to visit Dora the next day. Now it would have to be enough to have been thinking of her. The last matriarch, the oldest pillar of the family, had slipped away during sleep, leaving us all looking for support.

2

I knew Dora in the last decade of her life. That's not a very great span of time, and within that decade the actual time we spent together was miniscule. I knew her in the twilight years, in mid-winter, in slow motion. Still, the petite woman filled my time and space as well as anyone ever has. Time and space, and Dora. Her spatial life during our years together evolved around two poles of activity: her two-room apartment in the Westside Apartment Building; and the house of her only son, Martin and his wife Rita five blocks away. As those years progressed, she moved between those two axes of her spatial existence with decreasing frequency. She moved from a spry amble to a cautious methodical plowing of an every-thickening atmosphere surrounding her, then to a cane-assisted, broken ramble, and finally to a walker. With the walker, autonomy ceased. More and more, she sat or napped, and moved and spoke less than anyone could remember. Then in the weeks before the midnight call came, she rose from bed unwillingly, asked only for beer, and lay smiling out from under the covers where she nursed her mild high and waited patiently to drift off into the sleep after sleep.

Leslie went over to her apartment after midnight to see Dora for the last time, before the UCLA team came to claim her body for the medical school. Her nurse had washed and made up so that she departed from her home composed and graceful in the mind of those who saw her leave. My wife said she looked very peaceful, even beautiful, her head resting lightly on the pillow. *My own mother's face had been childlike in the restful simplicity of its final sleep.*

She was, we thought, ready to let go. She was surrounded by people who really cared for her. She had always had a rich social life in her apartment building. She regularly visited her great-grandchildren in the preschool adjoining the Westside Home for the Elderly where she lived. A circle of practiced caregivers orbited around her, lovingly making her days and nights as comfortable as was possible. She had the kind of steady soul that attracts loving care to it.

Her chief caregiver, Rita, arranged in the mid-80's for a special birthday party for Dora in the Westside Apartments. Rob Lempert, a Harvard physicist and pianist, and I presented a brief program of *Lieder*—Schubert, Schumann—in her honor. I have stored several impressions from that night. I will put aside the dry quality of the piano's tone, the slow tempi, and the crowded conditions. (The trained voice needs distance to work.) I will concentrate on Dora. She sat beaming like a queen ensconced on her cloth and wood throne, listening carefully to the sounds dedicated to her. How many would have such a concert given in their honor?

After the *Abendkoncert*, I approached Dora and kissed her. She introduced me to a seemingly reserved lady sitting nearby, who moaned to me as I took her hand. *Why* <u>Dora</u>? she said, her eyes clinging to mine soulfully. Bent over, still holding Dora's hand, I glanced momentarily into the lonely desert of self-pity that awaits a certain type of person in old age, then retreated into politeness.

She's the birthday girl! I said. Then I turned and winked at Dora, who had been trying to cheer her dour friend up.

Dora rolled her eyes toward the ceiling with comic allure. *Why not for Dora?* I said.

It couldn't hurt (pronounced hoit), said Dora, and she offered me a piece of cake.

Dora didn't pity herself and didn't complain. When questioned by a doctor, *Where does it hurt* and *How do you feel* she would reply, *You're asking me?!* You had to observe her to see what was going wrong; otherwise, you'd never find out. *The Doctor's asking me what's wrong?* she would say later, in understated outrage. She was not a squeaky wheel, a kvetcher.

Dora was dutiful and generous. She married a man who would also take her mother. She dedicated herself to one child and deprived herself to help insure his success. She took no credit when he succeeded, but enjoyed his success enormously, for his sake. She was a calm, full spirit from the old world who strove and cared for others in their need, and she was in turn cared for in her time of need.

I remember the strong impression that I got while singing to her: it seemed a natural and good thing to do. Her face smiled unceasingly as she lost herself in the music, in waking dream. It is clear in remembering that evening that there was a balance and depth to her life that this music echoed. It was an experience that went far beyond that evening. Dora was living proof of the simple nature of nobility. To me, she is also proof of the ability of certain human qualities to transcend space and time.

3

Photographs *are* reductive. Photos slow, even stop time's flow in our comprehension of the time-space continuum enclosing us. The photographic process approximates the mind's act of constructing, then preserving visual images. A photo does this by accomplishing a visual simplification of image or person in situ. Such a simplification destroys the complexity of real context and allows dreamers like me to make-believe as we study photographs, to recreate scenes and color them with our sentiment. And even if I know this mimics the mind—is probably even a lie of the mind—I enjoy time's arrest. Time is our worst invention.

I especially love black and white photos in which I have to warm the hard-edged forms with memory and emotion. In the mental and emotional effort the illusion of suspended time is created. I love this illusion. In a world dominated by machines, this activity offers a chance to take the product of the machine age and, by exercising imagination and intuition in relation to it, to actually explore the effect of such inventions on the human self-image—and perhaps the soul. Imagination arrests time while intuition is a facility that ties us in a spatial, historical—topological—sense to the deepest roots of the birth of self.

I have a photo of Dora, but she is not alone in it. My son Asher's two-year-old countenance is pressed against hers. Even shadowed—everyone points out the photo's flaws, as if this mattered to the heart of the imagination—the two faces beam like twin suns from the cage of dots and lines forming but only vaguely representing and at all enclosing their joy, their spirit. Two individuals, separated by nearly a century, form themselves joyfully, whole and complete, in my vision of this two-dimensional box.

It is around nine on a beautiful summer morning at Arrowhead. Dora had just finished her exercises, while Asher plays nearby. I've shot the lake, Asher, and a nearby squirrel weaving its energy around a pine limb. I had given Dora her privacy earlier, but when she approaches Asher and squats beside him, studying his play with fallen leaves and acorns, I can no longer resist. I say, *How about a photo of you two?* Dora immediately says, *Okaaaay!* and grabs Asher to her. I barely get the camera to my eye before the shutter clicks and the moment of their instantaneous huddling has passed. I hadn't focused or really considered the composition. *Oh well,* I ask myself, *I wonder how it would have looked if I'd been ready?* Dora smooches Asher before she lets him go, and the day melts quickly about her into the other restful, stressful days of an Arrowhead retreat. Asher returns to his play, Dora begins her daily knitting.

Later, I am amazed when I receive the prints from that day's shoot. In this particular photo, two lovely people, not at all separated by the eighty years between then, crush the raised cheeks of their faces together. They might be two beautiful children playing on a summer's day, children who paused then as Asher and his brother Joshua occasionally do now, for a moment to share the spontaneous blessing of the other.

Such photographs are for me the keys to the heart of memory. Pictures of the mind fade, along with the elasticity of the flesh; photos fade less quickly. Now that Dora has gone before us into that undiscovered country, I can only hold her so long in my mind, but Asher will have this photograph, this image of a summer's day he hopefully will not and I cannot forget.

Dora didn't share my love of illusion. Her sturdy sense of self didn't need to take arms against a sea of metaphorical troubles; she let metaphors and time wash over her. She'd seen enough of the real thing. *Hamlet,* she said, *Who would want to read it? It's about a loser.* Dora was not a loser. She kept her *Complete Works of Shalom Aleichem* at hand. She had escaped the castle of horrors that mauled and swallowed the Yiddish Renaissance and she never looked back. *You don't want to know,* she said. And shrugged time off her slight sturdy shoulders, shoulders grown a little weaker in later years.

As I study the photo, I see its many imperfections: the shadows, the focus. Still, there is something of a miracle about it for me. Dora's eyes are focused on the camera—on me—dark and true. Asher, in a manner reminiscent of my mother, glances away, perhaps into the future. The pair of them live so clearly in my vision of this crude image. There is a power that defeats with inherent grace the technical difficulties in the execution of the taking of the photo, as well as the enormous disparity of age between the two subjects of the photo. That photo emanates from strength of heart and steadfastness of soul. My hope to see my children develop this power is as clear in my mind as the knowledge that Dora possessed it.

4

Pouring over photographs, reductive clues to a wonderfully complex life story, a narrative full of mysteries emerges. One such mystery is the unknown woman who appears in several of the New York photos of Dora in the 20's and 30's. Who was she and what role did she play in Dora's life? Vast portions of every life are veiled in mystery. And we do somehow long to know the details of that life, even the dark details, no matter how innocent or terrible they might have been. These are the historical hallways we will not stride or waltz down ourselves, yet they are somehow a part of our personal past. Wanting to know about them is like longing to find about a long-lost part of ourselves. There were complex forces that shaped the calm, petite figure who was such an important part of our lives.

She was a source, a flower of the ancient, noble tree of Ruth and Esther. She represented those who did not escape the jaws of death in Russian and Polish pogroms and in the Nazi death camps in Europe and those who did not come to America to continue their family's life. And she did not want to be a Pandora for that family. She wouldn't open the box of her past. Perhaps she felt enough people had done that already. She summarized it all with *You don't want to know.*

Dora created our present time. She is the mother of my second father, the grandmother of my wife, the great-grandmother of our children. We will live on in the present she created, in our vision of that present. She also was herself a spirit of the present. *You don't want to know* was her way of saying, *Live now, enjoy this time.*

As a writer, I create and work in the eternal present. This is the mode of the creator. With each individual reader, a situation is recreated, every word uttered for the first time, every glance burns, every stroke gleams. This is the world in which Dora now resides for me, somewhere between dream and reality, in the soul of the imagination. I know these images of Dora will fade from my memory, but I will cling to them, for the artifice they offer will be more real than anything else I have. Images of Dora in time, even the limited time we shared, are powerful in my personal myth: the family gatherings, the concert, the Arrowhead photograph, the smattering of remarks that color my personal dictionary with their sweet plainness. All these were Dora in Time, and the Space she occupies within me is very large and full of solid and unspoken joy.

Los Angeles, 1994

GARDENS OF THE MIND

1

When I was a child, driven wild by physical pain and loneliness, I would seek out quiet places to be utterly alone. In these places, usually natural environments, I could cry and strike things without fear of ridicule or punishment, and then, when calmed by exhaustion, simply slump and study what was around me until hunger or some other need brought me back to the house where my mother, father and sisters waited. Once I began to frequent a particular place and sacralized it with suffering, it became crucial to my childhood world. I dreamed of it, imagined myself in it sometimes when I was not there; in short, I internalized such places and they became a pristine wilderness in my imagination. Such environments became crucial retreats for the wounded child I was and spiritual signposts for the adult I became.

Carl Jung describes such a place among his "island of memory" in *Memories, Dreams, Reflections* beside Lake Constance. There the young Carl is transfixed by the lake and "the idea...that I must live near a lake; without water, I thought, nobody could live at all" (p. 7). Jung's impression—a small part of a very happy and precocious childhood—of the expanse of water as having given him "inconceivable pleasure" was very different from what I experienced—which was *release*—in my secret places, yet he and I shared a parallel experience with regard to such secret places. These quiet places, or rather the impressions and actions experienced in them, became sacred in a way humankind comes to regard a place as sacred when invested with immanent powers of healing. Jung returned to water his whole life to recapture this feeling; he never lived far from lake water after that. His final home was directly on a lake.

I also seek out similar environments—by lakes, the Pacific Ocean, or fountains—knowing that these places connect me with something deeper and beyond my individual self. Carl Jung suggested that such places evoke archetypes, mythic patterns inherent in the collective consciousness—the internalized collective experience of the human race which is manifested at some level in each individual human consciousness. I think—and more importantly *feel*—there is a good measure of truth in this assertion. Once such space for me was the levee near a small pond on our farm in southern Arkansas where I grew up. There were others, but let me describe this one because its essential elements are archetypal, universe in nature.

Beyond the rolling pastures of southern Arkansas, lies the old weeded pond and brambled levee, and the mud that sucked deeply at my feet near the water's edge. I lingered for long moments to study the vague stirrings under the water, how the surface wrinkled and slid in vague patterns. Insects swarm over the shifting surface, each delicate leg a living needle. In bright July patterned cracks appeared far out from the viscous, writhing edge of the slime, and I gripped the fissures with bare toes, and dreamed of falling far into the earth.

As darkness descends, I retreated to slip under watery sheets in the breathless air of my room, where great black panthers played at the foot of my bed for endless moments before I flew, returned to the pond where in darkness I could finally see the bright fluttering landscape beneath the surface, hear insects scream in seething masses and prey upon one another, while the ancient pond sung in silent movement from its dregs of the mysteries of wetness and warmth hidden there.

I carry this particular place with me even today, and sometimes draw on its environment, the rhythms of its elements—wetness, warmth, bright darkness—and its symbolic connotations to release tension and to stimulate my imagination. The existence of this, and other environments within me allows me to, in Einstein's wonderful phrase, to "withdraw into the chambers of my mind." It is here that a certain fulfillment is possible for me, for it is here that nature and spirituality are inextricably intertwined within me.

Unlike Freud, Jung held that man's inner religious (by this word I mean *God-seeking*) drives were at least as powerful as, for example, sexual urges. Without getting into intensive analysis of archetypal or mythical plot, character or imagery, I want to simply say that my feelings and thoughts by this pond and in other similar places were my childhood visionary attempts to structure my inner world with a personal myth that would allow my self "a splinter of the infinite deity," to use Jung's marvelous phrase. I attempted to bring my nascent self into contact with the hidden patterns of true life, the patterns of need and meaning running underneath and through every civilized being's longing for understanding of and fulfillment concerning his basic condition. I drew upon the natural environment to create emotional and mental designs which were to sustain and empower me for life.

An important part of my maturation consisted in my learning that such gardens of the mind may complement fulfillment through a religious drive. The "inconceivable pleasure" Jung discovered and the peace I sought and found were, it seems to me, God-seeking activities of which my childhood was full. My embrace of this knowledge was to wait 40 years. This event occurred in another garden, the one in which my conversion ceremony occurred.

The gradual process of my conversion to Judaism involved a web of elements so complex that I am still discovering and exploring them. They were and are in essence a new land of self for me, and as I examine their richness I am led again and again to what for me has become *the* essence of my conversion process: the recovery of my belief in God out of the chaos of contemporary existence through love and the flower of memory. Without this spiritual rebirth of childhood I would never have converted. This is the story of how that recovery came about, how I rediscovered the presence of deity I felt so clearly as a child in nature.

A child feels innocent delight in the natural world. At seven or eight years of age, I loved to watch the rising sun turn our fields of sorghum and corn into glistening green and gold blankets. The rainstorms often swept up quickly and washed the field dust of Southern Arkansas from the corn I hoed and from my slender arms in a cool flood. The evening breeze that invisibly moved the leaves of the great red oaks surrounding our yard stirred my hair and caressed me like a grandfather's gentle hand. I sat for hours alone in the tall grass of our fields lost to the realities of life my father spoke of constantly, and dreamed within and about the flowing force of life enclosing me, which I felt so clearly on my forehead. There in the fields of our farm, I felt the numinous presence of God on my temples.

This awakening to the harmony of nature helped resolve a struggle taking place within me. By the time I awoke to this beauty of nature, I was a very unhappy boy, to whom natural beauty and its inherent power were a great comfort. I *felt* the rain and wind's power literally because I could not see well. At four I had lost the vision in one eye in an accident, and I was buried in pain and darkness—both my eyes were bandaged—for most of two years after that while doctors tried to save the damaged eye.

Worse than the physical pain during this period was the loneliness of a blind boy through the long weeks and months in the hospital. During this time both my eyes were bound with cotton patches and gauze. My mother was unable to visit me at all during this time, and I rarely saw my father. When he did come, his visits were very unsettling for me. I longed to be held and comforted, but he stood far from the bed and spoke gravely with the doctors about my condition and the expenses involved in the treatment. The unkind nurses were always nearby to complain to my father about the many "problems" I had caused them in his absence. I was not a "good boy." I was an embarrassment to my father and, I felt, to my absent mother. I was so far from any contact with nature and its healing power. It was the stuff of nightmares. I remember the entire two years as just that, seemingly endless nightmare, typified by operations during which I was both awake and powerless to cry out and the recurring ether nightmares of horrific power.

The loneliness of blindness after one has seen—and taken sight for granted—is a deep thing, and when my poor sight was again given to me (in one eye) all natural beauty struck me with an intensity close to ecstasy.

Little wonder that rainbaths and wind seemed to me the caresses a loving but absent God/parent. The landscapes themselves, the fields, woods, the pond's surface trembled in dimensions of morning or evening light. Above, the clouds blossomed in lenticular splendor.

I have come to see the inherent impulse that brought me to invest the environment of the pond with metaphysical relevance and the curious peace that invaded me there as essentially religious in nature. My love of the interplay of natural elements is a reaction to characteristics or qualities of God's benign presence in the world. It was through this growing awareness of the divine in the world about me that I survived the trauma of my childhood and adolescence. These special environments and the numinous events which occurred in them came to form the garden of my mind, a place where beauty and the strange sweet interconnectedness of all things could exist.

2

Before I describe my garden of conversion, I want to describe my "Certificate of Conversion," one of those external symbols I love. I confess that I need these objects because in a disorienting world they remind me of my duties. I agree with a stripped-down existence in principle, but in actuality I do not like bare walls where I live or work. I certainly want the walls of my mind rich in images and ideas. More than either of these, I want to cultivate a relationship between that which is good within me and that which needs help outside me. It is the nature of such symbols on my walls to link me to memories and ideas I value. The relationship between my certificate of conversion as symbol and my desire to do good works is strong.

The certificate begins with the Shmah: *Hear, O Israel, the Lord Our God, the Lord is One.* These words echo down through the centuries with great power exhorting the Jewish people to direct their hearts and minds to the one God. The certificate then continues: *This is to record that William George Wallis (Ze'ev Asher ben Avraham) having sought to join the household of Israel and promising to live by its principles and practices was received into the Jewish Faith on July 6, 1988 corresponding to the Hebrew date 21 Tammuz 4748 at Beverly Hills, California.*

Note that the text of the convert's certificate refers to the *household of Israel, the religion of Israel, its principles and practices*, and *the Jewish Faith*. Israel, both the land and the sacred ideal, is first a *household*, a living family, a family beloved and chosen by God to bear and uphold his sacred laws in the world. This family is instructed to be fruitful and multiply, while insuring the perpetuation of God's law through obedience to Torah's teaching. These laws are the basis for *the Religion of Israel* and direct Jews to study *Torah* (the law itself) and to perform *mitzvot* (acts of compassion and mercy). When one desires to be a member of such a *household* and abides by *the principles and practices of the Religion of Israel*, then one is received into *the Jewish Faith*.

The use of the two dates hints that an even greater and more complex change may be involved here. The date *21 Tammuz, 5748* implies that time is no longer to be demarcated by the birth of Jesus, but by "the first day of the creation of the universe." So the convert must not only change his actions to conform with the laws written in the Torah and derived from sacred teachings by the wise ones, but must begin to see time itself as a structure with new aspects. Halacha, Jewish law, requires that the convert radically alter his concepts of both space and time. This certificate suggests that this old religion requires a sea change, a new vision, a profound if sometimes subtle and gradual transformation of the self to conform with an ancient vision of moral life and spiritual ecstasy.

A part of my gradual transformation was demarcated by a symbol, my Hebrew name. My new name was created in the following way. *Ze'ev* is Hebrew for my own given name, William. It is also the name of the father of modern Israel, Hertzl. *Asher* is my first son's name, and I wished to share a name with him. *Ben Avraham* is the name given to all converts, for Abraham was the first convert to Judaism. My name thus ties me to the first Jew, the founder of Israel, my son, and my personal and complex past.

The certificate is signed by Rabbis Harvey Fields, Sheldon Donnell and Steven Leder, three learned and dynamic, gentle men who have influenced my life. The certificate then closes with the words: *Thy people be my people and thy God my God.* This quotation from the Book of Ruth was spoken by Ruth the Moabite—the Moabites were arch-enemies of the Israelites and idol worshippers—to her Jewish mother-in-law, Naomi. God has chosen Ruth to enrich the Jewish people and bear the father of the great King David, who will unite the Children of Israel in one earthly kingdom for the first time. So, the signature of God in the history of the Jewish people closes my Certificate of Conversion, reminding me that one of the great themes of the Tanach is the omnipresent hand of God determining the affairs of men.

Those who honored God with their presence in his own home, performing an act of many-leveled symbolic significance, not only brought me into *the household of Israel*, but into his own household as well. His trust and many gifts have empowered me with the courage and faith to change myself, to bring myself closer to God.

My wife Leslie, who patiently helped guide me to the warmth and acceptance of a life of Jewish family values, was at my side. We share a quiet pride in the gift of our togetherness, and our family. She is my helpmate and support in everything worthy that I do. She is my Rachel. My dear father- and mother-in-law, Martin and Rita Horn, were there, their quiet support of their daughter's marriage and of me as a person as evident as ever. Martin's cousin Steven Marmor and his wife Ruth (also a convert) lent their support and good wishes. The generations were represented by my mother-in-law's parents, William and Tessie Wenig, both of whom fled the pogroms and other diverse forms of terror anti-Semitism took in Easter Europe in the first half of the century.

And Peter Marin, the intense renegade champion of the underprivileged and dispossessed was there. This outsider who champions those shut out, this sustainer of the ancient tradition of compassionate intellectual questioning came bearing gifts other than his presence: he brought a gift born of his playful, passionate intellect and great heart: a poem celebrating the occasion. Here are a few lines from it:

> Listen: something draws close,
> Angels in caps clapping hands,
> Bearded men over the sleeper,
> Ghost fathers dancing on rooves…
> Players brotherly in embrace,
> Transfigured by triumph, aflame.

This was the group that gathered in the garden to bless the near-naked gawky child of forty-two as he submerged himself three times among the roses.

3

After a brief ceremony of prayers, we went to the pool where I was to submerge myself three times in accordance with the conversion ceremony's form. With each submersion, I rose a more complete and richer person. Before the first submersion, I was acutely aware that I was surrounded by loved ones. Then I submerged myself and I was suddenly surrounded by the sunny, cool silence of the pool's water. When I rose the first time from the water and it ran down my body like liquid fire, I felt a deeper circle about me, one of love and spirit. This was the circle of love I had always longed for. Suddenly, I was standing by the pool of my boyhood with the smell of wild flowers in the air and the peace of nature enclosing me. The impulses I first felt in childhood were being fulfilled. Each friend around me seemed a flower of sweetness and beauty.

Then I heard the words of the Rabbi and found myself in his rose garden again, where each bloom and each petal of each of his carefully cultivated roses stood out in its particularity and special qualities, reflecting in its clarity and complexity the miracle of creation.

As the water slipped over me for the second time, I felt the presence of my mother. I curled myself into fetal position and lingered a moment in the special quietude and light of the submersion, and in the moment before rebirth. Never had I felt greater gratitude or love for her, for her guidance, compassion and concern. There, beneath the surface of worldly things, I revived my oldest connections with nature and family.

As I emerged from the water the second time, I was blinded by the sun, the eye of God's sky. The idea of rebirth, of redemption began to form in my mind. I might be born again, be burned clean by holy fire. The words of the Rabbi seared my mind.

As I submerged myself a third time, an image formed from the black and crimson shields of my vision. It was a face, and on that face was etched longing and a great desire to be loved. It was my father's face. I slowly recognized my own face within it, and the face of my sweet son Asher. In that ecstatic moment I knew my father as myself. It was revelation, a pure gift.

4

When I emerged from the third submersion, I left the pool and put on my robe. I was calm externally, but inside I was flooded by impressions and emotions. As we shared food and drink, I was filled with overwhelming feelings of love for those present. I had taken an oath, and every thought now seemed a prayer, every virtual image a poem. The roses, the water and the sun were now within me, illuminating my personal history, fulfilling the vague longings which I now saw as the qualities of nature God granted me as a visionary child.

In the many busy days since this numinous event I have come to see that, for me, the essential garden is that one in which my childhood, with its pain and loneliness, again comes forward as a passage rich in meaning and reflecting God's design for a future rebirth. The blindness and pain I experienced as a child were the seeds of vision.

Yet this essential garden is not complete or final. It is the beginning of my understanding of the garden in which the household of Israel dwells and all life. It began with my boyhood need to experience viscerally, then understand the essential qualities of the severe garden in which I was raised, Southern Arkansas, and is also a key to understanding that part of myself that has embraced the spiritual. The pond levee of my youth with its blackberry brambles and dusty sun sustained me through the difficult childhood for which I was destined. Rabbi Fields' fragrant rose garden closed this experiential envelope, and gave me the emotional closure that I needed to experience such a revelation. The natural and social environments of the South etched themselves on me as archetypal experience and were the beginning of a kind of spiritual wandering the record of which I offer you here.

NEW BREATH

A powerful and cohesive series of incidents and images surfaced at an event that was to prove crucial to my conversion to Judaism: the birth of my first son, Asher David. When his head emerged from his mother and I felt his first breath on my face, I felt the components of a complex pattern of memories within me finally take a recognizable form. It seemed to me that as I felt his first breath on my face, I was experiencing the breath of God. Genesis 2:7 describes it:

> *The Lord God formed a being from the dust of the earth.*
> *He blew into its nostrils the breath of life,*
> *and it became a living being.*

The evening breeze that had caressed my forehead on a farm in southern Arkansas was an echo of the wind (ruach) that sweeps over the water (Genesis 1:2) preparing the way for the light of creation. It is also that breeze that moves daily through Eden heralding the presence of God, as it does just as Adam eats of the forbidden fruit (Genesis 3:8). God was recreating the world in me through my new sensitivities, preparing the way for my intelligence to understand the purpose of his creation. God is the divine breeze that moves through creation that in turn encloses man, that special creation formed in God's own image.

Early childhood is every child's first Eden. It was for me a pure world from which I was torn by several types of violence, the source of which I still do not completely understand. But this Eden in which I, even as an innocent child, sensed God's numinous presence, is as real to me as my second Eden, the one in which I now live. This second Eden is the garden of marriage. More importantly, this second garden is the garden of parenthood.

I consider marriage and parenthood to be twin aspects of a single reality, and every marriage has the possibility of recreating Eden. Man and woman discover the other as something original and new, and, as that other becomes identified with the self, the world surrounding the couple is recreated through their individual and collective vision. Darkness and light are more sharply defined. The sun and moon will acquire special powers and be likened to the lover and his beloved. The rhythms of their bodies will find cosmic counterparts in the circling of the heavenly spheres. The elements of water, sky, the earth itself, are more beautiful because filled with a new promise of sharing and familiarity. All these natural phenomena are part of the world in which love is shared between two inhabitants of a new world, a new garden.

This new world is not entropic; its does not withdraw and collapse inward when threatened. It projects its harmony and vision of recreative power out on the greater environment. Sunlight and moonlight illuminate the paths of occupation and intimacy. Seedbearing plants, with their fragrant blossoms and sweet fruit will be likened to the beloved. The grace and power of nature will imbue the imaging of the partner. Consider the *Song of Solomon* 2:17:

> *When the day blows gently*
> *And the shadows flee,*
> *Set out, my beloved,*
> *Swift as a gazelle*
> *Or a young stag,*
> *For the hills of spices.*

The couple will liken their emotions to the soaring flight of the creatures of the air. Each member of the family of nature—sea creatures and the swarms on which they feed, the creatures that creep or thunder over all the earth, even monstrous things—seems a necessary part born of a woman and a man who have chosen to create a new world together, a new garden of existence.

But this new world is, for all its harmony and joy, incomplete. The union with each other and the renewed links with the natural world are clearly the early stages of greater discoveries. Man finds an unanswered question in the warm breeze that moves the trees causing the ripe fruit to fall and unsettles his heart as it stirs the moonlit hair about his wife's temples. Woman finds her inner rhythms and desires echoed in the ebb and flow of the moon, and she seeks in her husband's breath the ultimate knowledge of creation. This knowledge God gives her grace as she and her husband join their bodies to enact the circular dance of moon and sun, night and day, sea and earth, of creatures of the air and earth. As the river flows into the sea, the sea rises to the clouds and the rain regenerates the earth, their bodies mix to create a new inhabitant for the garden they have created. At love-making and in childbirth, the husband kisses the sweet saltwater of his wife's tears away. And she kisses his tears of happiness. And the oneness of their garden grows through children, and through the sharing children by their nature demand.

Beginning in the deep inner darkness of the beloved, in the salt seas of her body a tiny living seed makes its way, then merges with another before beginning a swarm of prodigious activity. In paroxysms of growth and motion it finds its way to the warm sea where it can begin to learn to swim. This new creature swims invisible, then dances within the water of its mother's body for nine moons. It will begin to gesture in response to sound from outside, to turn toward the warm light streaming darkly in through its mother's skin, to dance as it senses the sunlight awaiting it after it emerges to a great sea change: it must learn to breathe air.

During this time the mother lives to satisfy the needs of their creation. Her universe is now the universe within. Her rhythms are the rhythms of her baby's sustenance and growth. And her lover's rhythms must change now to satisfy the needs of the mother and her unborn child. The moon-created tides of earthly oceans now are replaced by the movement of waters within the womb. And so all rhythms of the new Eden have moved from the external to the internal worlds, where the dynamic vision of creation, the real miracle of nature, is now occurring.

As a husband I saw all of this in my mind's eye, as I watched my wife's body swell, and the world within her took control of our lives. Here was an excitement we had never known. We had been given the great power to create another by joining ourselves. I was aware of the responsibility that had been given us, and like most expecting parents I wondered if I was up to the path that life had opened for me. I had wanted this all my adult life, but would I be worthy of it? Would we be good parents? Would I be a good father? Would our Eden be diminished by this newcomer? So many questions face the parents, the new Adam and Eve.

These questions were answered at my first son's birth, and reinforced by the second, third and fourth. Any children who follow will only augment the certainty of my belief in what I want to describe to you. It was a moment in which my childhood memories merged with the most positive feelings and intuitions I have experienced in my marriage. They were joined as my son's lungs first cleared the waters of his mother's inner sea and drew their first breath of God's air.

Like many men of my generation, I participated as fully as possible in the birth of my children. This meant intense involvement in every stage of pregnancy and delivery. I will not dwell on what you have read or experienced firsthand: the discoveries and discomforts of pregnancy, the shock of the water breaking, the frantic activity of getting to the hospital, the fight for control as the stages of childbirth progress from early labor to transitional stages.

The doctor and I watched the gradual emergence of my son's head from his mother. With the doctor's help, Asher's head turned upward and I saw his dark eyes beneath the blinking lids. His mouth pursed, drawing air for the first time into his sea lungs. In that brief moment of rest, I leaned over my son's tiny face and said, *Hello, Asher.* The eyes blinked, and I felt the first whisper of air from his little lungs. It seemed to me in that instant, and still does, that that little movement of air was the breath of God on my face. It echoed down to me from the dreaming fields of childhood, through the sweet breath of my wife-lover. It was a sweet echo of God's original garden that recognized the nakedness of knowledge and knowledge's necessary existence in the story of mankind.

Beside me, the doctor said, *Now push a little more*. And Asher's little shoulders appeared, and an instant later he was writhing whole and perfect on his mommy's tummy in the bright lights of the delivery room.

Hi Asher, his mother said.

The population of our Eden had been increased. Our ability to love, my wife and I have many times agreed, has been increased exponentially through having children. In this act, the most natural as well as the most wonderful act with which we humans are blessed, God had made himself known very clearly in my mind. I would begin now to seek God in all things about me, and find him most securely in reflecting on the power of recreating the original Eden that was lost so long ago.

Each child is the Adam or Eve we once were, and in their first breath is our first breath. In their struggle to be born is the struggle of our own birth, and our work to create as much of an Eden on this earth as we can for them. And in this struggle is the promise we can remember when it is time to give back our lives to God. For only God has the power to create directly from the dust to which we must all return: *The Lord God formed a being from the dust of the earth. God blew into its nostrils the breath of life, and it became a living being*. (Genesis 2:7). God has given parents a power that echoes God's own vast powers of creation. How could I fail to see the moment of my son's birth as a call to me to recognize God's presence. How was this presence to realize itself fully in the Eden we three now occupied?

With the precious warmth of his breath lingering on my cheek, I washed my son of the pale film that had kept him warm in the liquid darkness of his mother's inner world. He was tired from his struggle, but rested peacefully in my great hands. He only cried once, when faced directly with a bright hospital light.

Wait till you see the sun, I thought. Only wait till you see the moon. Our garden is waiting for you. You are so welcome. It is your garden now.

WILLY

You shall love the Lord your God with all your heart and with all your soul and with all your might —Deuteronomy 6.5

1

This verse inculcates spirituality and its essential place in human nature. It instructs us—as complex beings—to love, to worship God with our "hearts," which I take to represent both physical being and force of will. Contemporary philosophy, alienated as it is from every humane impulse, has simply discounted or ignored faith conceptually, so I shudder at the response this reference to "soul" may evoke among academic readers. Nevertheless, I am drawn to this verse and those like it because they provide common existential ground for both Jews and Christians alike. This verse is important to me as a Jew and as a former member of the Episcopalian faith.

I want to discuss several figures from whom I have learned about the role of Judaism in Modern Times. I believe that such a discussion can shed light on the problems a convert faces in three areas: from within Judaism itself; from Christianity, one of Judaism's historical rivals; and from human society generally. The first problem is a matter of Jewish pride, defensiveness, and fear of loss of identity in the flux of Modern Times. This fear is quite old; it is omnipresent in the Tanach, the Jewish Scriptures. The solution to this problem lies in both sustaining essential truths and ideals of Judaism, while admitting that the advance of the humanistic and pure sciences hold some relevance in the study of Torah. The solution to the second problem may hinge on the first: in discovering their common roots and influences, both Judaism and Christianity may arrive at a stance of "separate but equal" and begin working together to face up to and to solve the dreadful human problems we must soon face or suffer terrible permanent damage from. (Perhaps these two great religions can serve as an example for other religions.)

The solution to the third problem will only result from the education of the hearts, the emotions and will of mankind. Only by realizing that we share the human concerns dictated by Natural and Social Law, which I take to be God's primary presence in man, will peace and order come about. Our modern egos and instincts are too laden with emptiness, aggression and greed to approach such problems rationally. The lion will not lie down with the lamb in our time. Our minds are too victimized by the aggressive mechanics of sublimated need to think clearly, except in isolated moments that seem impossible to sustain. God's Natural Law is the only place for mankind to heal itself now. It is through the natural love of the mother for her child, the natural affection of father for his son or daughter, mutual respect among neighbors, the natural respect shown to traditional values such as wisdom and sharing that mankind might renew the earthly kingdom. It is the law drawn up in the Ten Commandments, essentially the law necessary for sustaining good familial and neighborly relations. It is the law of the intelligent heart.

But how do we apply these simple principles on a macrocosmic scale? We might begin by considering that every human is God's sacred creation, and worthy of the love and respect we give to our families and neighbors until they prove themselves unworthy of that love. There will always be plenty of lawyers to decide about penalties for the unworthy.

What is the condition of the modern human heart? I want to look at the journey of one honest heart in this century, then at some of the great minds that have shaped the way we see the world we live in. How can we love God in contemporary times? How have we come to this garden of sand? Let's look at both small and great Jews and learn what we can.

2

In October of 1990, Grandpa Willy died. William Wenig, my mother-in-law's father, was a sturdy unassuming man: honest and hardworking. He worked at many different professions without finding success or security. He was raised in the pale, that section of Central Europe predominantly Jewish before Shoah's agonizing flame consumed Jewish existence there. Willy escaped the nightmare that still haunts every lowly corner of the earth, through Vienna. He fled from the peddler's paths of Poland and Rumania, where he had called out his wares in six languages and multiplied six figures in his head; he fled to America, where he obeyed the commandment to be fruitful and multiply. He found his Tessie and raised three girls in Pittsburgh and Los Angeles. He lived to hold his great-grandchildren, my Asher and Joshua, on his knees before he died.

He would call out to his grandson in a warm, gruff voice, *So, Asher, What ya doin'?* And to me, *Bill, what's cookin'?* The three of us might sit on a Sunday morning and chat about the weather, what we had done the day before. He was good company. He was a plain man, but to his family he was special. During the eight years I knew him, I grew to respect and care for Willy. I respected him as a man who had struggled to raise his family in a new land. And I cared for him as a Jewish survivor of this tortured century.

I sometimes asked him about his youth and young manhood in the pale and in Vienna. Typical of so many with his background, he had chosen never to speak directly of the conditions and events that drove him from his homeland. He would usually say, *I don't remember all that.* (Grandma Dora, my father-in-law's mother simply said, *You don't want to know.*) But he did, and sometimes dark hints emerged in conversation with those closest to him. I understood enough Yiddish to follow what was being said.

■

In 1985, I performed for the last time in Europe, at the Raimund Theater in Vienna. Before I left Los Angeles to begin rehearsals there, Willy requested that I say 'Hi' to Prater for him. (Prater is a large section of Vienna featuring an enormous park. It was and is a temporary home to many of the Jewish refugees who pass through Vienna on their way to Israel or the United States.) Willy had lived there during the long months before joining his family in the United States. I had asked him about his time in Prater. He looked up at the Southern California sky and studied the cloud formations to the south. He said softly, *It all seems like a dream to me now.* There was a touch of wonder in his voice: *To have come so far from the home country, to have wandered so far.*

Our experience in Vienna, that stone bastion of anti-Semitism, is explored in my poems and prose elsewhere, but so much of what I experienced there was colored by my thoughts of Willy and what his dream of Vienna might have been. As I studied and read about the period following World War I, the chaotic dissolution of the Austro-Hungarian Empire, I have come to believe that this cold city, from whose political and social climate both Sigmund Freud and Adolf Hitler emerged, was the final step in Willy's agonizing ascent to America from hell. The political and social forces that clouded Europe during Willy's youth were to gather into the horrific storm of the WWII. Is this what Willy saw in the clouds sweeping east over Orange County that Sunday morning?

I wrote a poem for Willy during the time infant Asher, Leslie and I were in Vienna in 1985. It is first of a cycle of twenty poems that grew out of my study of the environment of Vienna.[i] The terrorism of the 1980s was at its height. The Vienna airport had been bombed several days before Leslie and Asher flew into Vienna. At the time, we lived in a little street called *Luftbadgasse.*

In der Luftbadgasse

In this plastic time, another suitcase
Has erupted in light and blood.
Visitation, domestic cares
Seem trite while the globe
Writhes about us. But even so,
Come outside on my shoulders, Asher.
Open your tiny arms to this land
Grown stiff in the tired fury of lost wars.

Grandpa Willy wandered these streets,
Waiting for passage to America.
He leapt, young and strong,
From Prater to New Jersey.
Now I return, full of your newness
To stride into an echo of dove wings
In the confined, liquid air of Luftbadgasse—
Where your sun-filled hair tosses,
Explodes in brilliance above me.

I saw Austria as a land—and especially Vienna as a city—as self-lacerating, depressed and guilt-ridden. Like every nation or people ridden with failure and guilt, this people needed and need scapegoats on which to project their deep insecurities. The Jew had served this purpose for Viennese society and its politics for hundreds of years. In such an history-ridden environment, with its repressed and concealed furies, the growing threat of terrorism made me fearful of my children's future. Gustav Mahler's words rang in my ears, countering the joy of my corresponding awareness of my own emotional growth through him. Perhaps Leslie's, Asher's and my closeness to each other was accentuated by the forces surrounding us in that great, cold city. *Recondita'rmonia.*

We, like Willy, have not returned to Vienna since our introduction to that great stone bureaucracy. I became obsessed with the anomaly of our presence in Vienna. I went in search of our meaning in Vienna. I carried Asher afternoons through the streets of Vienna and began to conceive the cycle of poems in which In der Luftbadgasse appears. As we walked, Asher perched on my shoulders, it was as if Willy was walking beside us. Later as Asher slept and I wrote, Willy looked over my shoulder, murmuring. *So, Bill, what's cookin'?* Willy is for me the personification of that aspect of mankind that is honest, straightforward, practical and survival oriented.

Our second son, Joshua Ari, was born about a year before Willy died, so in a sense Willy had was replaced. The spirit that was hounded from his Central European homeland and struggled to succeed in America is both at peace and beginning again. Joshua will also face his clouded times, and will also reflect on the seemingly chaotic patterns of the clouds over Southern California.

It is important to remember, to know on whose shoulders we stand. As a Jew, I stand on Willy's shoulders, and though he lies in the earth beneath me, he lives on in the garden of my heart's memory. This garden includes many things, even the stone streets and monuments of Vienna. They are further back and darker in the reaches of my memory and imagi-nation. They represent the traditions of Europe that have produced in the last four hundred years both magnificent, ennobling art, philosophy and scientific achievement, as well as the horrors of suppression, and almost continuous war and mass murder. The contradiction inherent in this image of Western civilization has had terrible consequences for thought and belief in this century. This century is the century of the lost. The "lost generation" were merely another step in a long stairway.

■

In my eyes, Willy has come to represent a Judaism that is straightforward and practical. It is a Jewishness that has for the most part passed away now. The new age of America—Jewish or otherwise—is far from straightforward. It is theoretical instead of practical, generous only when it pays, and predatory in business and social policy. Michael Milkin is the symbol of the new age: brilliant, hardworking, family-oriented, and unethical in business praxis. *Well*, says the Beverly Hills Businessman in the $500 suit, *Your Willy was a loser. What did he have to show for all his honesty? Nothing.* It's true. He had nothing in his bank account.

A colleague of mine at Valley College refers to his father as a *shmuck. The only smart thing he ever did was to die and leave me the money for a beach house.* Although I am burdened with remorse about my own failure to love my father, an intelligent but self-lacerating man who shaped his children's lives with emotional violence, I was disgusted by my colleague's remarks. I do not idealize my father or Willy. I do feel they were decent men who tried hard. They deserve my respect for their attempt. Neither had very much luck in this world. But Willy had a solid constitution, he accepted who and what he was, and he had a solid faith in God. I stand on their shoulders gratefully.

Willy is part of my new family. His personal history has become for me a part of the history of the Jewish people, and he has played his own role in my conversion process. Willy never spoke to me of conversion, never encouraged me to convert. At the time of my conversion, Willy and I were simply bound by a great love for two people—my wife Leslie and our first son, Asher—and for God. Asher will remember his great-grandfather, but Joshua will not. I hope they both will remember that they, too, stand on his shoulders and should honor him. Likewise, we stand on my grandfathers' shoulders. But I know almost nothing about them.

My father never spoke a single word to me about his father. I don't know the reason for this, but I can't imagine that my father's complete silence on the subject would indicate a positive regard for this father. It is sad that I know so little of my own grandfather's life, because it means that I cannot describe his life and accomplishments to my children. If one cannot talk about a person, describe them, it is almost as if they never existed, as if their existence has been erased by silence. I am forced to stand on a ghost's shoulders. That's not a very comfortable feeling.

3

My writing on conversion has related the birth of my first son and a concurrent spiritual awakening with my conversion to Judaism. This act of tying the cycle of birth and rebirth to divine redemption and revelation is a radical—though common—act of the imagination which I see as an echo of God's endless creative power. We are not only created in his image, but imbued with his endless capacity for creativity.

Yet this creativity can be source of agony, as well as of joy under certain conditions. I will not raise the question of image-making within the Orthodox confrontations by Chaim Potok in *Asher Lev* and other books. *I want to discuss the struggle of the Jewish artist to function in Western Culture to demonstrate a larger theme: anti-Semitism as social form, and its product—alienation–through the eyes of a convert to Judaism. Many Jewish artists and thinkers have been driven from the inflexible world of Orthodox or Conservative Judaism in order to fulfill their destinies as artists. These Jews may mirror the societies into which they have been driven. When a former Jew enters outside society, he assumes a role in non-Jewish society roughly equivalent to the convert's in Jewish society.*

First, let me say that I view God's gift of creativity in artistic modes primarily as a two-fold blessing: first, it is a means to self-realization and fulfillment for the artist, and, second, it is a means of furnishing the audience with delight in beauty and with enlightenment through instruction. Art is inherently moral in nature. To deny this—typical of contemporary aesthetics and criticism—is, it seems to me, extremely foolish and dangerous. If a work of art fulfills and enlightens both the artist and the audience, then God is inherently glorified.

This said, I want to discuss two great Jewish writers, neither of who were practicing Jews. Neither could be more different from Willy. Both were Germanophiles and intellectuals, and at the same time alienated and exiled by an anti-Semitic German society and culture. Both personify the typical position of the "assimilated" European Jewish artist, who was accepted neither by European society at large, nor—and here is the larger point—by European Orthodox Jewish society and culture. The Jewish artists of the 19th and 20th Century Europe share a good deal with the convert of today. Like today's convert to Judaism, they left one closed circle to seek entrance into another closed circle, where they were looked upon as intruders by the majority of those in the social groups involved.

Heinrich (Hayyim) Heine (1797-1856) and Franz Kafka (1883-1924) were cosmopolitan Jews, the products of well-to-do mercantile families of Duesseldorf and Prague, respectively. Both suffered from tenuous familial and social relations as a result of their temperaments and artistic talents, never married, and lived all of their adult lives with terrible disease and pain. (Kafka died long before his time.) The artistic work of both these men can be approached in two ways: as artists in the Western tradition, for both were brilliant, as well as original innovators; or as Jews who were to a large degree alienated from both Jewish tradition and community, and often self-lacerating where their Jewish origins were concerned. (Heine's letters indicate clearly his dislike of both Orthodox and Reform Jews, but he also condemned Jews who converted to Christianity—Felix Mendelssohn, Eduard Gans—virulently. In criticizing these two, however, he was exhibiting self-hatred, for he himself converted, merely "for an entrance ticket into European Culture.") The first characteristic is not subject to debate. The second characteristic is of special interest.

Both these extraordinary men were born into Jewish—admittedly, partially assimilated—homes, yet neither's artistic, i.e. fictional or poetic, work contains a hint of religious Jewishness. (The last year of Heine's life offers a small exception.) Why should this be so? I will not detail my discussion of these two tortured spirits of separate centuries who splayed their souls while denying their Jewish origins. My point is this: the tension was so great between Jewish tradition and the world in which they lived that both found it necessary, in their artistic expression, to deny or ignore their Jewishness. I believe that Heine—Heine condemned religion generally—and Kafka cultivated ambivalence toward, denial of, or indifference toward their religious origins, not as a matter of convenience, or of their survival as artists. I do not think that this denial was motivated purely by social conditions: i.e., anti-Semitism in European society; or the whirlwind of the Romantic Age in Heine's case; or World War I and the Weimar Republic in Kafka's. It was, in part, Judaism's rote exclusion of men such as Heine and Kafka, who sought to express themselves in media—poetry, drama, secular prose fiction; with both writers working in the German language—cultivated by Western culture rather than the forms cultivated by Judaic culture, that alienated these two great ones from religious and even ethnic Judaism. They excluded themselves rather than face exclusion.

The question I wish to ask is this: Why is this necessary? These two extraordinary beings embraced the classical traditions of Europe, and created art essentially devoid of religious Jewishness. Both were artists who happened to be born into Jewish families; neither was allowed to become a Jewish artist. It is a rare Jew—outside of upper academic circles—who now even knows that these two great secular intellectuals were Jews. One could argue that the Jewish people are punishing themselves by this ignorance. Heine is perhaps the foremost German lyric poet, while Kafka is one of the most imitated and original writers of all time.

I raise the question of the Jewishness of these two great men in relation to my general topic, because they were also converts. They were apostate Jews who converted to European culture. They left Judaism, in part, for the same reason that converts have difficulty entering Judaism: certain aspects of Judaism appear to be limiting and exclusionary. As Jewish artists, their expressive range would have been severely limited by adherence to Jewish religious law. Freedom of expression might well have been the major issue that caused the severance with Judaism in the case of each man. Personal freedom was the essence of the Romantic Movement which Heine typified; Kafka sought freedom from anything that limited his aesthetic longing, imprisoned as he was in familial, occupational and political/bureaucratic structures. Both men had examined themselves carefully in the secular mirror European Jewish History refers to as the Haskalah, the Jewish Enlightenment. Both men exhibited a destructive emotion commonplace among estranged Jews: self-hatred.

I raise this final point also because these two writers are minor figures in a much larger tradition of despair and denial that has tried to crush freedom of choice and expression in the 20th Century. That is perhaps the greatest tragedy imaginable: *that those excluded from the Jewish tradition— or those who feel they have to exclude themselves from it for any one of several reasons—are in some cases those who adhere to, if not establish doctrines dangerous to Judaism, and religion in general.* In particular, I am thinking of those disaffected Jews who have constantly been a part of the radical anarchist, socialist or communist fringes; e.g., Spinoza, Moses Hess, Ferdinand Lassalle (Lasal), Karl Marx, Leon Trotsky, Rosa Luxemburg, George Lukacs, et.al. These apostate Jews have in some cases helped fashion the anti-Semitic forces that have persecuted Russian Jews since the establishment of soviet communism. Even Heine, foreseeing the future his socialist friend Marx spoke of, utterly rejected revolutionary socialism and its virulent hybrid, communism. Marx is perhaps the most extreme example of Jewish self-hatred. He utterly shut Judaism out of his life, though some historians argue that the influence of Rabbinic thought was great in his theories.

George Lukacs was a Czech intellectual theoretician of Jewish parentage who strained to find intellectual and political meaning between World Wars I and II. He went very wrong in the repudiation of common sense and conventional morality; he rejected both tradition and normalcy because positive traditional values seemed to break down during this abnormal time. He mirrored rather than struggled with the deplorable values of this time. In contrast to this alienated theorist of empty dialectic, Jews like Rosenzweig and Buber found their way in Judaism on the path of the deracinated children of assimilated parents. They sought, in the words of Daniel Bell[ii], not God, but "the Godhead which was the fusion of the self with the absolute."

This latter, subtle apostasy—if it actually is meant as stated and I interpret it correctly—is a mistake I do not intend to make in my own work. Clearly, this essay is partially about my self, my development as a person and as a Jew, as well as about the role of revelation in that development. Under no circumstance do I consider my self as essential to God or that I have "fused" or become one with him.

Each of the Jewish figures mentioned above was to some degree a prisoner of the social and political forces of his times. Sadly, it was these forces, rather than the forces of Judaism that dominated their lives. They sought out aesthetic, scientific or political structural replacements for the moral structure Judaism would have given them. They lost, at the very least, the common sense and practical wisdom of Judaism. In the latter part of their lives, both Heine and Kafka expressed a renewed interest in their Jewish origins. In the pain of mortal illness, both men began to explore Judaism. Heine declared himself "a mortally ill Jew" and wrote several ecstatic poems on Jewish subjects; Kafka studied Hebrew for a time and enjoyed Yiddish theater immensely.

Willy, a common man and victim of European anti-Semitism, entered the second promised land, the United States of America. On the way to escape through Vienna, he passed through Prague, where Kafka was frequenting coffee houses with his friend Max Brod. Those like Kafka's sisters, who stayed behind the migration to Palestine, South America or the United States suffered one of two fates: they were persecuted and fled later, if they were lucky like Max Brod; or they were persecuted, degraded and systematically murdered. When Kafka died in 1924 of tuberculosis, only a few of his works had been published. His three older sisters perished at Auschwitz. Many of Willy's family also perished there.

One answer to the difficult questions that anti-Semitism poses is suggested by the existence of certain figures whose fragile but continuous presence provides a positive example for both Jews and Christians: Gotthold Lessing, the close friend of Moses Mendelssohn and author of *Nathan the Wise*; Goethe, Heine's close friend; and Thomas Mann, who married a Jew and cultivated a long and happy life with her. Mann also dedicated many years of his creative life to the study of Jewish history and tradition. He did not convert, perhaps because he had suffered enough alienation as a humanist in the German culture during the first half of the century.

Thomas Mann's great (and in large part accessible) prose work *Joseph and his Brothers* is an exploration of the ancient origins of contemporary culture, and finally formulates a plea for rational humanism and universal understanding. Mann explores the Joseph story with the hope of uncovering the common archetypal properties of all Western civilization's splinter religions and nations. Intellectually, he makes a good case. Lessing, incidentally, had performed a less ambitious but similarly motivated task in his *Die Erziehung des Menschengeschlechts (The Enlightenment of Mankind)* nearly two centuries earlier.

I want to stress that there have always been among the Germans great artists who have been *Judenfreundlich* (accepting to Jews). Among these have been Goethe and Mann, two towering figures of German Culture. Mann was forcefully estranged from German Society for his stand against Nazi gangsterism in the early 1930's. He never again lived in Germany. Sadly, such close relationships—e.g., Mendelssohn and Lessing's, Goethe and Schiller's, Mann and his wife's—are the exception in the land that perfected Shoah, and are seldom enough found in Western civilization generally. They are, nevertheless, the fragile historical bridges that I and other converts must study. We are ourselves such bridges.

Unfortunately, as several writers have successfully argued, the anti-Semitism and racism that tears at the collective psyche of Western civilization, is not a matter of the intellect alone. It is a sickness of the heart and values, the product of irrational fear of encroachment and exclusion, a fear of the unknown. If everyone would read Lessing's *Nathan the Wise*, or *The Enlightenment of Mankind*, Goethe's *Faust*, or Mann's *Joseph and his Brothers*, quicker progress toward healing could be made. But this is not likely to happen.

So what is to be done? Where are the answers to the difficult questions, those born of prejudice, to be found? How are the ancient forces that tortured Heine and Kafka and deprived Lessing and Mann of peace of mind, to be lessened and the psychic wounds healed? Now that Eastern Europe has opened to the West and we see the unhealed wounds of sustained anti-Semitism and racism that have festered under the communist—not that the thoroughgoing vileness of Polish anti-Semitism wouldn't have sustained itself under any government—mantel of suppression, what can we do to heal these wounds and make safe the lives of the million Jews lingering in Slavic lands, or in the virulently anti-Semitic Middle East? In the "new" unified Germany? In the anti-Semitic cities of Paris and Vienna?

Are a few scattered works of art—at what great cost!—all we have to show for Jewish acceptance in Western Culture? What are we now to do? The greatest danger may lie in silence and lack of involvement that characterized my father's relation to his family. Shoah has taught us this.

I am going to offer some suggestions as a convert to Judaism. I believe the convert can help both Jew and non-Jew to find answers, because to some degree we converts personify, embody the conflict many Jews and non-Jews have withdrawn from discussing. And the active, sincere convert is to one degree or another *living* this conflict, and seeking out gardens from which to offer help to both parties of the tragic struggle. We are truly, to the majority of believing Jews and Christians, persona non grata, except in our selves, in the strength of our non-exclusionary Judaism.

4

Behind discussions of conversion lurk a number of questions. One is, Why does the convert seek out and struggle to enter this painful Jewish existence in Western Civilization? What is the world of a convert like? It is my hope that the questions I am asking and the answers I have found will offer light and perhaps even practical suggestions for fellow-converts.

Conversion to Judaism requires radical changes in the serious convert. Imitating or even assuming to understand the existence of Grandpa Willy, which seemed so simple and unassuming, implies enormous challenges to the hearts and minds of those who were raised in the Christian tradition. The convert faces rejection from both orthodox Christians and Jews. He has entered a world between worlds; he exists in his own special diaspora. This condition is what I mean when I say that I embody the conflict between Judaism and Western culture. I myself am the conflict between Christian and Jewish principles, as I myself am the potential resolution of that conflict.

I began my studies of Judaism as part of a search for meaning in Western history and culture. Then, the slow understanding and embrace of Judaism began. Who cannot be sympathetic to a people who have been systematically disenfranchised, hounded and slaughtered throughout Western History? This hounding continued until the founding of two nations destined to become the material and spiritual bastions of Judaism in modern times appeared; the United States of America (1776) and Israel (1948). Until the formation of the United States of America from the North American British colonies, Jews had no land where their citizenship offered them safety from periodic disenfranchisement and where laws protected them in actuality, as well as in theory, from murder. Every other Jew in the world suffered the same injustices and unequal treatment that William Wenig did, before he came to the United States. He could be made perpetually homeless by a magistrate's whim or a mayor's political designs. Like Willy, the average Jew

93

wandered homeless, accompanied only by God and hope.

Willy, to my knowledge, never owned a house. He was not a man to whom success was attracted, though he worked hard his whole life. He died at ninety working as a caretaker of a small apartment building in West Hollywood. He left no wealth or land behind him, but he left something far greater: a family.

I married into Willy's family; I converted to his religion.

It is not what Willy left behind. I was and am what he was: a child of God. And Willy was Israel, an ideal that was manifested new existence in 1948 after two millennia of foreign occupation. For the Jew in diaspora, for the convert in diaspora, Israel is the essential symbol of God's blessing.

The greatest gift and challenge for the convert is to know that he himself is Israel, the idea and ideal, and to experience in his heart the 2000-year diaspora of the wandering Jew.

For I am sore afflicted
grieving unattended in a room
grieving unattended in an alien suburb
grieving unattended in a city I do not know:
Jerusalem, Jerusalem, golden in the heart.
—Peter Marin: *For Jim Henderson*

Jerusalem! How often does an ageless symbol concretize itself? How often does an ideal become real and open its arms to the victims of world oppression? Yet this great and ancient city is now the center of controversy in the present Middle Eastern crisis. As I write now, the world powers are attempting to bring Arabs and Jews to the negotiating table to settle the Palestinian question. The great problem holding up beginning negotiations concerns the representation of representatives be from East Jerusalem, thus legitimizing their claim to Jerusalem as the capital city of their nation. Israel will not allow this for many reasons, most of which concern survival.

This bright land, Israel, the hope and refuge of Judaism lives from day to day, surrounded by blood enemies, and supported in essence only by its single great ally, the United States of America. Israel and the U.S.A., Moses and Aaron.

5

I myself am Israel
In the heart of mankind.

The world is shrinking experientially, as the bands of instantaneous communication and profit-seeking activity tighten about the globe. Yet old hatred and fears continue to plague us. Interfaith and interracial tensions run high nationally and internationally because human goodness lags far behind media and commerce. The United States is now the (self-declared) only remaining superpower and the singular ally of a small nation constantly in danger of being inundated by the flood of hatred of its neighbors. And there is tension between these two allies.

The ever-persecuted Russian Jews stream from wounded Russia, that great self-lacerating land of pain, to settle in the disputed West Bank. It is not only the spiritual freedom that Israel offers victims of the diaspora, but economic opportunity as well. Some Jews choose the U.S. over Israel for what they consider to be its superior economic opportunities. Willy had no such choice. When he came to America, the world's bands of communication were just beginning to tighten. Jews were forced to flee oppression, even murder, to the arms of America. Even now Russian Jews wait for permission to flee to religious freedom. In the U.S., they faced and face another challenge: they were and are threatened by the materialism that is driving this nation to moral bankruptcy. In Israel, refugees face extinction at the hands of the enemy nations that surround them. Their hope, and the hope of the Western world, is that somehow the United States and Israel can work together—commercially, diplomatically, even spiritually—to protect and aid each other while waiting for millennia-old hatreds, emblemized presently by Saddam Hussein and Osama bin Ladin, to subside.

Both America and Israel exist within me. Both Christianity and Judaism exist within me. I am a practicing Jew and have embraced Judaism with my mind and spirit. I do not condemn or feel remorse for my past contact with Christian principles. I accept their existence and importance to others spiritually, even as I continue to love my mother's memory. To deny that part of my life would be to deny the intellectual/historical attraction to Judaism and certain events in my private life that brought me to revelation.

My children are Jews. I pray is that their generation will be less troubled by interdenominational tensions and the rage of dysfunctional relationships between the World's three great religions than mine has been. Children are pure: they should not be taught to hate or be conditioned to be suspicious. Yet this seems our primary preoccupation now. Imagine if the same effort were put forth in teaching tolerance and love. Is this too much to hope for? In a world in which intellectuals have begun to bemoan the end of ideological and political tension as "the end of the time," the last great irony of this century may be the discovery that earthlings are addicted to hate and intolerance.

It is always good for honesty and growth to look at the origin of things. Many times, enemies can find enough common roots based in patterns of self-interest to dissolve the blind hatred and patterns of conflict previously created in struggles for survival and dominance. The ideas and beliefs that separate Christians and Jews project from a single figure: Jesus. For Christians, he is the Messiah; for Jews, he is not. (Jesus was a Jewish reformer. John the Baptist, and all the disciples [except Luke, a Greek] were of course also Jews.) The Jews still await the Messiah, but choose to follow God's commandments to live fully in the world. Christians believe the Messiah has come and offers all answers, including eternal salvation; Jews do not. Shall these differences condemn Christian and Jewish children to estrangement from each other? Must each condemn the other to hell/gehenna?

Countering this source of conflict is the historical fact that Christianity has its historical roots in Judaism. Surely there is enough common ground to discourage the heavy burden of sustaining this conflict between us. Or do religions depend upon the very conflicts they claim doctrinally to deplore, for their existence? Can man be satisfied when striving for the continuity of peace? Can we find meaning in the exercise of constant compassion and love? Or have we become addicted to tension and conflict? Even if we are addicted to such conflict, must we pass this addiction to our children?

Children are a great concern of both Judaism and Christianity. Both religions see the purity of a child as worthy of God. When Moses addresses the Children of Israel at the end of the forty years in the Wilderness he speaks of the *little ones who have no knowledge between good and evil* (Deuteronomy 1:39). It is the children of the Hebrews who left Egypt who will conquer and settle Canaan. Echoing Moses, Jesus says, "Suffer little children to come unto me and forbid them not: for of such is the kingdom of God" (Luke 18:16). Though it is often difficult to sense in the translation of the Christian Scriptures (New Testament) from the Greek, the Hebrew Scriptures or Tanach (Old Testament) from the Hebrew (probably both Moses and Jesus spoke Aramaic), it is clear that the writers of the Christian Scriptures consciously drew heavily—as Jesus did—on the Hebrew Scriptures, and saw themselves as sustaining, as well as revising, Jewish Law.

In order to ensure our children a better world, the time is fast approaching when the Old Testament's "Eye for an Eye" must be seen by a united world as an improvement on its legal precedent, and the Christian Scriptures' labeling of some Jews as "Children of Satan" as the overzealous ragings of a revolutionary reformer. But to make such enlightened judgements, we must be able to consider the historical *as well as* sacred documents. More conservative Christians and Jews do not allow for this kind of activity. Some actively oppose it. Hopefully this will change, and the conservative centers of these two great religions will loosen the strictures of absolutism that bind them and exclude them from moving their congregations toward peaceful coexistence with all their neighbors in the world.

Shall we condemn all of Martin Luther's work without considering the historic context of his occasional anti-Semitism? Shall we condemn all the Western art created by apparent anti-Semites? There would not be that much to enjoy. I want my Shakespeare and Dostoevsky, regardless of the anti-Semitic attitudes reflected in some of their works. I will not sacrifice the universal poetic splendor of *Hamlet* and *The Tempest* because of the portrayal of Shylock in *The Merchant of Venice*, or the humanness and profundity of Dostoevsky's *The Brothers Karamozov* and *The Idiot* for questionable descriptive passages in *Crime and Punishment*. Those who condemn Shakespeare or Dostoevsky seem to me perilously close in spirit to those who burned books in Nazi Germany.

In Chaim Potok's *Asher Lev*, the title character paints a highly personalized version of the crucifixion. For this he is roundly condemned by the Ladover community, an Orthodox Jewish community in which his father is a central figure. Potok—himself a Rabbi—does not, however, allow his character to be destroyed in the clash of the powerful forces of Orthodox Judaism and the traditions of Western art. Asher Lev becomes, rather, an outsider from both traditions. Yet as an adult he functions successfully as both a major Western artist and as a member of the Ladover community. Like the convert, he is not accepted by many in the extremely conservative Jewish community.

We can learn a lesson from Rabbi Potok. We must take the better part of Western civilization, learn from it, then throw the worse away. We must allow for creativity in our own kind and for other manners of worshipping God in other religions. We must keep our own integrity, yet open our minds to the beliefs of others. We must sometimes simply agree to disagree—but with civility, humanely, without condemning the other. We should try to learn from Martin Buber that the other is always human, and is more like us than different from us: the other is not a *You* but a *Thou*. We must do this for the sake of our children.

Willy's Vienna and my Vienna still loom in Europe's moral fog as a bastion of anti-Semitism. On the High Holy Days in 1985, Leslie, Asher (then five months old), and I attended Temple in Vienna as the guests of an Israeli official. Austrian security forces were moving along the street outside the synagogue everywhere, nerves on edge, machine guns ready. I thought of Willy's uneasy, late night walks through the tensions of the post-war Prater district. As Willy walked, Freud was fulfilling his destiny as the founder of modern psycho-analysis as he healed the damaged sons of the cream of Austrian society. As Willy walked, Einstein labored over the early stages of his General Theory of Relativity. As Willy walked, Marx's principles were being given their first practical application in Russia.

And somewhere else in Vienna a young veteran of World War I—one of millions returned from the great front—slouched outside Karlskirche in central Vienna and formulated his plans to dominate and cleanse Western civilization. This image of the young Adolph Hitler has haunted me since we returned from Vienna. Perhaps he and Willy passed each other in the Ringstrasse. How much horror has passed through the world since these two lives crossed in Vienna, and sixty-five years later when Asher and I walked together before the opera house. And so little has changed. Dare we change it? Can we?

We are ourselves Israel. We must be, for the sake of our children. In the modern world, all Jews can no longer hope to physically live in Israel. We must carry her within us, for the sake of the little ones. *Their children, too, who have not had experience, shall hear and learn to revere the Lord your God as long as you live in the land which you are about to cross the Jordan to occupy* (Deuteronomy 31:13). We must cross a new Jordan for the sake of all the children of the world.

NOTES

[i] This cycle appears in *Asher* (Sherman Oaks: Stone and Scott, *Publishers*, 1991.)

[ii] *London Times Literary Supplement*, p.5, July 26, 1991

4

PERSONAL ESSAYS

LOVE AND THE FLOWER OF MEMORY

When approaching an oceanic subject like love, a concept with an infinite variety of shades, textures, and a remarkable ability to transform both object and subject, I am inundated by vast ideas, like the sublime in nature, and vast images—the rainbow, a sign representing hope and idealizing a certain kind of destiny uniting all humans, or the endless blue-green sea I studied as a child for so many hours on the east coast of Florida. Not only is love infinite in variety, it is abstract, irrational, and theoretical in nature; it is hard to find, harder to hold, and impossible to define.

The subject also, you doubtless have noticed, inspires long sentences, fraught with adjectives. Apropos thereto, theologian Paul Tillich, echoing one of his teachers, called love the *ultimate* concern of one being for another. As I examine my own life, I see clearly that there is a great deal I don't know about love—but at the same time, I recognize it absolutely when I see or feel it. And I believe that love is the answer—not to every problem, but to many. Here are a few thoughts on the quandary of love, as I know it.

As a concept, Love is impervious to analysis, to rational patterning. Neither is it chaos. The history of a love may appear to have a clear design, but its power to change lovers cannot be reckoned or explained. All love, it seems to me, is based in one kind of passion or another and is thus capable of either/or transformation and transmogrification of all parties involved. All love begins in passion—blood-love of family, erotic attraction, or deep need. It is possible for these loose categories to cross, as they do in individuals who change the way we think about ourselves, like a husband or wife. Those of us who have been betrayed by family or friends, or hoodwinked by passion examine, over and over with a growing sense of futility, the "facts" of the power emotions that has violently pulled our childhood legs out from under us like an Atlantic undertow. We are passion's victims and dupes, but at the same time, ultimately, its beneficiaries. I am not speaking simply of Romantic love. No affection ensures greater happiness than family acceptance and no rejection is more painful than family banishment. As a child, I was blessed with a family environment of great emotional ambivalence, yet I always sensed the loyalty if not love of certain immediate members of my family and ,occasionally, friends. This sense of abiding sympathy. saved me as surely as I love my children.

Love, irrational as my belief in God, is what I have sought all my life and it is what I need above all else in this existence. Since childhood, love has been, in my mind, equal parts acceptance and ecstasy, but the hard facts of my life attest to the impossibility of this over simplified and idealistic construct. The experience of love is not only severely limited to analysis, but within those limitations the experience of love may appear to be so intense as to be beyond reckoning. More than any other emotion, it is prey to the relativity of individual perspective.

Even so, I want to attempt to describe some of the love I have experienced. I am not going to attempt to list and classify the types of love I have felt, but rather describe some crucial persons or "things" I have loved. By "things," I mean primarily ideas or concerns rather than concrete objects, though I have necessarily been dependent on and concerned about concrete things often enough. I have difficulty using the term love with regard to "things," though I know people who honestly proclaim "love" things. I rationalize such proclamations as misguided attraction to the symbolic power of certain objects. They have become obsessed with such things because they invest a personal prestige in them. I do, however, recognize how safe such emotional investment is. Love experiences with people or ideas are not so safe. Things do not desert you. They may be stolen, but lifeless as they are, they cannot choose to escape.

My first love was in some ways the greatest gift of my life: the unconditional love of my mother. It is the first taste of love I received on this earth and it set a very high standard, one that was not equaled in my life until I was able to love my own children unconditionally. This love is so perfect that we use it to approximate the love divinity has for humankind. Mother-or fatherhood is not in itself the object of worship, though many of us carry a kind of luminous image deep within us for the opposite sex based in that first profound acceptance. It is also clear that the violation of that acceptance is enormously destructive psychologically to the person not so loved. Worse, the absence of such love or the presence of abuse are clearly forces that misshape the human personality.

My mother died in 1989, at the age of 74. She was a gentle spirit of another age, one that she saw as inherently more civilized and gentle than the one I was born into. I was her fourth child and, since she had lost her first boy to death after one short week, I was dear to her. While my sisters have since expressed envy for my being her favorite, I remember principally her criticism of my being unable to live up to the standards she had designed for me since her own relationship with her father had ended. My mother loved me with fierce natural acceptance as an infant; as I grew into willfulness, her love became naturally tempered with qualifications. The conditions of her continuing love, it appeared to me when I was an adolescent, marred my memories of her earlier complete acceptance of me. As I negotiate now with my own teenage children, I am visited by revelation after revelation concerning my own youth.

I remember my mother's father as a dear man, who smelled of the warm milk of his dairy. That I closely resembled the son he lost in a terrible auto accident must have added a bittersweet edge to his love for me, his third grandson. He and Grandmother, like my parents, had lost their first son in childhood and this had scarred their lives. The loss of my mother's younger brother in a tragic accident prepared my mother and her parents to treasure every male that appeared on the family tree. When my mother lost her first-born son, I became an intergenerational event. It is not that there were not other male children, but my parents lived with Grandma and Grandpa at the time of my birth, and I greatly resembled my uncle who had been fated to an early and accidental death. I was the golden-haired kid, the apple of my Grandfather's eye because I was a kind of ersatz for his own lost boy. All of this attention may have aroused the approbation of my reserved and self-isolated father, whose own father was not warm. His mother died when he was a young child. He and I were never close and had many conflicts.

In my mind, my father scarred the lives of his family—he poisoned the natural sweetness of his wife, the worshipful affection of his son and distorted the self-image of two of his three daughters. My sisters accused me of being unfair to my hard-working father in this assessment, and they may be correct. There is a tendency for the memory to cling to the negative and this is certainly the case with my memories of my father. He was, I thought, not only intelligent, straight-laced, prudish and strict, but mean-spirited, bigoted, racist, sexist and to some degree paranoid. I do not feel that I would ever have learned what father love is from him,… but I may be wrong. And I cannot say that I did not love him in some way buried beneath resentment for the depth of that love. I can certainly say that I hated him for long periods of my life.

He was not sexually abusive to his children. The Puritan blood ran much too deep in his veins for that, but he was a classic pater familias—emotionally stolid, volatile, judgmental and given to rages of verbal abuse. He deprived us of one aspect of love, familiarity, and abused his three older children emotionally. When the dam of his restricted emotions broke, he was dangerous; the strappings he gave me are among the most horrific events of my childhood. Once, after he ordered me to grab my ankles and before he began the white-hot onslaught that usually left me unconscious, he said through clenched teeth, "This is going to hurt me worse that it hurts you." There was not an ounce of truth in his tone, which rings in my head to this day. Yet it could have been much worse. Ultimately, his concern for us was greater than his need to order our personalities in his own image. Finally, I believe he saw our stubborn resistance to his suppression of us as the mirror of his own ability to survive an abusive childhood environment, one probably afflicted with variations of the meanness and estrangement my sisters and I had tasted at his table, but with one important difference: we had a mother to protect us from extremes.

I do not know to what extent a lack of love or abuse shaped him. The cycle of abuse is an awesome and terrible thing. I became acutely aware of it while teaching in the maximum security prison in Lincoln, Nebraska in the 1970s and 80s. Sooner or later a singular fact emerged from every student writer in my class: they had been abused and they had abused. I have since seen frightening statistics concerning the prevalence of abuse among habitual criminals.

Considering what I have seen in my wanderings on this earth, I have always been grateful that my three sisters married good men. I think my father would have ultimately approved of all three—he met two of them— and would have recognized the end of the cycle of abuse in which he was both victim and predator. He was a man who, according to my mother, "did the best he could." He married a noble, if timid, woman and was haunted by what I still see as a driven and brutish nature. I have tried to see him as a victim of misfortune, an outsider. (Our family name, Wallis, means in fact "outsider," according to British etymology.) He was a difficult man to love and made self-trust and a positive self-image among his children a near impossibility with his acid criticism and degrading remarks. Yet he drove us to a certain self-knowledge and to a terror of ignorance and failure. He taught me to deal with pain. This was his heritage of love. My sisters and I could have done worse.

I learned about Romantic love from books. I never heard my father say "I love you" to my mother or to anyone else. My first sexual experience, at 19, corresponded approximately to my father's death at 59. Since we had not buried our old hatchet, his being torn suddenly out of my life left me with an unhealthy remorse and painful guilt. I buried myself in erotic love and a corresponding passion for ideas and art. Fortunately, academia rewards the latter under certain conditions, and the unruly forces of my inner life were sublimated and shaped into professional accomplishment in great universities, beginning with the institution, Southern Illinois University— Carbondale, where my father had taught at the time of his death from cerebral hemorrhage. Insecurity and terror are interpreted as sensitivity, even brilliance under some conditions; it is possible, I have learned, for the life of the mind to transform an inscape of personal terror into intellectual accomplishment and recognition. My motivation to excel is as much motivated by the fear of failure before the razor strap of an invisible giant as it is by the need for recognition or the need to share.

In my wanderings I was supported and strengthened often by friendship. I have been blessed with several fine friends, the most important and permanent of which began in my twenty-first year. This man, David Landis, is the brother I lost and never had. I have no doubt but that I see in him not only a sibling, but something of an ideal father—to see him with his own son is a mythic pleasure. Such is the nature of friendship for me. After my father died, I sought father figures everywhere I went for two decades and, ultimately, found myself part of a group of young men gathered around an elderly, fatherless artist who was a marvelous ersatz Father in his own way. He gave me away at my wedding. Gradually, the hunger to replace my father has faded—the artist, Len Thiessen, died in 1989—I am certain that becoming a father myself has had much to do with the lessening of my destructive hunger, the old terrible raging search for something missing. Old wounds heal slowly, but old emptiness just stays on and on. Yet it, too, ceases.

In constantly seeking after love, I have chanced to discover some of its manifestations. I recognized the importance of my mother to my life as an emblem of unconditional love. Throughout my life, I have discovered release from fear, even terror, in two ways: wrestling with ideas and in the arms of women. My wife Leslie has become the center of my world of love. We have been blessed with four children, who have taught us—as all children teach adults—how to love. We must only listen, with care, to them. Children also inform adults of the presence of divinity in the world, it seems to me, for the creation and birth of children is the surest sign of God's presence on earth. Children are also, I feel, the nexus of all love, for they have their beginning in romantic passion and then blossom in the environment of marital/familial love. From the difficult wrestling of personalities in marriage and childrearing emerges much of the essence of responsible love. The great dimensions of love may lie in its potential for selflessness. Eros will ultimately be tamed by Thanatos, but the flowering of memory and art will preserve the variety and universal beauty of love long after we have ceased to try to grasp it in our hands.

THE PROCESS

Love is primary in most lives, but not all. Ambition and fear capably block or subvert emotional fulfillment. Highly successful professionals are sometimes unstable in the personal realm—some cases, like that of Marilyn Monroe, are infamous—but many high rollers have both public and private stability; for example, statistics tell us, in the upper management positions of the business community. I am not really concerned with this stratosphere of society. I am concerned with the wrestling of the average person to find a balance between public and private happiness, which usually involves happiness in love as the anchor for survival.

I am, so far, a survivor. With a modicum of luck, I survived a rough childhood and adolescence in southern Arkansas in a marginally dysfunctional but precociously tough milieu and family. I have also survived success in several occupations and in several long-term relationships. Based on observation during my lower middle-class—just where do sociologists place teachers in the hierarchy of American occupations now?—life experience, I find that success in most balanced lives is built on accepting love in both its passionate and sharing aspects *as a process* which requires much more than mere acceptance of the other "just as they are." (What on earth does that phrase mean?) *Happiness requires accepting the other as process*, for as individual social and spiritual organisms we are never static, not as long as we breath, see and feel. We strive all our lives long to fulfill ourselves. It seems to me that a great deal of what love is about is helping our loved ones fulfill themselves within the realm of a constantly expanding circle of potential. Survival teaches us this.

Ingmar Bergman's film *Touch* (1975) introduced the act of touching as a metaphor for the dual powers of eros, sexual passion. Bergman is intent on exploring the creative and destructive powers of erotic attraction in this explicit and less than profound film. Several scenes, however, touched me deeply—they are still clear in my mind twenty years after viewing the film—because they drew parallels between eros and its profound shadow between the tree of passionate love and its deep psychic roots: it made clear the male need to re-enact, on some level, the child-mother relationship with the lover. It is the desire for this initial, unconditional love that drives some men to and from women, like clouds that form storms or currents that form torrents; and it is the failure of wives and lovers to provide that longed-for touch of acceptance that accounts for a world of unhappiness among men and their mates. I am not acquiescing to Freud's point of view; I am saying that every child is wonderfully spoiled as an infant and struggles a lifetime to rediscover the initial primal awakening of powerful hungers and emotions discovered at a mother's touch and at her breast. If women cannot understand this and glory in it, I'm sorry for them; those who ridicule it seem to me fools.

I cannot experience the female's point of view, but I can imagine that it is similar in some basic aspects to the male's, to mine. My sisters and I share a common affection for and understanding of our mother, but disagree strongly about my father. They praise his unbending vision of how we should fit into society and the world; for them, he is the source of our most useful common values: industriousness, fortitude, faithfulness, emotional strength, and commitment. They see him, at best, as quasi-deific; at worst, as a strict parent doing his best under poor conditions. I have a great respect for my father and his values, but I do not love his memory and I did not love him during his life. Certainly, for long periods of time, I hated him. My mother said and did cruel things, yet I loved her. Her struggle was mine, for she somehow accepted me as a part of her life, her self. By always holding me at a distance, my father never seemed able to do this.

I no longer think about my father and my failure to love him in terms of whose fault it might have been. Perhaps our failure was predetermined by forces neither of us could control. I now believe that my father never saw me as a complete person—perhaps a promising possibility, but weak, fragmented or unsteady—according to his values and therefore unlikely to be strong and succeed. It is possible I saw him through a similarly fractured mirror as a frustrated, mean-spirited failure. I learned from both my parents' lives, but I loved my mother's ability to see the promise of my life as a process, a continuous flow. My father condemned my efforts in isolated moment after moment; my father saw the fragments of my life and condemned them. My mother felt my pain and touched me with encouragement again and again. My father lacerated my body and soul; my mother healed them. I never once heard my father say *I'm sorry* or *I love you*. Never. I know he must have said them to my mother, but not to me and not to my sisters in my presence. He never said *I'm proud of you* to any of us children.

My mother put up with a great deal from both my father and me because she sensed our shared, obsessive masculine need for healing. Woman's power is very great in relation to men, both as a wife and mother. Clearly, society requires that these two roles be carefully separated. Sexual ecstasy and the eternal hunger related to it is the realm of consenting adults, not mother and child. The absence of accepted touch from an adult love is tragic in many ways and may cloud a relationship. The process of erotic need can override even the overwhelming love of parent and child. Divorce is the messy aftermath of the battle between need and pride, intuition and frigid superego.

Pride and ambition are apparently linked to eros in some outstanding individuals. A great Yiddish writer, Mendele, drew inspiration from an unhappy childhood to write his satiric masterpieces, while his even more popular contemporary Shalom Aleichem drew his whole life on his father and mother's initial support of his creative efforts. My father eschewed all the arts as avocational exercises in futility. He seemed to neither recognize nor care that, after my mother, music and narrative were the greatest loves of my childhood and formative years. Doubtless there is some irony that I share my father's principle occupation—we were born teachers. And whatever our differences, we share in common one great love: my mother, his wife. It is with great pleasure that I watch my sons now shaping their relationship with their mother, my wife. I only hope that they will find mates who will have the humanity and wisdom to remember to touch the living child in them, to guide their ambition and assuage the crippling fears the world will throw into their way as they process along roads more or less taken.

March 3, 1997

A BOOKSTORE

I don't recall the circumstances that first brought me through the front door of Dutton's Bookstore, but I can't imagine it was the unassuming exterior of the building in which it is housed. Once inside, however, I was struck by the winding rows and stacks of books that enclosed me in spatial patterns that hint at mythic adventure. As I moved into the first room, walls of book enclosed me, each volume forming part of a complex vastness. I was in a labyrinth constructed by a contemporary Daedelus. Later, while exploring the science fiction section, I paused a moment in mid-perusal to construe Dutton's as a vast, primitive computer. I felt, from first contact, that I was part of an environment charged with imaginative power; I was part of a locus rich with energy of history, ideas and learning. That initial impression has not faded in two decades. Like every worthwhile creation in my life, however, my vision of Dutton's has suffered a sea change. I have recently grown to need Dutton's in its concreteness—as opposed to my image or imaging of it. Let me explain what I mean.

The building I have continued to enter for the last decade squats comfortably on the southeast corner of the juncture where Laurel Canyon intersects Magnolia in the San Fernando Valley. At this inauspicious juncture of concrete and tarmac paths, a friendly bank, a vile supermarket, a filling station, and a nondescript business building have settled in graceless, utilitarian proximity. Dutton's Books occupies the penultimate position on the southeast corner, next to the gas station. Generations of Valley dwellers have found it natural to pull over and go into the pleasant, quaint universe of literature and art that rests unassumingly under a less than sturdy roof. Even so, Dutton's is easy to miss.

Through the years, Dutton's has become a respite for wandering book lovers like me, especially on chilly days in February and during the hot, unforgiving weeks of August and September. Time slows magically in Duttons' and sometimes, if one can find a comely book and settle in a comfortable corner, time—our worst invention—stops altogether. I tried to capture this phenomenon once, in a poem dedicated to Davis and Judy Dutton:

> Time ceases here, where we pause to search through
> Other lives that lie, stand, hang about, above us here.
> Piles of books and prints are vague mirrors where
> The film of memory stretched out behind you appears.

As I have approached and passed my fiftieth year, my desire to loosen time's vise has become more pronounced. Books are one key to transcending my extreme dependence on time-awareness generally; the opportunity for constant self-examination. As I experience the worlds created in books, I can compare the patterned existence of writers of the past with my own, even if these writers happen to be writing, like an author I admire, Peter S. Beagle, about realms that exist only in the farthest reaches of fantasy. Books are mirrors for the imagination. I relive my past and discover sparks of the future in the pages I turn. Since I spend my present writing, I seek lonely patterns of conflict and resolution on Dutton's remote isle. In the maze of culture there, I have encountered the Minotaur of my past and made an unsettling truce with him.

The books at Dutton's are neither immaculately clean, nor are they always where I expect them to be. Dutton's is in this regard a kind of adult treasure hunt, the jousting field for a comic contemporary quest. Those who work at Dutton's, however, always seem to be able to find what is needed. (After working a Dutton's a while, the employee acquires a certain bemused smile, an expression that Merlin might have acquired while searching his tomes for a long forgotten spell.) There have been rare exceptions. During one bewildering year, eight separate books that I had special-ordered disappeared before I could pick them up. At the time, everyone was quite confused about the fate of my orders. I believe that now, a mere decade later, I have invented a possible explanation: the books were of such a high quality and so unique in nature that a passionate bookworm, or perhaps a spirit, shyly filched every one of them before I could claim them. Then, suddenly, my books stopped disappearing—probably due to a lapse in taste on my part. At any rate, someone has quite a strong row of books in their library now. On the other hand, it may have been the borrowers. Several years from now, those eight books may yet be found, carefully wrapped, deep within a secret lobe of the bookstore's crammed cranium.

I encourage my students to visit Dutton's, because I value it more each day as a safe house for ideas. I don't know how many such bookstores are scattered throughout the earth. I suspect there are many; perhaps they are countless. My students compare it to the bookstores of Yerevan, Seoul, St. Petersburg, Tehran and Buenos Aires; and they write about the importance of such bookshops to their youth. In my student days, I lost myself for long afternoons in the musty bookshops in lower eastside Manhattan. I don't remember the names of those bookstores. Their names are not important. They are all Dutton's.

One kind of people who frequent Dutton's are professionals, professionals from all walks of life, but especially television and film. I met the very cultured Charles Champlin there, and brilliant fellow-southerner Brett Butler. It's not the customers who tend to be talkative; many of them are there to escape professional pressure and, at the same time, gather material for work. Still, lively conversation abounds. And, if Davis, his wife Judy, or Carol, Judy's sister, are around, anything goes. Oh yes, then there are the occasional celebrities who come by looking for a copy of their biography. There is a kind of camaraderie that spring up in a store like Dutton's, a business that lives as much from recycling used books as from selling new ones. I feel that an interchange in Dutton's is based on a sense of honor and pride in understanding the spirit of the printed word. When in Dutton's, I can occasionally remind myself that it's not all about money. Where does the true lover of books go to rest? Dutton's.

That Dutton's is not carpeted or immaculately kept has less to do with money than with the types of books that live there. Most, I sense, have been read more than once. Each used book at Dutton's has a history all its own. I often fabricate the existence of those who previously owned the books I buy. I once bought a book because I was charmed by the handwritten dedication to its previous owner. The intimacy of sharing a book with an unknown friend from the nineteenth century, let alone experiencing the fine pungency of aging bindings, browning paper and auburn thought, entices me greatly. Books, under some conditions, speak volumes about their owners. But that, dear reader, is a highly personal matter and ancillary to my discussion.

Not only am I unaccountably unsettled in houses devoid of books, I am less attracted to bookstores that do not handle used books. I once worked in a huge, sterile commercial bookstore, and it was a miserable experience. The smell of old books charms me, perhaps because it reminds me of my own mortality. The life contained in older editions is ageless, but the binding is mortal—older books remind me of that. Bound as we are by language and memory, book lovers are part book. I disagree, however, with those thinkers who argue that our minds, even souls—is there a difference, they ask—consists exclusively of language. In a world flooding with infinite textures, limitless palettes of color and vast symphonies of natural and synthetic sound, such conjecture seems ratiocinative foolishness, metaphysical sign play. I mean that language is the timeless fire passing between us as we express what we know and are. The inked forms on this page and on all the pages I have lovingly studied or written are mere signs, yet essential to sharing the crucial connectors in the bridge across time's merciless flow. Time is our worst invention and presents us with our most meaningful challenges.

If I am honest, however, I am never completely at ease in a library or bookstore—even Dutton's. I am afflicted with a pleasing restlessness, for the same rows of books that hold escape and promise are also the vast iceberg of humanity's collected knowledge. How much of it can I know? Sometimes I feel I occupy *a tight corner in the convergence / Of lonely thought and dialogue,* and I know that where I sit spiraling among Dutton's books I will never grasp the vast majority of them, but must be content to study their awesome bulk from a near distance. Sometimes, the myriad flow of knowledge in great gatherings of books like Dutton's provides the same comfort for me that I find in gazing at the airy design of cloud formation and flow, or the patterns of ground-gathered rainfall: on the surface, appearance doesn't seem to mean anything; it is, simply, its own visually-engaging self. Like crystals, the countless fascicles that fill the shelves of Dutton's appear chaotic on their multifarious surfaces; but structurally the diverse disciplines they represent all share the common thrust of language dedicated to gathering information and the communication of knowledge.

Most bookstores, with their Aristotelian categories and ordered rendering of the complexity of history and evolution of each subject evoke ambivalence in me. I am reduced to helpless confusion by so much organization. I don't feel free to wander lonely as a cloud, to muse over a self-imposed assignment such as relating Peter Marin's humanistic anarchism to Plato's deep and true longing for the Good, as I search the philosophy section at Dutton's. Or I may desire to memorize a Shakespearean sonnet while perched on a stack of unpacked boxes in the large nook enclosing the poetry section. Like Faust, I want now in my most unsettling moments to know all things. How can I call myself educated, in even a single field, when I have read and understood so little? I prefer the dusty rambling and brilliant accidents of Dutton's to the sterile well-ordered world of the self-congratulatory commercial bookstore, which is peopled with searchers like me— poor forked beings searching for words to help us sleep better at night, dream deeper and truer in naive hope.

This kind of comfort, dusted with the silver afternoon light of the valley, is what I return to Dutton's for. My search has to do with my faith in the certainty and permanence of knowledge, and my relationship to that knowledge. It also has to do with where the true lover of books goes to rest. I wrote these lines for Davis Dutton: *A community of hands tends your fields of words. / The crown's trembling passes calmly forward.* Independent booksellers are the philosopher-kings of merchants: they are concerned with the bound volumes of the human voice and thought, which signify that which is permanent and worthy in us. They also grant those of us who find our wings in books the power to arrest time. Dutton's itself is a peaceful microcosm of how I imagine the Eden of words to have been. Perhaps, it is also a hint at the promise of eternity inherent in the evolution of this written record of humankind and the insistent striving for a perfection it reflects.

5

SCHOLASTIC PIECES

THE CASTLE

An Affirmation of The Theistic Existential View

The later works of Kafka oppose a unified self to authorial truth. The protagonist no longer has the dual nature of a Gregor Samsa with which to define his existence by metaphoric narrative.[i] In *The Castle*[ii], as in all of Kafka's stories, the protagonist presents the sole point of view for the reader. This point of view discloses the manifest content of the story of K. in the village. Yet there is defined in the actions of the protagonist and in elements omitted from the narrative a latent truth, the expression of which is the ultimate purpose of Kafka's art. The consciousness of the narrator is placed paradoxically in contrast with the authorial truth of reality in the text. The self is pretense.[iii]

The negative presentation of the truth of reality through unitary perspective may be seen as an affirmation of the theistic existential view of existence. K.'s failure to consciously realize the truth of his existence can be defined by his failure to establish it in existential terms. The philosophy of Paul Tillich will serve to illustrate this hypothesis.

The first move of existentialism (whether theistic or atheistic) is to make everyman aware of what he is and to make the full responsibility of existence rest on him. The process of self-conception or certainty of being, as defined by Tillich's type of existentialism, provides the framework for analysis by which to illustrate the narrator's (K.s) failure to perceive the truth of reality in *The Castle*.

In Tillich to *believe* in something is to *trust* in authorities that enlarge our consciousness without forcing us into submission. Trust is an element of *faith*, which is the state of being ultimately concerned. *Belief's* incomplete certitude may be undercut by criticism and new experience. The certitude of *faith* does not allow this; it is "existential" in nature—the whole existence of man is involved. The major element of faith is this: it makes one's existence certain, defines one's being in relation to something ultimate.

In the concept of *symbolic faith*, *faith* is defined as the acceptance of symbols that express our ultimate concern in terms of divine actions. The language of *faith* is a language of symbols, for man's ultimate concern is expressed symbolically. The fundamental symbol for our ultimate concern is God. God is the symbol for himself. *Ultimacy* is a matter of immediate experience and is not symbolic in itself. For Tillich, God is an ultimate symbol (a symbol for itself), unquestionable, nonexistent; Kafka makes such a symbol of the Castle. *Concreteness* concerns ordinary experience symbolically applied to God, the fundamental and universal content of *faith*. The idea of God within itself is certain (the Castle is such an idea for K.); and all the qualities we attribute to God—power, love, justice—are taken from finite experiences and applied symbolically to that which is beyond finitude and infinity. (The qualities K. attributes to the Castle—strangeness, remoteness, illogicality, cruelty—he acquires in the course of his relationships in the village).

K., in theistic existential terms, does not *believe* in or *trust* the authority of the Castle, though he does not doubt the existence or the power of it. *Belief's* incomplete certitude is not allowed him; criticism and new experience reinforce rather than undercut his disbelief (K.'s long talks with the innkeeper's wife are explicative of this point). Without trusting the authorities whereby his consciousness may be enlarged without forcing him into submission, K.'s existence is undefined; he has no positive *faith*, no certitude of existence. He may not define his existence in terms of something ultimate, for he does not believe in its authority.

Further, K.'s *anti-faith* distorts and reverses the concept of *symbolic faith*. In contrast to *symbolic faith* (the acceptance of symbols that express our ultimate concern in terms of divine actions), K.'s *symbolic anti-faith* projects his own uncertitude of existence on the ultimate symbol. And after his initial projection of uncertitude (K. asserts he was summoned to the Castle as Land-Surveyor of the village), the Castle continuously reacts in a nebulous and reflective manner to all other testings of its authority by K. Finally K.'s *disbelief* and *anti-faith* undermine his process of self-conception, or his certitude of being. He does not believe in himself because he does not believe in the authority of the Castle. K.'s existence is negative, and the unitary, solipsistic perspective (attitude) through which we perceive the story is equally negative in its relation to the truth of the Castle and *The Castle*.

The difficulty with textual explication of the hypothesis is obvious: the cart precedes the horse; we become intimately acquainted with K. before the uncertitude of his existence becomes obvious. If we keep in mind the hypothesis, however, supporting evidence makes itself known in the first several pages.

When the "young man" awakens K. and questions him, K. replies, "Let me tell you that I am the Land-Surveyor whom the Count is expecting. My assistants are coming on tomorrow…with the apparatus." He claims to have been called and appointed Land-Surveyor by the Castle which controls the village into which he has "wandered" that night. On the preceding page we receive a hint that K.'s assertions do not run parallel to his actions. He asks, "What village is this I have wandered into? Is there a Castle here?" He seems not to know that a Castle exists near the village, and, in fact, we are told that the Castle was "hidden veiled in mist and darkness" when K. crossed the bridge into the village. Then why does K. stand "for a long time gazing into the illusory emptiness above him" when he is on the bridge? Surely, he knows and senses the presence (the name of which he seems not to know) seems not to interest him, nor does the fact that it has a Count. Only when he learned he must have a permit to sleep, and only then, does he assert his supposed summons to service. Made aware of the presence of the authority of the Castle, K. asserts his self-conception in relation to it: he is the Land-Surveyor in employment of the Castle. He defines his existence in terms of something at this point very powerful and intimidating, if not ultimate.

A call for verification is made to the Castle. K.'s assertion is rebuked. Then immediately the rebuke is rebuked with a return call from the Castle. K.'s reaction is curious, and, to our analysis, crucial. Instead of being satisfied with the news of verification, he considers the Castle's recognition of his claim "unpropitious for him... for it meant that the Castle was well-informed about him, had estimated all the probable chances, and was taking up the challenge with a smile." This mental reaction to his assertion and the above inconsistency—K. recognizes the presence of the Castle above him when he is on the bridge, yet pretends not to know of its existence when first interrogated—suggest that K. has falsely asserted a self-conception (his definition in relation to an ultimate) to the Castle's authority. If this is true, then the Castle's acceptance of the "challenge" germinates K.'s *anti-faith*, for the Castle accepts his *disbelief* and *distrust* in its authority as if it were *belief* and *trust*, which might be fully "certified" by *faith*. We see by his reaction to the second telephone call that he is denied even the uncertitude of *belief*, and may project that the certitude of *faith* is replaced by the uncertitude of *anti-faith*. More evidence of his false assertion of self-conception follows easily.

K. stated (above) that his assistants would follow him by one day with the land-surveying apparatus. But the Castle sends two "new" assistants, Arthur and Jeremiah, who know nothing of surveying. K. accepts them immediately, suggesting he really never expected the "old" ones. K. is assured over the phone by a Castle official that these are the "old" assistants; K. lies—"'They are the new ones; I am the old assistant. I came today after the Land-Surveyor.'" "'No'" is shouted back at him. He is here confronted with his first false assertion as well as his immediate lie. The next four lines are crucial.

"Then who am I?" asked K. as blandly as before.

And after a pause the same voice with the same defect answered him, yet with a deeper and more authoritative tone: *"You are the old assistant."*

(p. 28, my italics)

Unlike the first vague confrontation with Castle authority, here we see K. openly lie to an official—and the official recognizes his second false assertion of self-conception (a sort of microcosm of the first) and agrees to recognize it, reinforcing the *anti-faith* resulting from the affirmation of K.'s claim to the certitude of being the Land-Surveyor.

In the concept of *symbolic faith*, we accept symbols that express our ultimate concern in terms of divine actions. But the quality of acceptance is functionally reversed and distorted in K.'s *anti-faith*: the Castle officials accept K.'s symbols (false assertions) that express his ultimate concern (defining his existence in relation to something ultimate—the Castle) in terms of K.'s own actions. The being attempting to define his existence thus becomes the ultimate symbol, and all his actions are seen as concrete symbols of that ultimate. The Castle will allow K. to seem to be what he asserts he is.

Further, it may be shown that the qualities K. as narrator (the source of unitary perspective in *The Castle*) attributes to the Castle, manifest themselves in him; this suggests that such qualities had their origin in K. and are merely reflected by the Castle. The reflections from the Castle are the manifestation of K.'s pre-conscious attitudes of *anti-faith* into conscious actions. To illustrate: the authorities of the Castle are remote and, from K.'s point of view as narrator, cruel. K. asks for himself "'When can my master come to the Castle?'" "'Never'," is the answer. It is clear that the Castle has "accepted" K.'s "challenge" and is playing a game with him from its remote position. The game forms the plot of the novel. K.'s false assertions are met with equally false recognition from the Castle. He is given no land to survey and is never officially given office. The document which verifies his appointment is never found; it is supposedly lost among the mayor's *Schwärm* of other documents. The assistants drive him to do what he accuses the Castle of doing; as the Castle cruelly repulses K.'s attempts at communication, K. locks out the assistants in the snow and refuses to let them come in to him. They suffer cruelly, as K. has. The qualities K. attributes to the Castle are, in truth, his own—a reflection of his *anti-faith*, which reverses the concept of accepting symbols that express ultimate concern in terms of divine action, and expresses it in terms of one's own attitudes.

The theistic existential view of existence, as defined by Tillich, offers concepts and terminology extensive enough to explore Kafka's negative presentation of the truth of reality through unitary perspective. More specifically, through K.'s failure to arrive at a true self-conception in existentialist terms, *The Castle* may be interpreted as a negative affirmation of the theistic existential view of existence. Finally, the seminal concept underlying Kafka's art and the work of existentialist thinkers is that of the metaphoric nature of reality. Johannes Urzidil suggests that Kafka's true greatness lies in the validity of his images.[iv] Urzidil's remark presupposes a critically balanced definition: that the metaphor develops meanings problematic or relative to time-space conditions, meanings which lacked any (or complete) objective correlates at the time of their origin. Kafka's ironic, yet seriously and stubbornly realistic concept of existence (as it is structured metaphorically in his art) readily lends itself to analysis in the terms of theist existentialism. This analysis would seem to affirm Urzidil's appreciative evaluation of Kafka, and, further, to re-indorse the superb artistry that typifies Kafka's literary creations. Ultimately, these creations do not merely form metaphoric constructs of reality, but offer the reality behind the constructs—there existence is manifest.

NOTES

[i] The "acting out" of the metaphor in the narrative's events; spineless Gregor Samsa is no longer "like" a cockroach with respect to his spinelessness, but is one.

[ii] Franz Kafka, *The Castle* (New York: Modern Library, 1969).

[iii] Much of this first paragraph is paraphrased from Walter H. Sokel's *Franz Kafka* (New York: Columbia University Press, 1966). For a more detailed study see Sokel's *Franz Kafka—Tragik und Ironie; zur Struktur seiner Kunst* (Müchen: A. Langen, 1964).

[iv] *There Goes Kafka* (Detroit: Wayne State University Press, 1968), pp. 31-32.

THE DARK SPEED OF LOVE

Death in Romeo and Juliet

JULIET: *O now be gone; more light and light it grows.*
ROMEO: *More light and light, more dark and dark our woes.* (III,v,35-6)
LADY CAPULET: *I would the fool were married to her grave.* (III,v,14)

When Juliet opens III,ii with the rough iambics of "Gallop apace, you fiery-footed steeds," she creates images and rhythms that typify the passions which victimize every character in this early tragedy from the master's pen. The action of these five great acts is of such a furious nature that we grow as dizzy as the characters from time to time. And the nature of this fury, this speed of decision and action in character, extends in both traditionally negative, as well as traditionally positive areas of action; i.e., people kill as easily as they fall in love, in fact more easily. This play has only one love relationship, but at least five deaths. There is an imbalance of emotional content in the play's environment that seems to, in part, determine the destiny of the title characters.

The characters themselves seem aware that they are hounded by death. Even as he hesitates before entering the Capulet ball, Romeo fears "Some consequence" which will "expire [kill, murder] the term / Of a despised life closed in my breast / By some vile forfeit of untimely death" (I,iv,107-112) before he marches on to Fate's drum. Death is mentioned as often as love and often mixed with images and ideas of the love between the two. Even though "Juliet is the sun" (II,ii,4) and a "bright angel" (26), and their passion a "yielding to light love" (105), Juliet praises the "mask of night" (85) which allows them to exchange vows of love. As the chief agent of the balcony scene, which ends as she expresses in an almost comical fashion her fear of "kill[-ing Romeo] with much cherishing" (184), Juliet has earlier expressed a slight fear of these words: "My grave is like to be my wedding-bed" (I,v,137). Her mother's similar, but intemperate utterance in III,v has a dreadful chilling effect: to wish an only daughter, "the fool," married against her wishes is one thing, but to wish her—even in fury—"married to her grave" (III,v,141) is quite another.

If we begin to monitor the imagery of the play, but especially the imagery the two lovers employ as their paths intertwine, we begin to understand the imagery of Eros and of Thanatos are intricately intertwined in this play from its beginning to its end, and that the rush of action precipitates the tragic melting of the two into each other so that ultimately the mixture is complete: Romeo discovers the somnambulant Juliet and utters, "Why art thou yet so fair: Shall I believe / That unsubstantial Death is amorous,… " (V,iii,102-3) and for her part Juliet will draw poison from her dead lover's lips: "Haply some poison yet doth hang on them" (165). The combination of the speed with which action rushes toward its tragic conclusion and the darkness of the cumulative character vision make this play a study in tragic momentum, and incident of dark speed.

A clear and typical expression of the youthful impatience—and the speed with which all expectations met—is Juliet's first 19 lines of II,v. Here her words not only embody one of Shakespeare's favorite themes, tension between the generations, but makes this tension the vehicle of the themes of impatience/speed and love/death and the images which carry them. Images of time—odd to think that the Elizabethans could be as obsessed with time as our century has been—inculcate Juliet's feelings of impatience. "The clock stuck nine" (1) as she sent the nurse and now it is "Three long hours" later (11). The "half an hour" has become three, and the "the sun's beams" (5) of her passion will soon cease to drive back the "shadows" (6) of fear. Love is "wind-swift" (8), indeed as quick as thought (4) itself, while the older generation are the opposite: "But old folks, many feign as they were *dead*, / Unwieldy, slow, heavy and pale as lead." (16-17). Were she young, the nurse "would be as swift in motion as a ball" (14) or some winged creature such as a dove (7) or Cupid himself (8). Youth flies, rushes, hurries to its fate, and even though the Friar begs his students to slow their rush toward eternity, it is of no avail. It is the rush of Romeo's friend to Mantua to inform the bridegroom of his bride's death that precipitates the final three deaths in the dark tomb of Verona. Here we relive the entire tragedy as Romeo discovers body after body, before adding two to the pile.

The shattering power of the final scene comes from our awareness as audience that the partners in a love that was initiated (I,v) and developed (II,ii), consummated (III,v) under the blankets of night, now experience concretely that which had previously been only words. There is a terrible irony in what we experience at Juliet's waking to see and kiss that which she has previously envisioned in III,v:

> God, I have an ill-divining soul
> Methinks I see thee now thou art so low,
> As one dead in the bottom of a tomb,

or falsely argued in III, vi: "Indeed I never shall be satisfied / With Romeo, till I behold him—dead—.... " The enormous power of the extended implicit metaphors surrounding these two as they rush and are rushed to their brief union is perhaps best contained in a bittersweet reading of Romeo's last thoughts. He drinks the terrible potion, and as he kisses his love, he notices the warmth of her lips. Before he falls away from her, he may think he sees her eyelids flicker; fascinated even as he falls back from consciousness, his hand records a slight movement of her chest as she draws a slight breath. Too late, a voice deep within him screams out. Too quick, too late! And then the darkness he feared above all closes over him, as it will soon enclose, with dark speed, his lover and his love entire.

A LANGUAGE OF ONE'S OWN

An ESL Student Publishing Project

An ESL student's life in America features severe ups and downs. This will not come as news to Americans who have studied for an extended period in a foreign land. No matter how accepting the environment, the individual occasionally feels severed from home—from the familiar customs and rituals that formed him. As an ESL instructor, I try to find ways in class to relieve the loneliness and to rechannel potential tension, not only by engaging the class in the normal process of acquiring technical skills but also by encouraging students to share the wealth of their diverse experiences in writing and sharing that writing.

We write a great deal in my ESL classes, and I make use of student compositions in as many ways as possible. One way I call *Student Publishing*. Student Publishing uses the editing and publishing processes to create a compilation of essays original to a single class. It aims to cause students—individually and in groups—to review the content of the course as they select, revise, edit, and prepare an original publication from the class's collected writings. Below I detail how Student Publishing functioned in my advanced-level ESL class at Los Angeles Valley College during the 1988 Fall semester.

This course emphasizes advanced reading and writing techniques. Although I deal with grammar through texts, handouts, responses to graded homework or quizzes and mini-lectures employing examples from the homework, the class as I taught it focused on process. Often we read our writing to each other, answered questions concerning it, and received the corrections and gentle criticism of our classmates. We also worked in pairs and groups, for this class, which met only twice a week (9:00-10:30 Tuesday and Thursday), and which was happiest when listening, speaking, and reading *together*. Each writing assignment became a creative act we looked forward to sharing with our classmates.

Throughout the course, I was as concerned with the process of how good writing is produced as I was with the final product of that process: solid academic prose as written by students of English as a Second Language. Clearly, there needed to be ways to measure reading comprehension and technical writing skills. The most effective use of reading materials, however, became evident in this class when the student discovered in the readings an issue or idea—sometimes even a natural event—about which they wanted to write. When the writer's imagination was engaged in issues gleaned from reading, new vocabulary and grammatical skills usually were apparent in the writing.

I will sketch below the method by which the Fall 1988 ESL class collectively selected a single writing topic and responded to my evaluation of the manuscripts produced. I will then discuss the roles of revision and publication in the writing process that produced the Student Publication. My ESL classes meet half the time in our Writing Center's Computer Lab, where my students not only learn composition but computer skills.

The sole purpose to create a volume of student writings is to deeply involve the student composers in both the creative and critical aspects of composition. The preparation of a publishable manuscript requires students to review every aspect of the course, including grammar and composition techniques. Editing involves critical thought as well as interpretation, because the students read and criticize the work of others as well as their own. From their own rewriting process students learn to accept and understand the critical efforts of fellow students and the instructor; from constructively criticizing the work of others, students learn to teach themselves and each other.

In such a project the teacher's role as guide and advisor grows in importance as the role as instructor lessens. As the students select the work they prefer to share with others (in print), the publication generally begins its organic evolution toward its final form, *i.e.* toward a "published," bound document.

Such projects, however, do not simply happen; they must be pushed and nudged with persistence and energy toward organization and publication. Generally, the chief organizer and publisher will be the teacher. Sometimes one or two students or even a small group will dedicate their time and energy to playing a major role in the project, but generally the instructor will also invest considerable time scheduling student work hours, working at the computer, proofing and correcting copy, dealing with reprographic services, and distributing the finished product.

A particular section of the *Student Publication, Fall 1988*, entitled "Volcano" came into being from our class readings and came to be the initial section of the Student Publication book through this process: (1) selection of topic and composition of a first draft; (2) revision of the first draft by the authors after the instructor's initial comments; and (3) further revisions (editing) by the authors after further commentary by classmates and the instructor.

Unit 4 of our text *Between the Lines* was concerned with plate tectonics. Because of this area's frequent earthquakes, I assigned a three-paragraph essay on the subject for the first class essay. Although it was successful, many of the essays were tinged with terror and sadness, reflecting life experiences best forgotten. The following week, the class found writing a shorter piece about a volcanic eruption more rewarding. These essays involved the visual imagination and were tinged with romantic adventure rather than personal tragedy. Only one student turned in an account of the earthquake for consideration (remember that the students choose the works they wish to publish) while several submitted their passages on the volcano.

(1) During the last three weeks of the term, we began reading selections of each student's work—first in pairs, sometimes in groups, then in class-as-editor sessions. This is where the students who have selected certain pieces to be considered for the publication create the penultimate draft. (Those who actually enter the documents into the computer serve as final editors.) Major editorial changes never occur at this point, except possibly when composers alter their own manuscripts a they type.

(2) In addition to self-consciously constructed paragraphs and essays, the publication may contain some less formal prose passages: stories and tales (some told perhaps for the first time in English), movie critiques, autobiographical essays (perhaps written specifically to meet application requirements at a university), poems, speeches (delivered in class or at a meeting), and journal entries.

I and the students editors made every effort through this entire process to preserve the author's original voice and style, even though they sometimes stretched the English language to its limits. Not all students in the class were through translating their thoughts from their native tongue into English. However, part of our work as ESL teachers is to accept the students where they are, while helping them to learn to think in—not translate into—English. All creative thought is precious, even that which is not fully conceived and framed in English by those struggling toward the educational standards we set. I don't feel that we should ignore this quirky treasure of expression any more than we should legitimize it.

The general thematic structure of this course's writing topics was "from the self outward," and such movement from the personal mode to the analytical and critical may well be reflected in the general grouping of the compositions in the publication. In our class, the topics ranged from the purely imaginative "Volcano" and "Dream" sections, through reflections on family and homeland in "The Old Country and the Self," to the United States in "Growing Pains and The New Land," and finally to still more analytical writing in "The Future." Many early one-paragraph assignments later grew into essays. Thus, the work of the class determines to some degree the structure and the content of the student publication.

The cover for the Fall 1988 publication was designed by the husband of a student in the class. The cover drawing of a unicorn related to the prose work I chose for the students to read at their own pace—Peter Beagle's *The*

Last Unicorn. Illustrations can be used to good effect in a student publication. If no class members are artistically gifted, the publication can be enhanced with photocopied newspaper and magazine materials and photographs. However, illustrations should be used with restraint and taste. Student Publication is about writing, about wrestling with words.

In addition to the pedagogical value of Student Publishing, the product of this composing process has other uses. It might function as a minor class text, offering examples, and perhaps, setting standards for excellence at a certain level. Good student writing in permanent or semi-permanent form establishes a tradition of excellence and documents contemporaneous students' educational and life experiences. Thus, I make sure that the LAVC library has copies of our *Student Publication*, which may serve in the future as collective slices of student life.

There are two essential characteristics of the Student Publishing process. First, it is a student activity. Although the instructor may serve a primary organizational and advisorial role, the students themselves function as both creators and critics, not only of their own work but of their classmates'. Second, it is a class activity. It demands the full participation of as many students as desire to take part in its full process. Ideally, it would involve each class member. Certainly, the work of every student in class should appear in the final publication.

Clearly, those students who follow through the entire publication process gain the most from it. I do give grade credit to those class members who make a greater investment in the project and whose involvement results in intensive familiarity with the course principles and materials. I see the essence of education as the communication of essential characteristics of the mandated subject matter. Seen in this light, Student Publishing is a useful educational tool in composition courses at all levels, for it facilitates intensive review and application of the essential structures of grammar and composition in a dynamic process. It also produces an educational document that can serve as an example for similar classes. It can also be fun.

Through the Student Publishing process the class creates a work that represents their collective growing writing abilities. The process not only provides a vehicle for personal expression, but it also encourages the students to make the English language their own.

6

AN INTRODUCTION TO LYRIC POETRY

AN INTRODUCTION TO LYRIC POETRY

Poetry frees language to create unforgettable visual images and emotion-charged ideas. It does this through special use of description, rhythm, rhyme and sound patterns. Poetry is the most intense and explosive use of language—I could even argue that poetry is a *dangerous* use of language in that every good poem is like a "thought bomb" that can blast open new dimensions of the reader's imagination. Certainly, both poet and reader take great chances in baring their soul. Poetry's influence, because of the intensity involved in both creating and analyzing a poem, can be a life-changing experience. Since poetry evokes the irrational, this essay's purpose is to give you the tools with which to read a lyric poem deeply and to analyze it as rationally as possible: in essay form. This essay is in two parts. The first part defines a lyric poem in terms of its elements; the second describes how one may interpret a lyric poem, employing the essay form.

I will be limiting my discussion to lyric poetry, a genre of short poem that differs from prose in both form and in its aim. The oldest and purest meaning of "lyric" is a poem to be chanted or sung, usually with instrumental accompaniment. In modern times, many short poems have been set to music by composers, even though the poet might never have considered that possibility as he wrote his poem. In pre-civilized societies, song and poetry were almost certainly inseparable. Certainly, it is probable that most poetry written during the Greek high civilization was meant to be chanted or sung—certainly this is true of Attic dramatic (e.g. Sophocles' *Oedipus Tyrranus*) and epic (e.g. Homer's *Iliad*) poetic forms and probably of the lyric poem as well.

The longer forms of poetry may tell a story. Epic and dramatic poetry share this aim with prose fiction, but the elements of plot (the arrangement of action) and character essential to epic and dramatic poetry are rarely crucial to lyric poetry, which is dominated by image, mood and meaning. There will always be exceptions, but these seem to me the three primary constituents of lyric poetry that come down to us from ancient times. One of the first great lyric poets was Sappho of Lesbos (612-? .C.), whose love poems, even in translation, have great power of mood and image. She speaks, for example, of her passion as a fire running under her skin.

To return to the idea of lyric poetry's oral tradition, it seems to me that most poetry has its roots in oral tradition and was meant to be spoken aloud or even sung. The ballad, a form of lyric poetry that sketches out a brief story, is written specifically to be sung. Ballads such as the Beatles' *Eleanor Rigby*, Leonard Cohen's *Suzanne*, or Bruce Springsteen's *State Trooper* may survive as lyric poems quite apart from their music because of their strong emotional content and striking visual images.

Poetry does more with less; it dedicates its rhythm and sound patterns to creating striking visual images, then to surrounding these images with a powerful mood or emotional charge. Because not all poems succeed for all readers and because not all images have universal meaning, make sure that when you choose a poem to analyze, you pick one that speaks to both your emotions and your intellect. Lyric poetry aims to involve all of your mental and emotional resources. It expresses strong feelings in a few words.

Here is a pleasant lyric poem, universally admired in the English-speaking world. It is by A. E. Housman (1859-1936), an English lyric poet.

Loveliest of trees, the cherry now
Is hung with bloom along the bow,
And stands about the Woodland ride
Wearing white for Eastertide.

Now, of my threescore years and ten,
Twenty will not come again,
And take from seventy springs a score,
It only leaves me fifty more.

And since to look at things in bloom
Fifty springs are little room,
About the woodland I will go
To see the cherry hung with snow.   *(1896)*

Most readers would agree that the strongest visual image of this pleasant poem is a cherry tree in bloom. The poet may refer to the cherry blossoms as "bloom," "white," and even "snow," but the tree in bloom is clear in our minds even after a first reading. The rhythm of this poem is regular and the mood of the poem is pleasant, but underneath all this regularity and pleasantry, the poem is saying something profound and unsettling about the human condition.

The visual image of a poem may work in a number of ways. The visual image of the cherry tree in Housman's poem is a symbol. A *symbol* is an object to which we attach special meaning; i.e. it is generally something concrete to which we assign an abstract meaning. The cherry tree might represent, for example, the beginning or springtime of life to the reader. To others, it may represent a figure, perhaps feminine, "wearing white for Eastertide," in which case the trees' symbolic power is used as *personification*, a figure of speech which allows us to attribute human qualities to inanimate things.

A *metaphor* is a powerful figure of speech, which is the substitution of one thing for another. This substitution amounts to an implied comparison between two dissimilar things. In the following poem by America's most original poetic spirit, Walt Whitman (1819-92), the persona creates a most striking metaphor in which the spider spinning its web is compared to the human soul reaching out to others.

> A noiseless patient spider,
> I mark'd where on a little promontory it stood isolated,
> Mark'd how to explore the vacant vast surrounding,
> It launch'd forth filament, filament, filament, out of itself,
> Ever unreeling them, ever tirelessly speeding them.
>
> And you O my soul where you stand,
> Surrounded, detached, in measureless oceans of space,
> Ceaselessly musing, venturing, throwing, seeking the spheres to
>   connect them,
> Till the bridge you will need be form'd, till the ductile anchor hold,
> Till the gossamer thread you fling catch somewhere, O my soul.
>
> (1868, 1881)

This poem illustrates how a well-chosen metaphor can dominate the mood and idea of a poem, and in such a good poem other elements must complement and augment that metaphor. Let's list the poetic elements and then I'll try to prove this thesis to you, dear reader.

Now that we've read two lyric poems and given examples of image, mood and meaning, we can discuss the elements of poetic language and form in more detail, using examples from poems by Housman and Whitman. The purpose in becoming familiar with these elements is to begin to use them as tools to unlock the secrets of the lyric poem itself—that unique combination of image, mood and meaning.

1. *Poetic Diction* is the use of words, phrases and figures of speech that are not current in the ordinary discourse of the time. Consider, for example the poetic syntax Housman uses in his line "About the woodlands I will go," which reverses the prosaic "I will go about the woodlands." This phrasing, like Whitman's "And you O my soul where you stand," an intense emotional utterance devoid of punctuation, is acceptable in poetry, but unusual in everyday conversation and certainly in expository writing. Poetic diction allows the poet to create patterns of rhythm and rhyme with which to work their magic. Diction is a very broad concept and includes essentially all the elements below under its wing.

2. *Rhyme* is the repetition of sound patterns, most commonly at the end of lines, i.e. end rhyme. Rhyme is one of the powerful forces the poet uses to shape the mood of a poem; it creates verbal music. *End rhyme* is the repetition of the last stressed vowel at the end of a line of verse and the

speech sounds following that line. Housman's poem illustrates end rhyme beautifully: "And since to look at things in *bloom* / Fifty springs are little *room*," (Please note the manner in which I quote from the poem). It is important to recognize that to use end rhyme in a way that complements, even augments the meaning and mood of the poem without drawing attention to rhyme itself is a great skill. Housman's use of rhyme complements the regularity of the bucolic scenery described and, perhaps, one might argue, in its regularity embodies the idea of passing time by echoing a ticking clock with its metronomic rhythm and regular rhyme.

Whitman's use of rhythm is much subtler than Housman's, though Whitman allows himself a partial end rhyme in the last two lines with the words "hold" and "soul." It is more fruitful to look for *internal rhyme* in Whitman, for example in the words "seeking" and "need" in lines 8 and 9. Although Whitman's poem predates Housman's by 30 years, the American was doing something much more modern in it. He was creating American free verse.

Alliteration is the repetition of speech sounds in a phrase, sequence of words, line, or even longer unit of the poem. It is thus a kind of rhyme. Housman's "seventy springs a score" and Whitman's "vacant vast surrounding" are good examples of alliteration. Alliteration is one of the great secret powers of poetry, because it allows the poet to create sound pattern to complement the sense of what is being described. Such poetic augmentations of description give poetry power to penetrate the unconscious of the reader and to reach deeper levels of consciousness than might ordinarily be evoked. Housman's use of sibilants—any kind of consonant making a hissing sound—lets us imagine the score (20) years being swept away by the wind, while Whitman's use of the complex patterns of "v," "n," and "s" separated by final "t" sounds creates a feeling of space, empty space. Skillful use of sound patterns expands the meaning of a poem immensely. Look for them, not only in poetry but in your own speech.

3. *Rhythm* is the recurrence of stress in patterns that complement rhyme and augment description and meaning in the poem. We call the recurrence of stress in regular units "poetic feet." There are six major types of feet. We take the names of these feet from the Greeks, who had many such categories, making their poetry enormously complex to analyze. The most common foot in English is the iamb or the iambic foot, which consists of an unstressed syllable followed by a stressed one. We write it this way: / - ´ /. The line "Is hung with bloom along the bough" consists of four iambic feet and, to demonstrate its meter, would be scanned in this way, "Is húng / with bloóm / a-lóng / the boúgh." Following the great Greek and Italian poets, most Western poets previous to this century have made meter as much a part

of their poetic form as alliteration. Most poets of this century have followed Whitman and Hopkins' examples and worked in greater rhythmic freedom than Housman allowed himself in the British tradition. Robert Frost said that composing poetry without meter is like playing tennis without a net. Most poets writing now don't play tennis, but they acknowledge the importance of rhythm in their work.

Other common poetic feet are the trochee / ´ - /, the dactyl / ´ - - /, and the anapest / - - ´ /. Another seldom-used foot is the spondee / ´ ´/, which is used for dramatic emphasis. The anapest and iambic feet are useful, for example, in scanning this line of the Whitman poem: "Till the brídge / you will neéd / be fórmed, / till the dúc- / tile án- / chor hóld".

What is the point of such scansion—analysis of rhythm? We do this for the same reason we observe alliteration: to discover how the rhythms of a poem complement that which is described or meant. Lovers of any art of sport do the same thing in study of an admirable object or performance. In answering the question, "Why is this thing an admirable or beautiful accomplishment?" Whether we are speaking of Placido Domingo singing *Tosca*, Sting singing *Desert Rose*, Kobe Bryant dunking from the top of the key, Mark McGuire's home run swing, or Walt Whitman capturing the America of his time in timeless poetry, we perform the same critical act when trying to understand it. After admiring the whole event, we take it apart and admire that same event in terms of the number of causes that created the final product: song, dunk or poem. In poetry, we do this by analyzing the poem's rhyming and rhythmic qualities and how these augment the poem's meaning. Patterns of sound and rhythm are powerful poetic tools, which can also be useful in everyday life. Certainly, the better we understand such patterns, the better we can understand a poem. Some poems are puzzles to be solved, intricate locks to be gradually released by a number of keys, i.e. poetic elements such as rhyme and rhythm.

The pure repetition of a word or phrase is a very potent if obvious tool of the poet and creates an effective pattern of literal rhyme and rhythm. Notice Whitman's repetition of the word "filament" in line four of his poem. The effect is to create a verbal counterpart to the spider's weaving—and the soul's seeking. Sound echoes sense; form follows function. Both Whitman and Emily Dickinson were influenced by the King James translation of the Bible and use biblical patterns of parallelism in their verse.

A *motif* is an idea, action or thing that occurs over repeatedly in a work of art, taking on a richer meaning with each occurrence. To illustrate, in Whitman's poem, we have the two entities of the metaphor actively "launch[ing]" and "unreeling" (the spider) and "throwing" (the soul) themselves out to fill the void surrounding them. Whitman describes this act as a dynamic function of each entity to evoke a comparison between them.

4. *Point of View* is the way the story of the poem is told or an emotional contour described and the elements presented. There are two broad perspectives, the first-person (I)—"about the woodlands I will go"—and the third person (he, she, it) narrative. The point of view, combined with rhythmic and rhyming elements, helps establish the mode—the manner, style—and mood—the emotional qualities, sometimes the atmosphere—of the poem. In some poems, the setting of the poem is important and approximates the point of view.

It is important to remember that the speaker of a poem is referred to as a persona and is not necessarily the poet. (Walt Whitman refers to himself in some poems from his masterpiece *Leaves of Grass* as "I, Walt Whitman," and such cases are of course exceptions to this rule.) You can understand, of course, that the poet might well want the speaker of the poem to be a character in his or her own right. Both the above poems have straightforward personas: Housman is straightforwardly first person, possibly autobiographical, and Whitman's persona is his typical "universal I," or omniscient persona—a sort of disembodied spiritual presence capable of being anywhere at any time. Both these personas are speakers of sensitivity and intelligence who share their thoughts with the reader.

A poem may also feature a character, a figure presented in a work of literature, usually described in third person. In the two poems above, we might consider the cherry tree, the spider, or the soul characters, but they are not meant so in the strictest sense. They are objects or qualities personified (Housman) or addressed in the second person (Whitman).

5. *Poetic Form* is the principle of organizing a poem, e.g. the number and length of lines in a verse, and the number and pattern of the rhyme. The most common poetic form, the quatrain, has four lines; the sonnet, another popular form, has fourteen. Two lines may form a couplet if they are end rhymed, three lines a tercet. Each of these poetic forms is a rhythmic, rhymed unit of verse.

The Shakespearean sonnet, for example, consists of fourteen lines of iambic pentameter, carefully divided into three quatrains and a couplet. Shakespeare ends many of his scenes with a couplet to give the scene a sense of finality, e.g. "The pláy's / the thíng // Whereín / I'll cátch / the cón- / science óf / the kíng." Note that this is iambic pentameter (five feet per line). Housman's poem is in iambic quadrameter (four feet per line). Whitman's verse, being free verse, is more difficult to scan. Rhyme is a structural principle in these forms. The Dramatic Monologue is a long speech spoken by a single person that explores a specific situation at a critical moment.

Blank verse consists of lines of unrhymed iambic pentameter. This verse form comes closest, perhaps, to natural speech rhythms in English. Marlowe invented this verse form and Shakespeare perfected it in his plays. *Romeo and Juliet* is his greatest poetic drama in terms of consistency and quality of its blank verse. You should look at Marlowe's *Doctor Faustus*, however. There are other forms that do not depend so heavily upon rhythm or rhyme. One—free verse—is demonstrated by Whitman's poem.

Free verse is poetry with an "open form," which consists of irregular line length and little or no end rhyme. Whitman perfected this form in the 19th century, inspired in part by the poetic qualities and line length of the King James translation of the Old Testament Hebrew, which is often in the Hebrew free verse very rich in imagery and rhyming/rhythmic variations. Free verse shifts the emphasis from the poetic foot to the phrase and line as primary rhythmic units, in part because the frequent use of parallelism in biblical language. Line five of Whitman's poem offers a striking use of parallelism, wherein words anticipating phrasing are repeated: "<u>Ever</u> unreeling them, <u>ever</u> tirelessly speeding them."

6. *Figurative Language* is a departure from the standard or literal meaning of words. The symbol and the metaphor are the most common figures of speech. Personification is quite common in poetry. The *simile* is a direct comparison between two distinctly different things using "like" or "as." There might be some confusion between a metaphor and a simile. "My love is a red rose" contains a metaphor, a substitution of one thing for another, while "My love is like a red rose" contains a simile, a direct comparison.

In summary, the images and mood of a poem attract us first and from this "first impression" an idea, the theme of the poem, emerges. The more knowledge of the basic tools—poetic diction, rhyme, rhythm, figurative language—used to create the poem we bring to bear on the idea and form of a poem, the greater will be the depth of our understanding of it. It is important to say that, while not valuable in itself, complexity (the number of elements) is, when combined with integrity (the skillful integration of elements), a characteristic of most great poetry. When a poem is both complex and well made, its effect is likely to be great. When imagery, rhyme and rhythm all complement the literal meaning of a poem, a rewarding understanding may be created in the reader to complement the creative effort of the poet.

WRITING AN INTERPRETIVE ESSAY

Lyric Poetry

Now that we have two examples of lyric poems and have been introduced to the tools poets use to construct them, let's look at the basic tools needed to construct an essay, the prose form often used to express our feelings and thoughts about poetry. The essay is a valuable tool for every student to possess, because it is universally used in higher education to define and to describe concepts. Knowledge of the essay form helps organize thought on any subject, but is especially useful in gathering and organizing thought into patterns which allow communication of that knowledge. It's a good thing to be familiar with. Here is a short essay describing the essay form.

The Essay Form

The essay is the most prevalent prose form in Western culture. Many radio and television advertisements are essays; the average conversation adheres to essay form. Most essays are explanations or descriptions; for example, the question "How are you?" may prompt a description. The subject of an essay should be clearly stated near the beginning of the essay: "I'm well, thank you." This statement of subject is called the thesis statement. The thesis of any essay should be clear: *This essay will describe how to write an essay.*

One characteristic of the essay is that the thesis statement is restated near the essay's conclusion to remind the reader of the essay's focus and purpose. This kind of repetition is part of most social communication. Most conversations begin with "Good to see you" and end with "See you later," or simply "Hello" and "Good-bye." These are verbal signals that open and close a communication sequence. In more complex forms, like the essay, which is meant to contain more than social discourse, we state the main idea at the beginning of the essay, then restate it, perhaps in variation, at the essay's conclusion.

We use the essay form to define, describe and otherwise develop the subject we've chosen. An essay is a kind of discussion. We have many tools with which to develop a discussion on whatever subject we choose. We know and use most of them already in our everyday speaking and writing. The writer can use an essay to define the subject. We may want to give *examples* of the subject—remembering to save the strongest examples for last—or describe it in detail. We may approach the subject as a *process* and *analyze* that process in detail. The writer may want to concentrate on *cause and effect*, or *compare and contrast* the subject with a similar one. We might want to approach the subject by asking a *question* about its nature, then answering the question. We can make any of these tools the only or central tool we use in discussing our subject, or we can use as many of them as seem appropriate. Such tools are called modes of development. They are *example, definition, description, process, analysis, question and answer, cause and effect,* and *comparison and contrast.* Every writer can develop their own strategies from these tools.

Every essay should become more dynamic as it progresses. This is a simple thing to do. Just save the strongest points until last. For example, if we are writing about racism and want to use examples of it, save the most personal and violent for last. If we are writing about Housman's cherry tree poem, we may want to write of how the poem moves toward its climax—the realization by the persona that "fifty springs are little room," i.e. time is flying, life is short, and he should get out and enjoy the cherry trees he's been describing to the reader of his poem. In Whitman's spider poem, the persona becomes increasingly ecstatic as he realizes he and the spider share a universal tendency to reach out into the void surrounding them to create a web of meaning.

The *paragraph* is the basic unit of the essay. Each paragraph is a "mini-essay" and should make one point of the thesis' development clear and have its own "thesis" which we call a *topic sentence.* Each topic sentence is an aspect of the thesis. The topic sentence can usually be found at the beginning of the paragraph and usually isn't repeated. The paragraph is also a unit of thought and as such should be developed. It should develop its own topic as well as the essay's thesis. The art of arranging the topic sentences of an essay is called outlining. It is a very useful *prewriting* activity in terms of organizing the essay's discussion. By the way, closing a paragraph with a concise statement can be very effective. Try it!

Outlining an essay is simple: organize the topics under the thesis and brainstorm—write down words, phrases related to the topic—about ways to support the topics/thesis. Bingo, paragraphs start to appear. Most writers encounter difficulty at some time during the composition of an essay. Many of us don't know exactly what we're thinking until we write it down: writing makes thought more concrete. For this reason, it is not unusual for an essay to go through several drafts. Such revision gives the writer a chance to edit out common errors, as well as develop the essay's structure. Typing a handwritten copy is also important; typing is an objectifying activity and an important stage of editing.

The essay dedicated to the interpretation of a literary work may use each of the modes of development mentioned above as they relate to the meaning and structure of the poem. For example, the thesis statement of an interpretive essay on Housman's poem might be *In Housman's Loveliest of Trees, rhythm and rhyme support the primary theme of carpe diem.* The essayist might then give examples—the most striking one last—supporting this thesis. The examples would necessarily involve short quotes from the poem and analysis of the quotes. Quotes should be used sparingly and analyzed fully in an interpretive essay. Any mode of development might be applied to poetic analysis.

The purpose of writing this essay was to make the reader familiar with essay form. I have used several modes of development in this essay. I hope that the essay's elements are clear now. The more essays we read and write, the clearer the form becomes and the more likely we are to exercise creativity when using it. Each of the above paragraphs has a topic sentence and each topic develops the discussion of the thesis. I have developed my thesis adequately. That's the major task of this or any other essay.

That's the end of the essay.

You will have noticed that both of the forms we are studying, the lyric poem and the essay, involves patterns of repetition. This is natural since repetition is one of the basic elements of design. It allows us to order things. Imagine, for example, a day not ordered by the rhythm of the sun's rising and setting, imagine a cherry tree on which every blossom is shaped differently, imagine a spider's web without regularity of form. A poem, too, is an organic thing; an essay may appear to be highly formal, but it also has its organic qualities. Certainly, getting an essay from mind to paper involves some creative thought. Repetition fights chaos and gives certainty; too much of it is, of course, dull. But just the right amount of it is necessary to communicate successfully. Remember to repeat the main idea of your essay close to its end, but in variation or, as the French say, *en passant* (in passing).

The interpretive essay is a special kind of essay. It clarifies a work of art—in our case, a lyric poem—for the reader. The point of an interpretive essay is to share meaning. The most successful way for me to share meaning is to describe what the poem has communicated to me and how that meaning is created by the poem. Suppose I say to a friend, "This is what the poem means to me." My friend then says, "Well, that isn't what it means to me. Why do you think it means that to you?" In order to support my interpretation, I must be prepared to explain my view of how the poem's elements work together to support the meaning I have derived from it. If I cannot support my interpretation in this way, then my interpretation is suspect.

So how do I do this? This is where the essay comes in handy. First, I may describe the poem in terms of its basic elements; for example I might begin, *Housman's poem consists of four quatrains of iambic quadrameter, carefully end rhymed and with patterned imagery containing subtle use of symbol, metaphor and personification.* To begin on solid ground, I might begin my essay with a description of the poem's scene and environment. I might begin with the cinematic scene or process the poem presents in my mind. Trust your visual imagination when you read a poem. It is a most valuable possession.

I am going to compose an interpretive essay on Whitman's lovely poem. In this essay I am going to share my interpretation that this poem is about the nature of the human soul. It can be helpful to talk out my ideas with a knowledgeable friend, so I turn to my colleague and office mate, author Rod Val Moore. He is nice enough to read the poem.

"The meaning of this poem to me is that man's soul is a dynamic entity that strives to share its essence," I say to Rod, "and this striving is a natural function, echoed by nature throughout the universe—even in the spider's spinning his web."

"But I suspect," Rod says, "that this poem is about the predatory nature of the human soul, which longs to possess and suck the life from others, like a spider does its prey. Prove your humanistic thesis."

"The poor spider is a part of harmonious nature," I say, shocked at his condemnation of both the arachnid and human kind. "Nature is not threatening for Whitman; on the contrary, it is a means of liberation for the universal self. That is Whitman's subject."

"You mean the spider is supposed to be positive?" says Rod, flexing his long fingers toward me. "Surely he meant to contrast the little creep to spiritual humanity. I'm afraid, dear colleague, you have some explaining to do."

You can see, dear reader, that I have a considerable task before me. I think Rod has been reading too much science fiction, but I respect his opinion and will try to convince him of my viewpoint *in my essay*. The following are the thoughts, ruminations and notes I wrote down while studying the poem. They may look coherent, but they are not meant to be. They are the raw observations that I will draw on when I begin formulating my outline and my paper. Now I am going to give the poem a close reading and try to formulate my ideas in an outline.

First, I'm going to try to support my interpretation by describing the outstanding visual images of the poem. This is my favorite thing; many times I consider a poem a short film. Visualizing the poem is my way of getting into it. Every reader finds his own way. While I am engaged in this natural but highly individual approach to interpreting a poem, however, I must remember that I must convince Rod, the reader. The best way to do this is to use what we both can experience: the poet's own words. An interpretation of a poem must be grounded in the poem itself. I will use the poet's own words to make my argument whenever I can.

The first image is of a spider "launch[ing]"—notice that when I alter a quote to fit my grammatical framework of my prose, I acknowledge the alteration by enclosing the alteration in brackets—filaments "out of itself" into "the vacant vast surrounding." The persona—I remind myself that the speaker may or may not be the poet, Walt Whitman—does not say *why* the spider performs this act. He assumes we know the answer: Spiders spin webs because that is what spiders do. At any rate, Rod and I agree that this image is striking, maybe a little unsettling. (It is also inaccurate: a spider does not launch filament out of itself; it pulls it out as it moves or spins, using its body weight to do so. But never mind.) Spiders do not delight either of us, but we agree that the image of the spider in this poem certainly gets our attention. This is important.

What interests me about the first image is that the spider "explores" its "surrounding" with filaments launched "out of itself." There is something impressive about his spider. It seems to have certain human qualities, like curiosity and self-determination. I believe that Whitman, knowing the image of a spider would be creepy, perhaps a little shocking to most readers, has given it human characteristics. And the image of the spider is very dynamic: it doesn't simply weave its web; it "launch[es] forth filament, filament, filament." This spider is personified.

As I formulate the second image, I begin to see Whitman's strategy. The second image—the human soul—is abstract, even spiritual in nature. I'm knocked out by the poet's daring and begin to understand the poem a little better now. The humanized spider sketches a picture of the soul's activity. The soul, like the spider, "stand[s]." the soul, like the "isolated" spider, stands "detached" in "space" and actively "throws" its own filaments, its "gossamer thread," out to form "the bridge" it "will need." To help me visualize this abstract identity, the speaker has given me the visual form of the "sphere," a form which hints at the spider's body, from which it launches its filaments, and the perfect shape of the circle, which form represents divinity.

"I see," says Rod. "So Whitman uses the spider image to introduce the image of the soul. It's a striking visual idea."

"That's part of it," I answer. "I think the essence of the poem is in the soul's action. The spider's spinning prepared the reader for it."

"If you're right," replies Rod, "Then my interpretation of the spider as the bad guy won't work."

"I think it's our tendency to think of spiders as bad guys that makes Whitman's use of the image so effective," I offer.

"Still, don't you think it's dangerous, choosing a creepy spider to introduce the idea of something so precious as the human soul?" asks Rod.

"Poetry is a dangerous business sometimes, I guess."

I thank Rod for his help. Listening and arguing intelligently with someone is a big favor. I do the same for him.

So these images are complex and amount to a metaphor: I am to replace the image of the spider with that of the soul. Frankly, I have had easier tasks. Now I must ask myself, does this interpretation of visual images support my interpretation of the poem, my thesis that the human soul is a dynamic entity that strives in natural patterns to share it essence. Does my visualization of the metaphor support my thesis? Certainly this soul is dynamic and shares its "throwing" pattern with one part of nature, the spider. It is clear to me now that it is the actions, rather than the beings performing the actions that we are to compare. In this poem, a thing is what it does. Both the spider and the soul cast out, but for different reasons: the spider casts out to form a web, one function of which is to catch food, while the soul throws a threat to catch somewhere and form a "bridge" that will be "need[ed]." The spider wants to eat; the soul wants to communicate, possibly cross over to another entity or place. There is a difference as to why each performs the action they do; yet both do it to survive. Whitman knew this; we have to discover it through his poetic vision.

Visualizing a poem is a rewarding activity. Now, let's relate our visualization to the other elements of poetry and see if they support our thesis about the nature of the human soul: that it is dynamic and its actions are natural. Remembering the striking metaphor comparing the actions of the spider and the soul, creating an exciting tension of meaning. It also served to get my attention. Figurative language provides a visual dimension to poetry and creates a tension that allows the reader to see things in a new light.

Now let's consider rhyme, rhythm, point of view and poetic form to see if the poet's use of them will support my thesis. If not, then the thesis is not a very good one. I'll see. Earlier, we noticed how Whitman is after subtle, musical effects in his rhyme. End rhyme is too unsubtle for Whitman; it constricts his free verse longings. He wants to cultivate a long line and a broader rhythm in the phrases of that line. Remember how he creates the alternately whispering and moaning sounds of the emptiness of space in the phrase "the vacant vast surrounding" in line three? He also creates the ocean's waves with sibilant sounds in the phrase "in measureless oceans of space in line seven. Whitman is creating a shifting void, a background for the action of his two entities: the spider and the soul. This is sound complementing sense, a major tool of the poet.

End rhyme, so evident in Housman's poetic form, is a powerful element of traditional poetry. Whitman avoids it because he is shaping a new form. In interpreting a poem, I must remember that end rhyme is obvious and its purpose is also obvious: it determines poetic form and gives special emphasis to the words rhymed. Many people find the certainty of end rhyme reassuring. Whitman doesn't desire, I believe, to reassure us; he wants some other tone. Whitman replaces end rhyme with the constant, quiet music of his alliteration and internal rhymes. Notice how he flirts with end rhyme in lines one and two, shuffling letters in the words that rhyme on the first syllable only: "spider" and "isolated." This is the kind of subtle verbal music Whitman is after. Such subtle rhyming is more horizontal than vertical, so that the poetic form is more fluid, more a process, more organic. This verbal music describes the "measureless" space surrounding the spider and the persona's soul. But this is background. I need to analyze the actions of my spider and soul to see it their rhyme and rhythm support my thesis.

As Whitman describes the actions of both the spider and the soul, his rhythm is pronounced and exact, even in his long lines. Part of this is gotten by the exact repetition of words, as in "filament, filament, filament," a wonderful series of dactyls (´ - -) capturing the feel of casting out rhythmically, or in the parallel phrases "Ever unreeling them, ever tirelessly speeding them." The soul is given its own rhythm and sound patterns. So Whitman emphasizes the action of each entity with dynamic patterns of rhythm and alliteration. And he does this against the very dense regular patterns representing space. It will be interesting to see how the patterns interact. I sense that Whitman gives the actions rhythms that will prove natural in terms of fitting into the rhythms of the "background" of space and time. Whitman always gives the reader enough variation in sound and rhythm, but uses many patterns of repetition that do double duty as both rhyming and rhythmic devices. The interplay of rhyme and rhythm is, after brilliant imagery, the most powerful poetic tool. When combined, the two are remarkable.

Whitman not only revolutionized poetic form with his use of rhyme and rhythm; he revolutionized the role of the persona in poetry. Whitman's persona is a "universal I"—his vision of the American individual. Whitman wanted to lessen the distance between himself and the reader. He did this by baring his soul. Whitman's free verse form—though carefully structured—complements the very idea of a free soul, an entity with free will, a human dimension free of bias and prejudice. This poetic soul is as free as the verse with which it confesses its innermost workings. It is in the very act of writing that the soul of Walt Whitman reaches out to the reader through the poetic medium. Whitman is himself both speaker and poetic soul reaching out to us as we read his poem. The point of view of the persona is then a part of the very nature that the soul should reflect in its actions.

I feel that my thesis is supported by the central images forming the metaphor and probably by elements of rhyme and rhythm. Both spider and soul cast out lines to structure the emptiness, perhaps loneliness surrounding them. I've not yet shown how Whitman's description of the spider and soul's actions relate to nature as Whitman conceives it and thus whether the active entities are a harmonious part of that nature or not. I must show how the striving of the soul to communicate resonates with the universe around it.

Well, up to now I've been gathering information for my interpretive essay. I have a thesis I like and it seems like I have supporting material. The lowest aim of an interpretive essay should be to give a good close reading of the poem—by this I mean an intelligent, detailed discussion of what the poem literally means—and I feel like I'm beyond that now. I can also do better than that. I'm familiar with the elements of the lyric poem by now and I'm beginning to understand how Whitman uses them. Now I want to show my vision of the poem's visual flow of images and the meaning I derive them that flow are complemented by at least two other poetic elements. I'm not going to worry about the title of my essay; I'll let it grow out of the discussion. Okay, I'm ready to outline my essay in the most general terms.

I.   Thesis statement: the nature of the human soul according to Whitman

II. Metaphor and action: a striking comparison and the choices involved

III. The alliteration of emptiness and the rhythm of action: the lonely space to be filled with meaning

IV. The rhyme and rhythm of action—how the universe works

V.   Restate thesis, put all together, re man and nature in union

I'm thinking of each one of these sections as at least a paragraph in length. I will want to quote and analyze, as I did above, short passages of the poem that illustrate my points. I may well use some of the ones I've already analyzed. I will try to find passages that serve a double or triple purpose, passages that have a powerful or brilliant image and also supporting rhyme and rhythmic patterns.

Notice that I'm still playing with ideas here, leaving myself room to change my mind, expand or contract any ideas that I've had or might occur to me. In the past, I have occasionally altered or even changed my thesis as I have composed an essay and continued to analyze the subject of the essay. If that does happen, I don't give up and feel I have to start all over. I simply alter my thesis as the supporting material indicates I should. If my thesis was somehow totally incorrect, then I may actually have to start over. But I still will have learned a great deal and I will probably be able to use some of my analysis with a new thesis.

At any rate, I'm ready to compose. I'm going to assume that my outline is generally good, but if I need to alter it I will. I will begin my essay as most essays begin, with a general statement, and close the first paragraph with my thesis statement. My essay's opening may be general, but also enticing and intelligent, <u>not</u> something like "Walt Whitman is a well-known

143

American poet." I can do better. My first draft may be handwritten and smeared with coffee and mustard. It's a first draft, so anything goes. Just to discipline myself, I'm going to underline my thesis statement and topic sentences.

My First Draft

Walt Whitman's poetry is concerned with the American spirit, so it is natural for him to speak of the soul and to expect us to understand what he means. Whitman's short poem *A Noiseless Patient Spider* takes great pains to describe the nature and function of the human soul. In this poem, the persona compares his own soul—which is, by nature, internal and invisible—to a spider—which is, in nature, external and visible—and this striking metaphor is developed in such a way that the basis for the implicit comparison is a single repetitive action which both elements of the metaphor perform. (It is also clear that the spider serves as a referent, not only for the soul metaphorically, but for all living things in that it represents the urge of each natural thing to fill the void surrounding it.) Whitman's poem describes the soul as a dynamic entity reaching out with a need to define the "measureless oceans of space" that surround it and to form a "bridge" the soul will require. The poem implies, I believe, that this "musing, venturing" need defined first by the spider's action, then the soul's action is a universal longing shared by all natural things. It is as if Whitman is gloriously exploring the theme "Nature abhors a vacuum." *Whitman's use of metaphor, rhyme (including repetition) and rhythm all support the theme of the soul as a dynamic entity reaching out to define the environment that encloses it* (as a function of qualities which are universal in nature). *(thesis)*

The singular metaphor of the spider and the soul dominates the visual landscape of the poem. In the following essay, I will show how rhyme and repetition enhance the visual aspects of the comparison. Whitman's use of rhythm then helps the reader to focus on a repetitive, defining action of both the spider and the soul. It is this parallel action that is the real basis for Whitman's implicit metaphor. *This shared action indicates the essential theme of the poem, the soul's dynamism, which is reflected in an inner need to "bridge" the emptiness surrounding it. (repeat thesis, focusing)*

The persona begins by setting the "little" scene where a "noiseless patient spider /... stood isolated". Whitman is careful through his use of adjective to humanize the spider by attributing "patien[ce]" to it. (He echoes Greek myth in his choice of a weaver to embody patience.) Then the speaker observes ("mark[s]") how the spider "explore[s]" its environment by creating its web. But through alliteration and rhythm, the poet makes the nature of the environment clear. With the phrase "it stood isolated" in line two, the great craftsman has begun to hint with sibilants at the nature of the "vacant vast surrounding," the environment enclosing the spider. This setting, which isolates the silent spider, has the white, shifting sibilants of interstellar wind, demarcated by the slight moans of "v," "n," and "d." The final "-t's" puffs of sound create little spaces of silence to give relief from the moaning loneliness of the poem's environment. *This environment is a lonely, empty space, which isolates and tries the patience. (topic sentence)* In this environment, each entity defines itself by action. This poem is about two entities that act: the spider and the soul.

The carefully placed final "-t"s in this phrase also prepares the way for the action of the spider, which 'launch'd forth filament, filament, filament out of itself." The use of the initial, accepted "f"s and the final, unaccented "t"s n this wonderful line rhythmically defines the spider's repetitive action. Note the use of patterns of repetition with the whole word "filament," a dactyl suggestive of the mechanical motion of spinning. Note also the parallelism of the phrases in line five, each phrase with its echo of the "filament" in the dactylic line above: "ever unreeling them: and "tirelessly speeding them." Whitman also rhymes ("-reel-" and "speed") the phrases at their point of greatest accent, cementing the rhythmic expression. Finally, it is important that the spider's action was "launch'd" "out of [the spider's] self." Volition on the part of the personified spider is indicated. *And the spider's rhythm is dynamic and insistent, as the more dynamic alliteration and the strong rhythms of lines five and six augment.* But we do not know why the spider "speed[s]" its filaments out into the vastness surrounding it. (The second stanza will answer this question.)

Now the persona sets his soul, "detached" ("isolated") and "musing" ("patient") like the spider in verse one is and in a natural environment similar to the spider's. The soul, too, is surrounded b "measureless oceans of space." More importantly, the soul, too, throws out "thread" into the enclosing emptiness. But the soul "venture[s]" and "seek[s];" i.e., it has a purpose, a "need." It must construct "the bridge" from its "threads" that "catch somewhere." A bridge is made to cross over. *The soul needs the connection and it strives in the dynamic rhythms of alternating iambs and dactyls, augmented by repetition of sounds in line eight*: "Ceaselessly musing, venturing, throwing, seeking the spheres to connect them." While the spider has an inborn need to "explore," the human soul has a greater drive: to construct a means of passage. This need is manifested in the insistent, repetitive activity of both the spider and the soul, but the reason for the soul's activity is made clear in the final end rhyme of "hold" and "soul," which places emphasis where the poet wants it: on the soul.

The dynamism of the soul and, to a lesser degree, the insistent arachnid is clearly indicated in the repetitive rhythms indicating their activity, each in their own verse. Alliteration first helps create the yawning silence of the void dreaded by both the spider and the soul, then indicates the warmth of the insistent motion working to define the void with structure. Nature, which includes both the spider and the soul, does indeed abhor a vacuum. As we see Whitman throwing his own poetic lines out to us, we might surmise that his ultimate aim is self-knowledge and that the study of nature—perhaps best characterized here by the spider's involuntary energy—lead to a knowledge of one's own soul and the deepest human need: to "catch somewhere" and build a "bridge" to answer the distinct needs of the human soul. For Whitman, the study of nature leads to self-knowledge. After the initial shock of Whitman's choice of metaphor wears off, one need only contrast this celebrant of nature with another New Englander, whose vision of arachnids was much less positive, as was his view of nature generally.

    That's the end of the first draft.

    Obviously, I have a lot of work left to do. I haven't explored my thesis satisfactorily, though I've made some headway—and my topic sentences are not clear. Perhaps I'll simply limit my thesis to what I've been able to prove in this draft. At any rate, I feel a title coming on, a title that adds its own creative dimension to my essay. I like it when the title of an essay *appears* from my drafting work; suddenly, it's just there. Most of my work now is technical. Certainly, I need to clean up my paragraph structure, revise and clarify some sentences, and rethink some ideas that got too broad or just wandered off a little on me. This is the hardest part for me, but it has major rewards. Revision is when intuition as a higher mental function comes into play.

    The first thing I'm going to do is to take a copy of my first draft and mark it up as much as I want. There is a lot in it that is important to my vision of this poem, but I know it can be improved on. Still, I can't let pride or laziness get in the way of refining my writing. I must be prepared to defend my analysis against anyone whom I might ask to critique it, including the editor of a publication to whom I might want to submit it in the future. Anyway, I'm going to set it aside for a few hours or a day and do something entirely different for a while. I know it will be on my mind, but I need to get away from it for a time.

Final Draft

Knowing the Spider

    Whitman's poetry has as its primary subject and greatest concern the American spirit, so it is natural for him to speak of the human soul and expect his reader to understand what he means. *A Noiseless Patient Spider* describes the nature and function of the soul, as it relates to the universe at large. In this poem, the persona implicitly compares his own soul to a spider, and this striking metaphor is defined primarily through parallel actions that the spider (the tenor) and the soul (the vehicle) perform in the context of their environment. It is also clear that the spider serves as a referent, not only for the human soul, but for all living things in that it represents the urge of each natural thing to fill the void enclosing it. Whitman's poem describes the soul as a dynamic entity reaching out with a need to define the "measureless oceans of space" enclosing it and to form a "bridge" over that void that the soul "will need." The poem implies, I believe, that this "musing, venturing" need defined first by the spider, then the soul, is a universal longing shared by all natural things. It is as if Whitman is exploring the theme "nature abhors a vacuum." Whitman's skill as a poet is complete. His use of metaphor, rhyme, repetition and rhythm all support the theme of the dynamic soul reaching out to explore the environment that surrounds it.

Since the striking metaphor of spider and soul dominates the visual landscape of the poem, this essay will also show how rhyme and repetition enhance visualization of the description. Further, Whitman's use of rhythm helps the reader focus on the repetitive and defining parallel action that is the real poetic ground for his comparison of spider and soul. This shared action indicates the essential theme of the poem: the soul's dynamism, its *need* to "bridge" the emptiness surrounding it. Whitman has purposely chosen a highly recognizable visual vehicle for his metaphor: the spider and its web is not only a striking choice of visual subject, but immanently accessible as well. It prepares the way for the reader to visualize a much more demanding phenomenon: the soul's weaving.

The persona begins by setting the "little" scene, where a "noiseless patient spider" stands "isolated." Whitman is careful through his use of adjective to humanize the spider by attributing "patien[ce]" to it. (He is echoing Greek legend in his choice of a weaver to embody patience.) Then the speaker observes, "mark[s]," how the spider "explore[s]" its environment by creating its web. Through alliteration and rhythm, the poet makes the nature of the environment clear. With the phrase "it stood isolated" in line two the great craftsman has begun to hint with sibilants at the nature of the "vacant vast surrounding" enclosing the tiny weaver, earlier described as "A noiseless patient spider." This setting, which isolates the silent spider, has the white, shifting sibilants of interstellar wind, demarcated by the slight moans of "v," "n," and "d" in the "vacant vast surrounding." The final "-t"s puffs of sound create little spaces of silence to give relief from the moaning loneliness of the spider's environment. The auditory environment of the poem is subtle and effective.

The carefully placed "t-t"s in this phrase also prepares the way for the action of the spider. It "launch'd forth filament, filament, filament out of itself." The use of the initial, accented "f-"s and the final, unaccented "-t"s in this rhythmically defines the spider's repetitious action. Note the use of patterns of repetition with the whole word "filament," a dactyl suggestive of the mechanical motion of spinning. Note also the parallelism of the phrases in line five, each phrase with its echo of the "filament" in the dactylic line above: "éver unreéling them" and "tírelessly speéding them." Whitman also rhymes ("-reel-" and "speed-") the phrases at their point of greatest accent, cementing the rhythmic impression. Finally, it is important that the personified spider's action was "launch'd" "out of [the spider's] self." Volition on behalf of the spider is indicated. And the spider's action is dynamic and insistent, as the more dynamic alliteration and the strong rhythms of lines five and six indicate.

Here the persona sets his "soul," "detached" ("isolated") and "musing" ("patient") like the spider was, in a natural environment similar to the spider's. The soul, too, is surrounded by "measureless oceans of space." More importantly, the soul, in an action echoing the spider's, throws out "threads" into the enclosing emptiness. The soul needs connection and it strives in dynamic rhythms of alternating iambs and dactyls and repetition in sound in line eight: "Ceáselessly músing, vénturing, thrówing, seéking the sphéres to connéct them." While the spider has an inborn need to "explore," the human soul has a greater drive: to construct a means of passage. A need is manifested in the insistent repetitive activity of both the spider and the soul, but the reason for the soul's activity is made clear in the final rhyme of "hold" and "soul," which places emphasis where the poet wants it: on the soul's nature and need.

The dynamism of the soul and, to a lesser degree, the insistent arachnid, is clearly indicated in the repetitive rhythms in both verses. Alliteration first creates the yawning silence of the void dreaded by both the spider and the soul, then the warmth of the insistent motion working to define that void with structures. Nature, which includes both the spider and the soul, does indeed abhor a vacuum. From this poet, who is both physical (the patient weaver of poems) and soul (the "musing" spirit) and who casts his own poetic lines out to us, we might surmise that study of nature—perhaps best characterized here by the lowly spider with its ceaseless energy—leads to a knowledge of one's own nature and the soul's most human need: to "catch somewhere" and build a "bridge." In venturing out, we may answer the distinctly dynamic needs of that soul. And so, for Whitman, study of nature leads to self-knowledge. After the initial shock of the poet's choice of metaphoric material wears off, the reader need only contrast this celebrator of nature to another New Englander, a poet whose vision of arachnids and view of nature generally was much less positive, to fully appreciate the positive aspects of Whitman's universal spirit.

7

OPERA AS LITERATURE

SOURCES AND ELEMENTS OF OPERA

It is not surprising that Romanticism, an artistic movement marked by emphasis on emotion and the imagination, should be associated with opera. That opera should also be associated with the "Romance" genre, with love stories, is also natural. The greatest operas have as their principle subject the success or failure of a passionate relationship. Consider Otello and Desdemona, Tristan and Isolde, José and Carmen. But opera not only celebrates passion, Eros; it asks why passionate relationships succeed or fail. Romantic opera is ultimately concerned with the romantic obsession of its characters and with the interlocking themes of Eros and Thanatos, sexual passion and death.

This first group of essays discusses how opera's four elements—Literature, Drama (including Dance), Music, and the Visual Arts—work in combination. Traditionally, the ability to understand a character's emotions and thought in theatrical art is based in language, so we will begin our discussion with opera's literary aspects. In opera, language is piggybacked on music to charge it emotionally. Visual aspects then round out the performance experience. My approach to understanding and enjoying opera is to read the libretto and any appealing ancillary materials about the opera, listen to a recording of the opera—text in hand—and then see a staged performance or view a video/film of the opera.

Music is primary in opera; music is opera's aesthetic glue, combining and charging its quartet of elements into a musical-dramatic whole. Literary elements are, however, essential in understanding the complexity of opera. And even though musical and visual elements (lighting, physical action, costume, dance and other aspects of spectacle) may help us understand a character, it is often through language—poetic dialogue or soliloquy—that a character continues to live in our minds long after the performance has ended.

The originators of opera sought, late in the sixteenth century, to recreate the literary and dramatic values of ancient Greece. Taking their cue, we begin our exploration of opera with the values of the Classic Greek drama described in Aristotle's recipe for poetic tragedy, *The Poetics*. Aristotle's concepts will help elucidate opera's complex beauty.

Greek poetic tragedies continually invigorate Western culture with their unforgettable characters and the depth and complexity of their plots and imagery. It is through our empathy for the suffering heroes and heroines of these dramas that we are drawn into the striking dimensions on the stage before us. Instrumental music was a small but crucial element in Greek performance art, but it was a mere complement to the universal and essential musicality of poetic language. The essential elements of Greek tragedy—

character, plot and meaning—are language-based. This is rarely true of opera, in which music is the determining force. Opera and Classic Greek tragedy use the same elements in different proportions.

Opera allows us to vicariously experience the emotions of greatly diverse characters in extraordinary and sometimes exotic circumstances. That is one of opera's melodramatic charms. Early opera was based thematically in the essential ideas explored in ancient dramatic literature—mythic exploration/conquest, mankind's relations with divine forces, and historical events—but since the eighteenth century, opera has been increasingly concerned with obsessions like sexual passion and jealousy, and the psychology of human character under stress. This is the case with three nineteenth century masterpieces *La Bohème* (1896), *Carmen* (1875), *La Traviata* (1853) and to a lesser degree with *The Rake's Progress* (1957).

Literary Elements of Opera

Opera's dependence on literature is obvious and intimate. Most of opera's characters, plots and themes have literary sources. From the perspective of this book, the literary sources of opera are a matter of secondary, although fascinating importance. Many opera texts (*libretti*) are patterned after dramas, though many operas are based on novels, short stories, or narrative poetry. Giacomo Puccini's *La Bohème* is based on Henri Mürger's drama and novel *Scenes from the Bohemian Life*. Georges Bizet's *Carmen* is based on Prosper Méremée's novella of the same name. Giuseppi Verdi's *La Traviata* is based on Alexander Dumas fils's novel and play *Lady of the Camellias*. All these sources are readily available, and exploring them may cast light on the complex literary aspects of not only these masterpieces, but most other operas as well.

It is not necessary, however, to be familiar with an opera's sources to understand or enjoy a performance. *The Magic Flute's* plot was derived from a number of exotic tales, but enjoyment of this *Singspiel* ("play with singing" or "sung play") does not rest on that knowledge. Sometimes a libretto may have a more esoteric source; for example, the source of Igor Stravinsky's *The Rake's Progress* is a series of paintings/engravings by William Hogarth (1697-1764).

Sometimes, familiar literary/dramatic themes and characters become the property of opera for, as we will see in the following pages, opera has tended to imitate dramatic and literary forms from its birth and has continued to cultivate a close relationship with them throughout its evolution. For example, operatic form was greatly influenced by the nineteenth century's longing for the continuity inherent in prose narrative, i.e. the novel form. Most operas are based on narrative; they tell a story. Familiar universal themes and corresponding imagery patterns are constant in opera, tragic or comic; for example *the dream of love fulfilled* is a constant in the inner worlds of most Romantic operatic heroines. Romantic opera is female-centered and in general sustains the worshipful attitude toward female characters established in Renaissance culture, especially painting. Following Puccini, I refer to such idealized characterizations in opera as *luminous images.*

Most important for the purposes of our literary discussion, however, are the manifestations of the literary elements (1) dialogue, (2) lyric poetry and (3) description in opera, because all three are essential to the creation and performance of opera. My primary interest is in the chief elements of dialogue and poetry, since the libretto's use of description often appears as stage direction, which is to be read, not listened to. Let us consider how dialogue and poetry—including poetic description—play essential roles in opera. Both are usually chanted or sung in most operas.

(1) *Dialogue*, dramatized conversation, is an element of most literature. In nineteenth century opera, it is usually poeticized—written in rhythmic units, often rhymed—then set to music as recitative, chanted speech. Recitative has two forms, both of which have been present in opera from its inception.

First, *recitativo secco* is dialogue like its name—dry, non-melodic, and functional. It is accompanied by a keyboard instrument like the harpsichord. It moves the action along between musical numbers in most operas composed before 1850, but was still being used selectively by Puccini and other composers well into the twentieth century. It generally rolls along as quickly as stage dialogue would, sometimes faster. It finds its greatest fulfillment in Mozart's comic operas in the Italian (*opera buffa*) style, although Donizetti, Rossini and Verdi employ it later with great skill. Almost any scene from Mozart's *The Marriage of Figaro* (1786) provides superb examples of this type of operatic dialogue. Always fascinating, Igor Stravinsky— "the last great composer"—uses *recitativo secco* extensively in his masterful contemporary opera *The Rake's Progress.*

Second, *recitativo accompagnato (stromentato)* or "accompanied recitative" is another approach to setting dialogue altogether. This form of dialogue in opera is accompanied by full orchestra and may be melodic. Orchestral elements and the availability of melody make this form of dialogue expansive and allow the composer to make the opera's action flow seamlessly from one scene to the next.

Gluck (1714-87) theorized about it in mid-eighteenth century: His aims were to "restrict music to its true office by means of expression and by following the situations of the story." *Recitativo accompagnato* was the means by which he made his musical-dramatic creations more fully continuous.

In the capable hands of Giuseppi Verdi, accompanied recitative became a principle means of the uninterrupted flow of dramatic action so sought after in the post-Romantic period. Following Gluck and Verdi, Wagner made his unique contribution to operatic form with the continual flow of the *Gesamtkunstwerk* (unified work of art).

The myriad possibilities of interaction between the engaged orchestra and the dramatic action of the stage's realm have yielded incredible riches in musical-dramatic form. The entire first act of Puccini's *La Bohème* before Mimi's entrance, for example, is a flood of witty dialogue/*recitativo accompagnato*. Each following act was meant to be a ceaseless flow of musical drama. Composed fifty years earlier, Verdi's first act of *La Traviata* is a stunning achievement of continual musical action.

(2) *Lyric Poetry* is the second major literary element and is of great importance because its rhythmic units allow language to interface with musical units. In most Romantic operas, all the text is a functional form of poetry. The rhythmic units of poetry called "feet" approximate music units called "measures;" and through the amalgam of these units, words and music are joined. Most opera texts adhere to a functional poetic form. The unit of the lyric poem—a short poem of an emotional, often contemplative nature—is especially important to opera, since it serves as the literary component for the *aria*, a crucial means of operatic characterization and a chief source of opera's unique beauty.

An aria is a song, generally of great power and beauty, demanding not only a performer with an extensive vocal range but with an understanding of the delicacy of dramatic nuance. It is accompanied by orchestra and contains melodic power representative of the character's emotional state. In opera, an art form in which music is the chief glory and the human voice the chief expression of that glory, the aria is a crucial element. It is the aria, composed of a unique combination of a lyric poem and the voice in melodic flight supported by full orchestra, that offers the listener the clearest picture of character inscape—the character's desires, fantasies, ideals, needs. Opera is about character.

It is the in-depth appeal of character that brings us back to opera, again and again, after the lights fade. A great aria contains all the emotional striving of the human soul for completion. The aria invites us, through its unique combination of poetry and music, into the intimate depths of shared human experience. An aria's melody may take our emotions soaring, but it is the fact that this melody represents an aspect of human *character* with which we can empathize that makes opera meaningful. The empathy we feel for an operatic character brings our own deeper emotions and thoughts into play during a performance. Poetry mounts on music to achieve this effect.

The aria is the equivalent of a soliloquy in drama or a dramatic monologue in poetry; it is a revealing of the soul and generally stops the stage action or, perhaps better said, *internalizes* it. In an aria, we are telescoped into the inner world of character. At the end of *La Bohème*'s first act, Rodolfo and Mimi's arias do little to advance the plot; *such arias are primarily pure outpourings of character feeling and thought.* They demand the cessation of stage action—and a surrender to musical glory. Generally, crucial plot movement *follows* an aria. For example, the brief duet that immediately follows the two arias in *La Bohème*'s Act 1 arias determines the remainder of the story and action of *La Bohème*. It is an intense declaration of passion. The arias that preceded this duet are essential dramatic—and psychological—preparation for the duet; they help us understand Rodolfo and Mimi's later actions. The remarkably condensed lyric of the duet can do its work so quickly because the preceding arias have been so revealing of character qualities like loneliness, insecurity and desire.

As an aria's text, the lyric poem provides us with the narrative of the character's thoughts. Music then charges this thought to instill it with emotional intensity. Generally, poems that serve as aria texts do not stand alone as good poetry in the eyes of literary critics; such poetry is fulfilled only in partnership with music. There are, of course, exceptions to negative generalizations concerning the special type of lyric poetry of which a libretto consists; for example, portions of Auden's text for *The Rake's Progress* are lovely verses that stand alone as pure poetry quite nicely.

(3) *Description* is an inherent part of lyric poetry and is, to paraphrase Aristotle, so obvious an element as to not need definition in dramatic context. Characters describe what they see or feel and we take it at face value. Whether it is the scentless lilies and roses Mimi sews or the cold wind that sweeps through Rodolfo's apartment, we understand that poetic description has deeper meaning than literal description.

Study of any opera should begin with its text. Generally, this is where the composer began to appreciate the librettist's skill, and we could do worse than follow in the footsteps of Giacomo Puccini, Georges Bizet, Giuseppi Verdi and Igor Stravinsky.

Dramatic Elements of Opera

Aristotle's *Poetics* points out classic drama's three great gifts to opera: character, plot (the arrangements of events) and thought (meaning or theme). One approach to character from the dramatic perspective is to discuss a character's *internal*, or *personality-driven forces* (desires, dreams, needs), as well as the more obvious *external*, or *plot-generated forces* that shape character. *Carmen* is an excellent opera to demonstrate opera's dramatic qualities. One might carefully trace the patterns of forces that shape both Carmen and José in Bizet's masterpiece.

It is the three minor elements described in Aristotle's *Poetics*—*melos* (music), *lexis* (poetic elements) and *opsis* (spectacle)—that are most likely to attract us to opera initially, but it is character and plot (and their musical representations) that bring us back. These are the two great elements that enrich our internal lives. We sympathize with operatic characters initially because of the extraordinary power of music to portray character mood and emotion, but we grow to empathize with them because of the unique power of the word combined with music to represent common experience and thought.

The plot of an opera is the chief means by which a character is given the chance to change, to fulfill itself aesthetically: character change, growth is an important initiator of character depth and complexity. Such character development involves the audience's mind as well as their emotions.

Dance, primarily ballet and folk dance, functions in most opera as an optical decorative element, yet its abstract patterns may effectively enhance local color, echo plot and illustrate character. Operatic characters rarely dance, though Carmen and Salome do so effectively as an aspect of character. Dance generally functions as a part of the setting or local color, greatly adding to the atmosphere of a specific scene; for example, in Act 2, scene 2 of *La Traviata* or the opening of *Carmen*'s second act. Ballet is one of the elements of opera that ties opera firmly to the tradition folk dance, the source of most Western classical musical form.

Musical Elements of Opera

Music is the most essential element of opera, the voice the primary instrument. The aria is its most effective musical form in terms of creating character. Our interpretation of opera will be largely character-centered, but will also explore how each discipline is employed in the creation of character emotion and thought. Music complements to the furthest degree imaginable the amalgam of literary and dramatic elements already introduced.

Opera's purpose is remarkably fulfilled to a great degree when one simply listens to, rather than sees an opera. Listening is, of course, not the final step in opera exploration and appreciation, but the informed *listener* is, perhaps, in a position to best appreciate the pure power that opera exercises over the imagination. Listening is the very rich and important second step in the full appreciation of an opera.

The orchestra, whose initial role in opera was to accompany the singers, has increasingly encroached upon the singer's art—beginning with Gluck and, in fact, in part because of his theories—and has taken on additional duties: creating stage environment, even local color, and portraying character mood and conflict. This encroachment seems natural as we scan the history of opera. Still, it was a hard shock to audiences when Richard Wagner made the singing voice yet another orchestral dimension and formalized the symbolic power of music through musical motif structures (repeated musical ideas). With Wagner, subtlety in orchestral form became a great psychological tool and thus a chief means of characterization. Still, most critics agree that Verdi's skill in balancing the orchestra and voice in creating character in musical-dramatic flow in his final works is unsurpassed.

The orchestra also portrays the inner world of character. This is one of its chief tasks.

The major musical elements are (1) *the orchestra*, with its string, woodwind, brass and percussion sections, (2) *the chorus and the solo vocal artists* in all their uniqueness and diversity, and (3) *the musical-dramatic forms* of which opera is shaped.

As important as the aria is to character, the duet, trio, quartet and ensemble usually are to plot. When more than one character sings simultaneously, the action usually advances. As pointed out earlier, Rodolfo and Mimi's love duet at the end of *La Bohème*'s first act may appear outwardly static, but the rest of the opera's action flows from its dramatic consequences. Consider also the lovely quartet that closes Act 3 of *La Bohème*, in which Mimi and Rodolfo stand frozen in the emotional memories ruling their imaginations, while Musetta and Marcello act out their frustrations with life and each other.

Some of the most striking moments in opera come during ensembles in which most stage action ceases and each character withdraws into his or her own world. Plot time ceases and as listeners we can relax and more fully appreciate the complex beauties of opera's unique musical forms. *La Traviata*'s Act 2 Finale is, for example, a remarkable union of literature and drama enhanced by musical form.

The Visual Elements of Opera

Of the visual arts, painting provides the large-form visual stage environment in the form of flats (very large paintings which are framed and fastened together), backdrops and cycloramas. (Both these terms describe large paintings used to approximate scenic background, e.g. a landscape.) These large paintings fill the background of the scene, while plastic arts are employed to shape smaller forms, such as trees, boulders and other natural or man-made objects. Costumers, wigmakers, jewelry and property makers, and make-up artists create the living statues that sing before us. Finally, light—that visual element sometimes indicative of the spiritual element on the stage, and the aural equivalent of musical harmony—unites all the elements of the four disciplines mentioned above with its synaesthetic power.

No other art form involves so many diverse elements as opera and no other art form integrates these elements so effectively in an aesthetic tapestry portraying human character. How does the person who is attracted to opera find an entrance into this brilliant castle? It so happens that the easiest way to become familiar with opera in contemporary society is not only simple; it also echoes the creative process of the librettists, composers and performers of opera.

First, begin with reading the libretto that is usually included in every opera recording. *Second*, listen to the opera—text in hand, if you can—and initiate the engaging, imaginative acts of consciousness that opera evokes in the listener. *Finally*, watch a taped performance or filmed version of the opera, or, best of all, see a live performance.

Each of us comes to opera possessing varying degrees of familiarity with literature, drama (and dance), music, and the visual arts, if only through the world of media—television, film and the computer. Most of us are novices in one way or another in most of the arts and media. This need not concern us in our desire to experience opera. Even if we have little experience in any of these areas, this approach is designed for the reader who will work at his or her own level toward a more complete understanding of opera.

Those who are more advanced in one discipline will work at learning the relationship of that discipline to the others that constitute opera. In this way, the reader's understanding of their home discipline will be enriched. The greatest challenge and fun is in discovering how two or more disciplines interlock to create a meaning more complex than any single discipline is capable of attaining.

Remember that these great operas were not written for the professional musicians who perform them, or for the designers or stage directors who make their performance possible. They were written for an audience and for the heart and mind of any individual who has an interest in them. In short, they were created for anyone who cares to open themselves to the experience of opera through reading, listening or viewing.

THE ARISTOTLE CONNECTION

There is good reason for employing Aristotle's *Poetics* in discussing opera. There is considerable evidence that the creators of operatic form, among them a group of literary *dilettanti* who met at the house of Bardi in late 16th Century Florence, endeavored to recreate Attic drama in the experimental presentations which began to codify a new art form called "opera".

The works they produced were the forebears of opera. They were also a far cry from Sophoclean tragedy. These *dilettanti* did, nevertheless, envision *Oedipus Rex*, Aristotle's example for poetic drama in the *Poetics*, as sung or chanted drama. They may also have understood that the sole purpose of music in Sophoclean drama was to underscore and heighten the dramatic content of the dialogue. Whatever their understanding, desire or intent, the product of their efforts to recreate Greek poetic tragedy created a unique and complex art form ultimately dominated by musical considerations. Opera's unique interdisciplinary nature invites widely varied interpretive approaches.

One approach to understanding and enjoying opera is built on literary and structural considerations rather than more specific musical ones. There is more than one way to set a finely cut gem so that it may appeal to a wide variety of tastes, and so it is with appreciation of opera. Any of the four disciplines may serve as a gate to the realm of opera. This approach begins with literary considerations, but seeks a balanced interdisciplinary appreciation of opera's dramatic, musical and visual aspects.

In Classic Greek poetic tragedy, highly structured verse was chanted or sung by soloists and chorus. The performers were accompanied by a small ensemble of instrumentalists—a harp or lute, a flute and drums. Every movement of the chorus was probably choreographed, while the soloists had more individualistic freedom of movement and vocal expression. A performance was highly stylized, i.e. choreographed to the highest degree. The highly stylized verse forms imply this and what we know of Greek performance praxis supports this theory.

The Florence group, also called the *camerata*, aimed at a performance genre they described as *dramma per musica*: "Drama *through* music" placed music at the center of the camerata's presentations. Partially because of their worshipful appreciation of the source of their inspiration, they often based their earliest efforts on mythic subjects. Peri's *Dafne* (1597) is considered the first opera. Out of the performance of the first operas came an emphasis the language-conscious Greeks would never have allowed: the musical element of melody combined with verse to create songs and choruses. The effect of this union was called *arioso*. In this form, music took command of the literary arts, which were supreme in Classic Greek poetic tragedy.

Musical sophistication in the new art form took a great step forward in 1607 with Monteverdi's *Orfeo*. This work made music the essential glue of the operatic formula. As sometimes happens in the development of artistic form, one gifted individual like Monteverdi may determine through his unique musical-dramatic gifts the development and the formulae of a major art form. The elements were uniquely combined according to his taste and gifts.

It may seem retrogressive to reach back to the eras of Aeschylus, Sophocles and Euripides for the terminology and definitions to describe a musical-dramatic form that emerged between 1580 and 1607 in Florence and Padua, but in fact the taproot of opera—and, indeed, almost all Western drama—is Attic in nature. In his *Poetics*, Aristotle (384-322 B.C.), an admirer of Sophocles' poetic tragedy *Oedipus Tyrranus*, gave Western Civilization an aesthetic recipe that provides terms and values that describe the artistic urge and structure constituting most literary and dramatic genres. Since opera is formally a dramatic portrayal of character, Aristotle's terms for the ingredients of tragic drama provide us with a general, flexible structure for an in-depth discussion of operatic form.

The terms he gives us define poetic tragedy as "the imitation of an action that is serious and complete in nature in itself." Here are the three major elements of poetic tragedy, in the order of importance Aristotle gives them.

Aristotle's Major Elements

(1) *Plot* is, according to Aristotle, the life and soul of poetic tragedy. It is the arrangement of incidents in the story according to probability or logic. The general structure of the plot is that of rising ("knotting up" or complication of action) and falling ("loosening" of action), such large-form structure, easily echoed in small-form elements like verse forms or melodic lines, with a predictable rise and fall, satisfies an inherent sense of balance in the audience.

Here, briefly, is Aristotle's description of the plot's structure:
The complication is the part of the plot from the beginning up to the point which immediately precedes the occurrence of a change [peripitae] from bad to good fortune, or from good fortune to bad; the denouement is from the beginning of the change down to the end.

(XVII,2)

Aristotle's division of the plot into "constituent parts"—prologue, episode, exode, and choral song—has rough structural counterparts in opera's musical form, especially during the first 250 years of opera's development.

Aristotle distinguishes between plot and what we would call "action," including the literal gestures of character—for example, a sword fight. Such action might be caused by either a character's inner needs or by a character's reaction to a plot twist. By action, Aristotle means the flow of energy out of or in between characters caught within the plot's mechanism.

This is what Aristotle says concerning the primacy of action as a dramatic element: "Tragedy is not a representation of men but a piece of action, of life, of happiness and unhappiness." Character gives us qualities, but it is in our actions—what we do—that we are happy or the reverse. The best structure of tragic plot is "complex, ... one that represents incidents arousing fear and pity" in the viewer, which emotions are then purged through the plot's workings. Even the story of the plot alone, as is the case with *Oedipus*, should be capable of arousing fear and pity.

(2) *Character* is that which makes us ascribe certain moral qualities to the agents. According to Aristotle, character should be (1) "good," a quality shown when the character makes choices either through dialogue or action (earlier II,1), Aristotle states that characters—"objects of representation"—must be either "good" or "inferior," as distinguished by their "ethical differences"; (2) "appropriate" or well-defined in terms of type, e.g. manly or womanly, without mixing characteristics; (3) "like," as in the traditional portrayal of a given character, e.g. Odysseus should not ever be portrayed as being stupid; "consistent" in action and dialogue, or "consistently inconsistent." Further, a "good" character should have "some flaw [*hamartia*] in him," through which he falls into misfortune.

Aristotle is very clear where the motivation of a character is concerned. *Character is that which reveals the moral purpose of the agents*, i.e. the sort of thing they seek or avoid, where that is not obvious. As I have stated, the aria is one of the great means of developing character in opera. During an aria, the character's inner world opens to us, and they often speak directly to us of their deepest desires, feelings and fantasies. As important as action may be in illustrating character, truth may often exist in brief, still moments of intimacy. So it is with the aria. Aristotle compares the drawing of a character to the painting of one on canvas, stressing the necessity of clarity of form and values. The aria is such a literary-musical canvas.

(3) *Thought*, (meaning or theme) is all the character says when proving a particular point or enunciating a general truth, i.e. the power of saying whatever can be said, or what is appropriate to the situation. More importantly in terms of dramatic conflict, thought is "an argument that something is or is not."

Under the head of Thought come all the effects to be produced by the language. Some of these are proof and refutation, the arousing of feelings like fear, pity, anger and so on, and then again exaggeration, and deprecation.

In summary, Aristotle places each of the three major elements in a formula which echoes his analytic approach to art.

Thought and character are the natural causes of any action and it is in virtue of these that all men succeed or fail—it follows then that it is the plot which represents the actions.

In another sense, meaning emerges from a character's wrestling with her or his personal destiny, which is determined by the unique nexus of that character's internal forces (dreams, desires) and the external forces represented by the plot. Oedipus is manipulated by forces beyond his control. Aristotle collects such supernatural and natural forces within his concept of plot.

Aristotle's Minor Elements

Aristotle's three minor elements are *lexis* (diction), *melos* (musical elements) and *opsis* (spectacle). He neatly summarizes his approach to these three elements. "We have, then, a natural instinct for representation and for tune and rhythm—for the meters are obviously sections of rhythms—and starting with these instincts men very gradually developed them until they produced poetry out of their improvisations" (IV,7). It is fair to say that Aristotle shared his master Plato's disdain for poets and artists generally; these great thinkers considered an copy of reality a dimension of shadows. Plato also addresses song in the following manner in *The Republic*: "You certainly, I presume, have a sufficient understanding of this—that song is composed of three things, the words, the tune, and the rhythm?"

(4) Diction (*lexis*) is "the expression of meaning in words, and this is essentially the same in verse and in prose"; further, it is the composition of the verses, the expression of the character's thoughts in words (in opera, the libretto). Specifically, Aristotle says that "diction" is "the metrical arrangement of the words; and a part of the process of 'song-making'" (*melos*). Books XIX,8 through XXVI, 16 of the *Poetics* are primarily concerned with diction, *lexis*.

(5) Music (*melos*) is song, the most immediate characteristic of which—melody—according to Aristotle, is too completely understood to require explanation and is the greatest of the pleasurable accessories in tragedy. *Melos*, as used here refers, as in the above quote from *The Republic*, to the unique combination of poetry, melody and rhythm that was the aural medium in Attic tragedy. Later, Plato says that "the music and the rhythm must follow the speech," an idea which we will discuss more later. We know that "melody"—now used in the sense of "tune"—became much more

important in the post-Renaissance music which was used to set the first operatic texts.

(6) Spectacle (*opsis*) is the stage appearance of the actors and the dramatic setting that surrounds them. This includes scenery, costumes, make-up and masks. "Spectacle, while highly effective, is yet quite foreign to the art and has nothing to do with poetry." Aristotle's austere intellectualism insists that "The tragic effect is quite possible without spectacle, which is more a matter for the costumier than the poet." In short, the essence of poetic tragedy is for Aristotle in the words and the dramatic values that shape the plot, characters and thought inherent in the poetry—not in the staged performance. We should begin the study of opera, as Aristotle suggests, with reading. But we also want to become good listeners, as well as good participants at visual performances

These are the major and minor elements Aristotle gives us. In the following essays, these six dramatic values or constituents will be referred to in contemporary terms approximating their original meaning: plot, character, meaning, text (libretto), music and stage setting. Some philosophers say that most of the deep thinking of Western civilization occurred between 500 and 300 B.C. Others say that all Western philosophy is a footnote to Plato, Aristotle's teacher. At all accounts, Aristotle is our deepest dramatic-literary taproot, partially because we have (in relatively good condition) the play which Aristotle chose to use as the paradigm of classical tragedy, Sophocles' *Oedipus Tyrranus*.

Imagine the Greek chorus circling the orchestra—the circular area before the staired, pillared *proskene*—in graceful steps, their heads thrown back in controlled ecstasy as they move to the throbbing of the drum, linked invisibly by the musical web of lyre and flute. The great, meticulously trained voices are carefully modulated to the ensemble sound. Their form, when they slow, turn and cease their motion has the dancer's grace and expressive power. Their robes drift after their lithe forms in the Aegean breeze.

See them far below you in the great theater of Athens, moving as one in the September night. From a distance they are like a living ivory necklace, their sung words somehow recreating, encompassing your awakening evening dream, forming a woven crown on the bare earth. They encircle what was once an altar, representing the hero's crown—for where he stands, towering above the chorus in mask, robe and cothurni, you also stand. His voice rings out and their dance ceases. The old pain becomes new, the old secrets are again charged with the mythic divine.

We have, then a natural instinct for representation and for tune and rhythm—   Poetics, IV, 7

THE POETIC IN *MI CHIAMANO MIMI*:

Aria as Essence of Character

Mi chiamano Mimi's text is very effective dramatic dialogue in that it involves Rodolfo—and the listener—deeply with its revealing qualities, but it is much more than dialogue. It is poetry, self-consciously rhythmic and rich in images. Such poetry is natural in the world of opera, for opera is image-making activity. Mimi's aria is also a dramatic utterance, a study in calculated ingenuousness and as such indicates character depth. Mimi is not the most complex of characters in *La Bohème*, but in this aria we see into her depths. She poeticizes simple things, yet there is calculation in her naiveté, for example she is careful to inform Rodolfo three times that she lives alone (sola) in lines 3 and 7 of stanza 2. This is the first time Mimi mentions this word, but she will sing it a great many times before her hands finally grow warm in the final scene. This aria has a touch of genuine personality about it; it is a confession and has the unique power of visionary utterance. There are clear points at which the speaker of the poem opens utterly—almost as in a dramatic soliloquy—to Rodolfo (and to us) like a rare flower and unselfconsciously bares her soul to us. This aria is meaningful drama, in part because it is charged with the emotional power of lyric poetry.

Clearly, Rodolfo's outpouring of poetic fancy in his aria *Che gelida manina* has affected Mimi, and his compliments have not been lost. Her lovely eyes have robbed him of his "castles in the air," but also filled him with hope. Although Rodolfo is a poet, his words are less affecting than those he evokes from Mimi. In Mimi's dramatic monologue, as in many arias, we enter into the charged inner world of the speaker, in this case an operatic character.

In this form of poetic utterance, symbols and other images will indicate the complexity of the character's internal world, involving desires, needs, hopes, fears. Although it is impossible to separate the verbal and musical constituents within the aria form—so inseparably are they welded as sung text in opera—it is possible to discuss the aria's text as poetry and to point out the role of the purely musical aspects in approximating the density of sound pattern and imagery native to lyric poetry.

Elements of Lyric Poetry

The text of Mimi's aria constitutes a lyric poem of a very special kind, one designed to complement the rhythmic units of music, as well as the singer's art. It is made up of two verses, the second verse of which is irregular; having an additional six-line unit that approximates the rhythm and the content of lines 9-13 of the first verse. Each verse is closed by a line or two of dialogue that becomes secco recitative. The form of these verses is certainly dictated by considerations of musical form—it may have been, in part, written after Puccini composed the music—yet the verses have a certain power as poetry. This power emanates primarily from its images, for its form is dictated by musical necessities and dramatic truth.

The elements of a lyric poem are as follows. (1) The *persona*, or speaker of the poem gives us the point of view of the poem. In opera, this is almost always the character who performs the aria. (A ballad or song might be sung by one character about another. This is not an aria in the sense I mean it.) Mimi's poetic utterance is dialogue that grows into heightened dramatic monologue, at times almost soliloquy. (2) A lyric poem may have *a line of action* that approximates a plot, but it certainly has *an emotional contour* that moves toward a high point and then away from it. The emotional contour of the poem will be complemented by figurative language, rhythm and rhyme; these poetic elements in combination constitute the literary equivalent of a melody complemented by harmonic and rhythmic patterns. (3) *The theme or meaning of a poem* is its emotional truth, intellectual point, or moral significance. (4) *Figurative language* consists of images, especially metaphors and symbols. The density of figurative language may be compared to harmonic complexity and/or orchestral web, the multiplicity of colors furnished by the orchestra.

(5) *Rhythm* is the pulse of the poetic unit, with the poem dividing itself into stanzas, lines, phrases, and metric "feet." These feet can constructively be compared to the musical rhythmic division of "measure." Phrases and stanzas also have relatively exact musical counterparts. (6) *Rhyme* consists of patterns of sound repetition, especially standard (end) and internal rhyme, and alliteration, which is when patterns of sound recreate the rhythms and sounds of the thing described or evoked. An example is *chiacchierna le fontane...* from Act 3 of *La Bohème* which sound patterns imitate the "chattering" of fountains. Musical harmony is approximated by the interplay of sound patterns like assonance (patterns of vowel sounds) and consonance (patterns of consonant sounds), though in single phrases the flow of a particular sound pattern might approximate counter melody. (7) *Mood* is the emotional feeling we derive from a poem. It is a product of the interplay of the poem's images in our minds with the total effect of the poem's sound tapestry on our emotions.

Interpreting the Poem

Remembering that music will affect each of these elements, let's look at *mi chiamano Mimi* as lyric poetry. First, note that the poem is in first person and is confessional in nature. Mimi begins with the simplest act of self-definition: she names herself, twice. There is also a candid quality about her revealing her real name, Lucia. She then describes where and how she lives, then quietly moves through verbal gesture in an almost distracted manner toward the complex image of flowers, then *particular* flowers, the lily and the rose, which she fashions with her hands, then to spring, *la primavera*, where melody lifts her (and the listener) onto a higher emotional plane. In particular, the image of the rose is developed in such a way that it comes to represent her inner life, her self. Having begun to create the idea of spring, with its light and dreams, Mimi pauses to ask Rodolfo if he understands what she means. Moved, he answers simply, *Si*.

Mimi continues, perhaps a little nervously, for verse two begins exactly as did verse one, then while continuing in the same thematic content as in verse one, offers more detail. In the second verse she describes her sensuous joy in springtime's light and warmth and in the fragrance of flowers not once but twice in ascending melodic lines. The first ascent is an account of how she claims spring as her lover: *il primo bacio dell-aprile è mio*. "April's first kiss [light] is mine!" she exclaims ecstatically. Then for a second time, she—as in the last six lines of stanza one—she withdraws into the chamber of her mind and shares the ecstatic visions of her despairing soul with Rodolfo and us.

In stanza one's brief passage (lines 9-12), she personifies the flowers she creates, as if their voices were the voices of kindred souls, their faces and visions (*sogni e... chimere*) her own. Lines 14-19 of stanza 2 are graced with a similar music treatment and are even more revealing.

Her ecstasy with the natural beauty of an opening rose is wonderfully captured in Puccini's setting of the lines *foglia a foglia la spio!... / Cosi gentil / il profumo d'un fior!* The unfolding of the rose petals is revealed in *foglia a foglia la spio*, the poet's subtle combination of rhythm and alliteration. Puccini captures the triple rhythms of the words in duple measures, creating a lovely tension hinting at Mimi's melancholy observance that the flowers she creates with her hands have no fragrance of their own. She sadly contrasts the ecstatic fragrance of the natural blossom to those scentless ones she creates with her hands. The works of her hands are poor imitations of the natural essence. She can not create spring; she can only dream of it, then create an imitation of it with her cold hands.

Mimi here voices the essential French Romantic doctrine: Nature ennobles and completes mankind. In her longing for spring's light and appreciation of nature's beauty, Mimi is, poetically, the essential Romantic figure. Puccini's rapturous orchestral settings raise the emotional level appreciatively, but for the reader of libretti, there is much more than music at work here.

Poetic Elements at Work

Here is how the poetic elements work in the poem. (1) The persona is a character in a drama, who begins in the dialogue mode but quickly moves to a much more poetic, confessional mode. (2) The poem's action or plot is descriptive, emotional and revealing. Mimi describes how she experiences simple pleasures and performs simple tasks. (3) The theme of the poem is the descriptive truth of Mimi's existence. She is at first calculating and conscious of what she says, but quickly moves into a personal and momentarily unselfconscious revelation of her fantasy world. (4) I have earlier discussed the figurative language of this poem in the context of the universal and local imagery of the opera. This poem establishes the image patterns of spring, with its vital ancillary images of light, warmth and flower fragrance. It also associates these qualities with Mimi's character.

Metaphoric density is replaced in this (and most) arias by orchestral web, both in terms of orchestration and harmonic complexity. (5) One has only to listen to the aria to hear the perfection of the rhythmic properties of this poem for musical adaptation. Generally, a musical phrase requires two poetic lines in this libretto, except in the climactic, stretchy phrases where heightened emotion justifies the melodic expansion of phrase. (6) End rhyme sometimes unites consecutive musical phrases, but as often as not occurs within a musical phrase. It may also tie musical phrases together. The flexibility of Puccini's compositional technique allowed him to accomplish a subtle interplay between the units of the poem and his musical phrases.

In general, music's melody, harmony, rhythm, and other formal considerations complement poetry rhythm and rhyme so effectively as to replace them in the listener's ear. Melody, rhythm and orchestral color can vivify an image, as in Puccini's subtle, repetitive setting of the phrases *che han si dolce malia* in stanza one and *foglia a foglia la spio* in stanza two, each preceding the build up to the climax of each stanza: the musical/poetic ecstasy of *di primavera* in stanza one and *il profumo d'un fior* in stanza two. The subtle turning of the notes in the *foglia* phrase accents the melodic unfolding of the rose, already captured in the poetic rhythm of *fóglia a fóglia la spío*. (7) The mood, the emotional content of the poem is completely shaped by the music, though imagery is a very powerful tool. Just as musical considerations have usurped poetic elements (complex rhythms, sound patterns, the weave of metaphor and symbol), the action, theme and mood of the poem will be augmented by melodic and harmonic interchange.

The complex image of spring creates an image cluster that clearly signals the character's state of mind. Further, the interplay of figurative language and melody creates complex images descriptive of Mimi's inner world. The greater complexities of rhyme are assumed by musical elements in opera, principally by harmony and orchestral color. Although density of word sound is not unusual in opera (see Rodolfo's text in the Act 3 quartet), the poetic effect of this device, when sung, is minimal and, from the standpoint of the singer and listener, undesirable. Consonants interrupt the pure flow of vowels from which the stream of legato vocal line lives, and beauty of vocal line may be preferred in some cases to perfect projection of text. Melody lives from assonance as in lines 9-15 of Mimi's second stanza. The extensive use of consonants as poetic descriptive and rhythmic elements is to some degree replaced by harmony and orchestral color in Mimi's aria. The many-voiced orchestra assumes the role of sound density expected in pure poetry. Melody augments the idea, the sense of the poem, while harmony approximates poetry's density of imagery and word sound, and the corresponding atmosphere conveyed.

Clearly, poetry and music function to complement dramatic purpose. Poetry is more precise in specific matters—imagery, description of detail, and subtleties of character development—while music is more immediate in the presentation of emotional states and shades of character, as well as of environment. It is largely through music that we understand the emotional depths of character in operatic performance, but in opera, literary elements help form the basis for music's power to transport us into the inner world of character.

ACT 3, SCENE 3 OF THE RAKE'S PROGRESS

An Interpretation

The nineteenth century opera composer's striving for continuity through musical forms resulted in crucial development for opera. This growth was initiated primarily by Mozart's compositional and dramatic emphases in his *da Ponte* operas, and nurtured through the continuity established by both Haydn and Mozart in the symphonic form during the Classical Period. Mozart was concerned with this continuity of musical-dramatic form from his first operatic works. His later works developed certain characteristics encouraging continuity, from which such diverse works as *La Traviata*, *Carmen*, *La Bohème* and *The Rake's Progress* all benefited: subtlety of characterization, extension of the complexity and integrity of the orchestra's role in opera, subtlety in recitative, and general ennoblement of the *opera buffa* form.

Each of these four operas has a distinct great arc of action, usually with a quickly rising dramatic tension, that ties the acts together. This arc of action reflects classical values, with an emotional turn occurring within the character of the protagonist about three-quarters of the way through the plot. This feature reflects primary concentration on character in opera. (A climax of stage action occurs closer to the end of the opera.) The musical climax of an opera usually occurs along with the emotional climax, e.g. *Carmen's* Act 3 Finale, or *La Traviata's* Act 2 Finale. This coincidence of character and musical form is a logical consequence of the music's primary role in opera and its special power in portraying the emotional lives of the characters.

Musical, literary and visual sub-arcs consisting of repeated musical ideas or melodies and spoken or visual images tie the scenes and acts together. These sub-arcs are an extension of character in that they may reflect a persona's moods, dreams, desires, and needs, but especially their fantasies and memories. The recurring musical motif is especially important since, when used to represent memory of a particular character, it allows the listener to experience the inner world of that character.

Musical sub-arcs may also represent ideas or concepts of a more abstract nature, such as the "Fate" motif of *Carmen*. Alternately, some sub-arcs may be primarily structural in nature, as is the opening motif of *La Bohème*. (Needless to say, this motif and many similar structural ones contribute to the musical atmosphere of the opera. Structure and function are intertwining, inseparable concepts.) Musically knowledgeable listeners will find the use of such sub-arcs elegant and will regard them as the essence of structural integrity.

Within the structure of an operatic act, the divisions of the actions into musical units—recitative, aria, ensemble and chorus scene—were further subdivided by the composer into smaller, more plastic units sharing interrelated features and thus overlapping easily. This development was, in part, facilitated by the growing rhythmic and harmonic freedom embraced by composers of the nineteenth century. In this regard, Act 1 of *La Traviata* provides a stunning example of continuity, on which example Puccini's *La Bohème* builds. Curious milestones appear as we enter modern times. Wagner had by mid-19th century set as his goal "unending melody" as the musical-dramatic ideal. A full century later, Stravinsky's modern intellectualism and wit finds its form in broad stylistic parody of Wagner's ideas, as well as of Baroque and Classical opera forms in *The Rake's Progress.*

The orchestra's role also grew and diversified in operatic performance, thanks primarily to the influence of Mozart, Beethoven and Wagner. Each of these masters to some degree served as the musical model for his successor. An individual instrument's qualities came to represent specific moods and emotional values and thus acquired implicit dramatic content. Musical elements such as dynamic antithesis were used to complement theatrical effects, providing new means of subtle emphasis in developing character and creating logical dramatic sequences by clarifying rising tensions.

There was a move to embrace and imitate literary form. This tendency has always been evident in opera's relation to the literature of its time. The opera composer generally takes his inspiration from a literary work of fiction or a drama, then begins his own unique creative process with a poetic reduction of this work, a short play in verse that must be fleshed with music. The tendency to complement literary form is thus natural, as is the struggle between word and music in the musical-dramatic environment.

The treatment of character and plot became more realistic in opera as a result of two influences: the subtleties of character motivation demanded by Romanticism (a reaction against the effusive formalities of eighteenth century classicism) and the down-to-earth plot portrayal evoked by naturalism (a reaction against the excesses of Romanticism). Both of these influences gave Realism, the essential aesthetic mode of all ages, new emotional and environmental integrity. This integrity carried over from literary into dramatic and musical-dramatic forms, and has the effect of engendering believable characters like Carmen and José, both of whom carry the power of archetypes within them.

Yet it is unquestionably the musical element of Bizet's *Carmen* that defines and ennobles these two embattled peasants captured by the writer-historian Mérimée in his novella in 1845 and lifts them into operatic immortality. It is in the elegance and subtlety of the motivic weave representing aspects of character and plot that Bizet's music—culminating in the watershed final duet—lifts tragedy to the level of Attic inevitability without a whisper of the determinism which will soon dominate literary and philosophical circles in Europe. In the greatest operas, music inevitably asserts its claim as opera's primary element.

Romantic and Ideal Love in Opera

Siegmund:
Du bist das Bild das in mir barg.

Sieglinde: (den Blick schnell abwenden)
O still! Lass mich der Stimme lauschen—
Mich dunkt, ihren Klang hort' ich als Kind.

Die Walküre, Act 1, scene 3

Tom and Anne:
Rejoice, beloved: in these fields of Elysium
Space cannot alter, nor Time our love abate;
Here has no words for absence or estrangement
Nor Now a notion of Almost or Too Late.

The Rake's Progress, Act 3, scene 3

These two passages are singular apices of profane and sentimental love in opera. The first passage was written in the mid-nineteenth century and the music composed some years later. The second verse was written 100 years later. Each is extreme in its tone and form, and in the role it plays in opera history. *Die Walküre* is in some respects the height of Romantic expression, while *The Rake's Progress* is a twentieth century hybrid—and the result of remarkable poetic and musical integrity.

Wagner's lovers are brother and sister; their love is fated by power beyond themselves, a power that manifests itself in the lovers' anguish-bound passion. Auden's lovers are, by contrast, pristine. In Act 3, scene 3, of *The Rake's Progress*, they are united by a philosophical love that transcends the madness into which one partner has descended. Time and space have no power in this realm of absolute love, in this quasi-religious ritual of confession and forgiveness. Wagner's lovers flee from the beginnings of human civilization into a spring night where their emotions break forth in imitation of nature's inherent chaos. Auden's lovers could not be further from the nature they idealized in the pristine wilderness of their past; they sit on a straw pallet, an unworthy altar on which a mad hero will expire at play's end. They are in Bedlam, London's subterranean asylum, and are fated to enact the tragic ritual of priest and sacrificial victim.

Wagner's lovers are capable of union with nature, and their passion is grounded in earth and flesh; they are creatures of blood and passion. Tom and Anne's passion is of air and fire, as fragile as the ideal of love, or of any similar philosophical dictum; for example, Hegel's notion that we mortals must always wear the spectacles of time and space when we think rationally. Anne will, of course, think rationally in the *Rake*'s final scene, and will desert her beloved—something Sieglinda is not empowered to do.

From a purely literary standpoint, a careful examination of the two texts and the dramatic context will show Wagner's blank verse phrases are a product of the doctrines of primitive mysticism, and draw upon the darkest hue of Romanticism for their power. A chthonic mythic force dominates the entire *Ring*, hinting at man's deepest psychic roots. Auden's refined stanzas reflect layers of sophisticated philosophical thought and classical values, representing far more space and time than the one hundred years separating the two librettists imply.

Both aesthetically and philosophically, far more than one hundred years separates these two works, whose climactic moments reflect the formal values of the artists who created them. These compositional criteria manifest themselves in Romantic and Neoclassic forms, respectively. Auden and Stravinsky's opera is a masterpiece of poetic, dramatic and musical design. The final scene is a remarkable summary of the opera's plot. Consideration of the setting, verse and music as they define and affect character and shape the action—among the complex of lesser units of which operatic form consists—within the great arc of plot's resolution will demonstrate the musical-dramatic integrity of the scene.

The Final Scene as Summary and Conclusion

The final scene is both a conclusion of the opera's story, containing the climax of the stage action and a summary of all the opera's individual constituent elements, gathering those elements together in a familiar tapestry. This latter phenomenon is subtly accomplished by Stravinsky through the reiteration of previous motifs now vastly augmented by rich, new material, and by the repetition of image and idea by the librettist Auden.

When such repetition occurs, we are initially more affected by the feeling of *deja vu* than by conscious recognition of musical or poetic/mythic ideas. With repeated listening and viewings, however, the integrity of such careful structuring of the literary and musical sub-arc yields multi-faceted and -leveled meanings. Such subtlety of poetic and musical patterning is unusual—though not rare in great opera, as we have seen in this book—and both Auden and Stravinsky prove themselves masters of it.

The final scene is a summary of the opera in several senses. First, the characters now act out the allegorical roles they previously alluded to in the opening scene. In this bittersweet distortion of a Romantic vision—the "future state / Ever happy, ever fair"—Tom now believes he is Adonis. In compassionate response, Anne *pretends* to be Venus. The literary irony is especially apparent in a contemporary setting. It accents the opera's under-pinnings of despair and pain. Purely literary allusions in the first scene now become the histrionic basis of a disturbing play-within-a-play in the final scene.

Second, musical ideas from earlier in the opera are used, bringing with them an emotional charge recreating the former mood or the previous emotional state of a character in the listener's memory. Tom's confession to Anne, for example, begins with orchestral figures in the strings similar to those that introduced 2,2, where the instrumental accompaniment express-es Anne's loneliness and anxiety in London: Anne's loneliness is now Tom's, musically speaking.

Tom's vocal line in the confession is, however, fervent, and builds on the orchestra's coloring somewhat autonomously, rather than being restrained by it. There is an uneasy quality to the accompaniment, which atmosphere creates an effective interplay of tension between voice and orchestra reflecting the disparity between what we know to be real and what Tom is experiencing in his demented state.

Finally, the instruments that captured the "birds and beasts at play" in the natural environment of the opening scene of *The Rake* appear again, but this time either curiously subdued as in Tom's music, or else striving (sometimes shrilly) upward to break from the cage of madness, as in the cho-rus's response to Anne's lullaby. Stravinsky's use of woodwinds, especially oboe, English horn, and piccolo is, as always, noteworthy.

Immediately before 3,3, we have seen the power of good and evil amply demonstrated. Anne's love has saved Tom's soul, but Nick has used his remaining power—or, conversely, Tom's remaining vulnerability—to curse him: "To reason blind shall be your mind. / Henceforth be you insane!" The strength of Anne's love was futile to prevent this curse, and Nick's great power was echoed in the driving rhythms and heavy brass of his fiery exit aria.

The tremendous contrast between Nick's final powerful vocal efforts and Tom's child-like verses that immediately follow couldn't be more extreme in terms of dramatic or musical content. In Tom's nursery rhyme, Auden and Stravinsky have prepared the most pessimistic implication of the opera:

> *With roses Crowned, I sit on ground*
> *Adonis is my name,*
> *The only dear of Venus fair:*
> *Methinks it is no shame.*

The music that immediately precedes and follows these phrases is the music of the duet that will join Tom and Anne for the last time, later in

3,3. The occurrence in this passage would forestall any idea that the duet might represent a return to order (sanity) or be of lasting comfort for Tom. This music is carefully defining madness in terms we ordinarily ascribe to beauty, i.e. aesthetic order. Tom is from this point purely mad and no sense is to be made of it. If we attempt to make sense of it, Stravinsky seems to be saying, we are as mad as Tom.

Anne's act of compassion in 3,3 is found in her willingness to descend to meet Tom on the only level possible for him, the level of symbolism somehow common both to normality and the hopelessly insane, long enough to say good-bye to her "beloved." That this level is typified by music of the highest classical purity—Gluck at his finest—is a puzzling stylistic statement on the composer's part. Perhaps the ecstasy of great joy and the utter irrationality of insanity share certain formal characteristics that may be expressed, in Stravinsky's view, only in highly structured forms. Is he implicitly condemning Classical form by implying its relation to insanity? Or is he simply creating music to typify the mythic level of consciousness, no matter in whom it occurs? Or is he asking us to completely separate form and content at this point in the opera?

With such tensions established within the foregoing scene, 3,3 opens with the stately poetry and elegant music with which Stravinsky wishes to define the symbolic state on which Tom now exists in Bedlam.

The Stage Setting

The last visual impression of 3,2 shows Tom sitting on the grave of his sanity: (*The dawn comes up. It is spring. The open grave is now covered with a green mound upon which Tom sits smiling, putting grass on his head and singing to himself in a child-like voice.*) This raised mound becomes a raised eminence, a raised pallet in the following and final scene. On this makeshift altar, Tom will expire, the victim of his own weakness and failure of will. 3,3 returns us to the pure impulse of Greek theater with its altar in the middle of the circular *orkestra* area. The Greek orchestra was originally probably centered by a sacrificial altar, where victims were brought to propitiate the Gods of planting and harvest. Tom is clearly the victim here, but to whom is he being sacrificed?

The most striking aspect of the stage setting in the final scene is the enormous contrast its melancholic, dark mood and closed Baroque musical forms with the surroundings of the first scene and its bright, hopeful colors, dancing orchestral figures, and playful, open musical forms. Romantic love blooms for Tom and Anne in the country. In horrifying contrast, the final scene's dreadful and disorienting environment signals the death of Romance in a way singularly contemporary and pessimistic.

The comparison of the opening and closing scenes of the opera is unavoidable and enormously important if one wishes to get at the dark beauty at the opera's center. Tom and Anne express their love for each other only in these two scenes. Anne and Tom are never absolutely alone, so perhaps they are deprived of the necessary intimacy to develop their love. The final scene is their intimate reunion and their ultimate parting. In the preceding scenes, love has failed to save Tom's sanity from Nick's vile grasp, and Anne must now surrender to circumstances beyond her control. She does this by accepting Tom's confession and by singing her swain to sleep with a heavenly lullaby, the verses of which contain the extraordinary patterns of imagery that range from the Greek ("islands of the blessed") to the Peaceable Kingdom so heralded in art and literature of the eighteenth century.

Most importantly, the first and last scenes of this opera are similar in action. The lovers meet to enact a seasonal ritual of love—Adonis has risen from the cold earth to be warmed in the arms of his Venus—but the final scene's atmosphere is as close to hell as the creators could devise. "Poor Tom's a-cold" as he attempts to instruct his court of madmen in the initial lines of 3,3.

> Tom: *Prepare yourselves, heroic shades. Wash you and make you clean. Anoint your limbs with oil, put on your wedding garments and crown your heads with flowers. Let music strike. Venus, queen of love, will visit her unworthy Adonis.*
>
> Chorus: *Madmen's words are all untrue; / she will never come to you.*

Great power of contrast is found in the tension created between the music given to each of these statements, as well as the contrast between the dark, hellish estrangement enforced by Bedlam's stone walls and iron gate, and the "fragrant odors and... notes of cheer" (1,1) of the opera's opening scene. Tom and Anne never regain the tenuous union with nature briefly established in the opera's first scene. In the first scene, Tom leaves Anne (at her request); in the final scene, Anne deserts Tom.

Tom has called Nature his "green unnatural Mother" in 2,1. After Tom enters the dread city, his contact with Nature is distorted. Anne, the virgin queen herself, is seemingly helpless in the face of the city's corrupting influence, although we might have sensed this possibility in the sylvan opening scene when she looks evil itself—in the figure of Nick Shadow—in the face and does not comprehend the tear that will dim Tom's and her dream of "joyous design." The closing scene shows the full consequence of each character's blindness to the possibilities of evil in the world.

The Characters

There are three major characters in the opera's final scene: Tom,

Anne, and the chorus. Here the opera chorus functions as its counterpart in a Greek poetic tragedy, serving—even in its collective madness—as a source of indirect enlightened comment and order. Most touching, the chorus serves as a true middle-ground between Tom and Anne, for its members respond honestly to both the lovers. The classic chorus functions as narrator, commenting on the action and interpreting it in light of civilized values. Here the chorus is used as an element of dark distortion and projects its restless unease onto the protagonist; its insistence that "No one has been here" after Anne's exit is the final blow for Tom. His "heart breaks" and he "falls back on his pallet."

Ultimately, it is for the chorus and not Tom or even Nick, to indicate the ambiguous nature of Fate in *The Rake's Progress*. The chorus cruelly punishes Tom in his madness, and only after the little light of Anne's lullaby and the event of Tom's demise, can it be moved to "mourn for Adonis," thus fulfilling its ritual function of purifying the emotions of fear and pity so expertly aroused in this scene. The chorus also has an expository function. Its first solo action is to dance before Tom with *mocking gestures* while singing a "Chorus-minuet." The chorus Minuet is framed in driving rhythms where stinging brass accents the blind fury of madness and the oboe cries out for release. As the chorus prophecies, this study in chiaroscuro and distorted perspective will indeed be a deterministic "night that never ends."

The chorus here functions in classical elegance, rationally and to inform. But between this passage, with its ominous, descriptive elegance, and the final bereavement, the chorus also functions as the hopelessly insane, lacerating Tom and responding ecstatically only to the simple beauty of Anne's lullaby. With one exception, they hound Tom like the Furies until his death. The imagery here is of the darkness, strangeness and sameness of existence in the society in Hell. They are a vital force of truth in the scene and we cannot help but be reminded of Aristotle's insistence on the chorus's central importance as character in ascertaining tragic effect.

The contrast between Anne and Tom in the final scene is exceptionally strong. In portraying Tom's state of insanity, Auden and Stravinsky drew inspiration from Hogarth's secondary characters in Plate 8 of the series: one madman believes he is a king, another believes he is the Pope. Rather than portray Tom as a jabbering idiot, he is made to believe he is Adonis, the mythical character he prefigured in the opening scene; and he is made to act accordingly. A much sadder, wiser Anne agrees to assume momentarily the role she had earlier dreamed of playing in the bright sweetness of nature and not here in the frightful underworld—the role of Venus.

Stravinsky initially chose to depict Tom musically with a formal Baroque arioso, noticeably free of discord. His vocal line is ornamented and secure in its riding phrases. The melody's approach to the upper register, the rising of which could reflect hysteria, is instead gentle and well prepared, reflecting inner peace and certitude. But it is the peace of illusion and sanity lost. The world of madness is a world of Baroque musical order, of concord. In this world, *reality* is discordant. The oboe, bassoon and clarinet's reedy melancholy seem to debate and search hesitatingly within Tom's fragmented soul, yet all is ordered by Stravinsky's cool aesthetic in the Baroque structure.

Tom's arioso is accompanied by strings, with the piccolo and flute joining the orchestral palate only on the word "love." These two instruments also accompany Anne's lullaby. The flute is expressive of feminine images, and the emotions and ideas of female characters. Anne has become here a female Orpheus, descending to Hell to reclaim her mate. All Tom's lyric moments in the opera have been accompanied primarily by the string choir, with occasional woodwind colorations.

The arioso, music and word, is a vision inspired by madness, having its own order. The chorus cruelly responds and Tom can only murmur, "Come quickly, Venus, or I die." She does come, but cannot save Tom; thus Tom's notion that Anne could save him is relegated to the status of the madness enclosing him in Bedlam. The orchestra's agitated, teasing figures and the uneasy harmonies of the choral writing in the dialogue following Tom's arioso highlight the effect of this spiritual and physical tension on Tom: after his contrasting section, he falls back in despair, prefiguring his fall into death.

Anne, who at this juncture represents compassionate reason, enters but is helpless to correct the evil loose in this hell-generated nightmare and tries only to bring comfort where possible. She hears Tom's confession and as priestess/goddess brings "solace to tormented brains" in Bedlam. With Tom and Anne's duet, a confession and absolution of sin, the main action of the scene is accomplished, and the audience attains its catharsis. The lovers are together again and Tom/Adonis declares his love for Anne anew. The music is lovely—as the Alfredo-Violetta duet in *La Traviata*'s Act 1 is lovely—but this romance is no longer possible.

The bitter twist of Anne's liberated exit and Tom's subsequent lonely death are more a projection of modern existential emptiness than a matter of dramatic verisimilitude. Tom's madness is dramatically problematic in that it offers the audience no real release of tension, except for that which may be gotten from Stravinsky's divine music or from the Epilogue. We are left with the problem of death and no clear relief for Tom or release from our fear through empathetic identification that such a restive fate might await any of us. The only satisfaction must be intellectual or literary; thus, the necessity for a moralistic Epilogue, ala *Don Giovanni*.

The final scene of *The Rake* presents the themes, characters, and situation of the opera's opening scene. It is in effect a dream re-enactment of the first scene's action and content in a hellish setting. We see this scene through Tom's eyes, from his point of view. It is the tormented chorus that tears us back again and again to the reality of the scene. Anne's acquiescence to Tom's distorted vision of reality augments involvement on the listener's part.

Anne: (softly) *Adonis.*

Tom: (raising his head and springing to his feet) *Venus, my queen, my bride. At last. I have waited for thee so long, till I almost believed these madmen who blasphemed against thy honor. They are rebuked.*

With Anne, we also want to believe that "this dream, too, this noble vision" will not prove "as empty as the rest;" but the chorus is the cruel instrument of reality and never lets us or Tom forget that the real world pounds on, regardless of what we want to believe.

Confession, Duet and Promise of Release

So much do we empathize with Tom that we believe his earlier contention that he will die if Venus does not come, and because she does indeed come we must pinch ourselves later, when he does die. The chorus has warned us throughout this last scene that "Madmen's words are all untrue," but we are like Anne: our first response is to say, "Adonis" and to pretend with her to enter Tom's sylvan vision. Auden's words and Stravinsky's music make it easy for us. After Tom's disordered existence within the reality of Acts 1 and 2, the ordered beauty of the music assigned to him in Bedlam makes a deeply ironic statement about the nature of the reality "in the city overhead." It seems Tom has retreated into "the beauty of insanity."

The gentle rhythms of Tom's second arioso "I have waited" contain such longing and sweetness that in our hearts we cannot help but applaud Tom's "They are rebuked." We do not want the chorus to be correct about the idyllic world in which Tom now exalts. Then the horns and woodwinds accompany Tom's invitation to Venus to mount her throne and hear his confession. These horns are the same ceremonial instruments that accompanied Anne on her crusade to save her beloved in 1,3. Like Micaela's horns in the wild mountains of Spain, their rich tone is the voice of religious fervency. Breaking Romantic music-dramatic tradition, they are utterly ineffectual here in Bedlam, which defines its own, highly formal musical beauty.

In the next duet, the worlds of madness and love mix in a religious and musical ecstasy. Anne has become Tom's luminous image.

Tom: (he kneels at her feet)
O merciful goddess, hear the confession of my sins.

In a foolish dream, in a gloomy labyrinth
I hunted shadows, disdaining thy true love;
Forgive thy servant, who repents his madness,
Forgive Adonis and he shall faithful prove.

Tom's voice intertwines with a *dolce* English horn and flute while the string choir pulses underneath in familiar patterns. His vocal ecstasy is that of the true believer. Stravinsky's delicate instrumentation complements Auden's words. The melancholy English horn now chimes in with Tom's words "Gloomy labyrinth," while his "foolish dream" is shadowed by Anne's sweet flute. These three voices—sincere Tom, the melancholy English horn, the sensuous flute—murmur confession and ask for forgiveness: "Forgive Adonis and he shall faithful prove."

Echoing Tom's newfound faithfulness, the English horn then phrases the question plaintively in a rising, inclusive pattern after Tom's voice quiets, seeming also to ask, "Will you forgive?" If we follow our hearts here, the music would lead us to believe that Tom's madness has not reduced him to senselessness, but rather has freed him from the world's disorder. Such is not the case, however.

With an increasingly strong pulse in the lower strings, Anne's ecstatic absolution is supported by both Tom's strings and the woodwinds, including Anne's faithful flute. The two lovers are finally united musically.

Anne: (rising and raising him by the hand):
What should I forgive? Thy ravishing penitence
Blesses me, dear heart, and brightens all the past.
Kiss me, Adonis: the wild boar is vanquished.

The flute and English horn join in harmony as Tom and Anne kiss. Because "the wild boar [lust] is vanquished," Tom and Anne can now sing sweetly in thirds, "Rejoice, beloved" to celebrate their bittersweet final reunion.

(Rakewell suddenly staggers. Anne helps him gently to lie down on the pallet.)
Tom and Anne:
Rejoice, beloved: in these fields of Elysium
Space cannot alter, nor Time our love abate;
Here has no words for absence or estrangement
Nor Now a notion of Almost or Too Late.

With the words, "Too late" the strings fall away in gentle patterns, even as Tom's consciousness fades. Tom then asks to be taken to Anne/Venus's breast and to be serenaded. He is secure in his absolution, his calm joy, his assurance that "the heavens are merciful, and all is well."

Anne's Lullaby and the Chorus's Longing

The ecstasy of the following verses provides *The Rake's Progress* with its only real emotional turn, a dramatic fact accomplished by the most tasteful poetic and economic musical means. Anne's words paint the Peaceable Kingdom in pure lyrics, and the chorus responds with couplets of great longing and beauty. They are given merciful respite through Anne's compassion. Like Tom, they are weary unto death.

Anne:
Gently, little boat
Across the ocean float,
The crystal waves dividing:
The sun in the west
Is going to rest:
Glide, glide, glide
Toward the Islands of the Blest.

Chorus: (off in their cells)
What voice is this? What heavenly strains
Bring solace to tormented brains?

The accompaniment of these antiphonal responses contains the throbbing strings of Anne and Tom's duet, but now in cross-rhythms with the chorus's straightforward pulse. Combined with the strings is the striving oboe, always rising questioningly, perhaps begging at the end of each verse, asking for more and more peace and forgiveness.

The flute in the lower register and the piccolo accompany Anne's verses adding quaintness and a crystalline quality to the visual harmony she describes. Anne's clear lyric soprano voice and the simple, mounting melodic lines, joined by the flute and piccolo, create the "sacred music of the spheres," the musical absolution and evidence of harmony for which the inhabitants of Bedlam long.

Duettino: The Stalwart Desertion of Tom.

While the chorus reaches an emotional release in the lullaby, Anne gathers the strength to obey her father and leave Bedlam and Tom. She then addresses Tom, but more importantly, the audience with the verse below, *tranquillo ma resoluto* (peacefully but with resolution).

Tom, my vow
Holds ever, but it is no longer I
You need. Sleep well, my dearest dear. Good-bye

Then, as her father joins her with a supporting melody, she bids Tom farewell:

Every wearied body must
Late or soon return to dust,
Set the frantic spirit free.
In this earthly city we
Shall not meet again, love, yet
Never think that I forget.

These words, which imply her understanding that Tom is close to death, the only possible release for him, are accompanied by a resolute march rhythm in the low strings. It is a final farewell and a stalwart desertion of unfortunate Tom by Anne. The marching basses indicate her resolution to go. The vocal line is set firmly in the rich middle register of her voice, reflecting the firmness of decision and emotional control.

In contrast to the great bulk of Stravinsky's score, Anne and her father sing in rhythmic union with the orchestra, creating the idea that her decision is, in terms of musical form, universally acceptable. There is, however, syncopation in the bass line. Anne has saved Tom's soul in the graveyard, but the scorpion's tale of fate has claimed him in Bedlam. Only death can release Tom.

Finale: Tom's Release into Empty Ecstasy

Tom: (wakes, starts to his feet and looks wildly around)
Where art thou, Venus? Venus, where art thou? The flowers open to
the sun. The birds renew their song. It is spring. The bridal couch is
prepared. Come quickly, beloved, and we will celebrate the holy rites
of love.

Tom's tortured spirit might perhaps be released in the ecstasy of the vision he shares with us, but he has slept for a moment and Venus has disappeared. The mad chorus crushes his fragile vision, without intent or purpose: "Madman! No one has been here."

Tom responds with despair, presaging death in his imagery and idea:
My heart breaks. I feel the chill of death's approaching wing.
Orpheus, strike from they lyre a wan-like music, and weep, ye
nymphs and shepherds of these Stygian fields, weep for Adonis the
beautiful, the young; weep for Adonis whom Venus loved.

Tom's passage ends in mythic truth: "[I am] Adonis whom Venus loved."

Anne—Venus, the Virgin Queen—is the real source and emblem of love in the opera. For whatever reason, no matter how richly and lyrically accompanied by regretful strings or romantically-appealing the woodwinds, Tom's nature is weaker than his music and incapable of returning Anne's love except in the mock reality of madness. Although we know not to expect realistic qualities from an allegorical character like Tom, the extraordinary moral strength of Anne and the pity we feel for Tom lead us to expect more of a conclusion than this scene gives us:

Mourn for Adonis, ever young, Venus' dear,
Weep, tread softly round his bier.

Conclusion

The power of Stravinsky's music in this scene cannot be overestimated. Here is found some of the most beautiful music of this century, music that ranks with the best of Mozart, Haydn and Schubert. In Tom's final passage, the voices of the woodwinds fall away one by one: Tom's English horn fades last of all to leave him alone with the heart of the orchestra, the string choir. Finally, they, too, are silent. There follows the chorus's dirge with plunging bass, ceremonial brass, mournful English horn, and a final, lonely trumpet fading as the ritual ends.

Aristotle's ideal complex plot requires that a deed be perpetrated in ignorance and a tragic discovery be made afterwards. This is the pattern found in *Oedipus Tyrannus*. Tom commits no heinous crime of his own volition. He is the victim of supernatural forces, personified by Nick Shadow. Tom is merely a naive, flawed young man. Or perhaps Nick is simply the destructive machine, and Tom merely another victim of irrational fancy. Yet we are moved profoundly by Tom's plight, due primarily to the exquisite power of the music the last great composer has given us which describes in detail not only his moods but the wrestling within his guilty soul throughout this late masterpiece.

It is to Auden's and especially Stravinsky's credit that we can become so much involved in Tom's plight. In maintaining the necessary balance between external (visual-dramatic) and internal (verbal-musical) motivational forces, the two writers have projected a musical-dramatic vehicle that thoroughly engages without negating the necessity for scenic effects and stage action.

The opera never grows sentimental through the excess of music or obscure through verbal vagueness. Stravinsky's enormous skill at creating environment, complementing and vitalizing Auden's lovely and well-crafted verse and ennobling Auden and Kallman's dramatic situations, and above all his ability to capture character inscape is the primary source of greatness in *The Rake's Progress*.